125-

Careers in Social Media

Careers in Social Media

SALEM PRESS
A Division of EBSCO Information Services, Inc.
Ipswich, Massachusetts

GREY HOUSE PUBLISHING

Cover Image from monkeybusinessimages (via iStock).

Publisher's Cataloging-In-Publication Data
(Prepared by The Donohue Group, Inc.)

Title: Careers in social media.
Other Titles: Careers in--
Description: [First edition]. | Ipswich, Massachusetts : Salem Press, a division of EBSCO
          Information Services, Inc. ; [Amenia, New York] : Grey House Publishing,
          [2018] | Series: [Careers in--] | Includes bibliographical references and index.
Identifiers: ISBN 9781682176665 (hardcover)
Subjects: LCSH: Social media--Vocational guidance--United States.
Classification: LCC HM742 .C37 2018 | DDC 302.231--dc23

First Printing

CONTENTS

PUBLISHER'S NOTE

Careers in Social Media contains twenty-four alphabetically arranged chapters describing specific fields of interest for those with a desire to work in the social media in marketing, advertising, fundraising, research, writing, editing, or digital design and production. Merging scholarship with occupational development, this single comprehensive guidebook provides social media students with the necessary insight into potential careers and provides instruction on what job seekers can expect in terms of training, advancement, earnings, job prospects, working conditions, relevant associations, and more. *Careers in Social Media* is specifically designed for a high school and undergraduate audience and is edited to align with secondary or high school curriculum standards.

Scope of Coverage

Understanding the wide scope of jobs for those with a passion for social media is important for anyone preparing for a career that plays out on a variety of social media platforms and networks, including Facebook, Twitter, Instagram, Snapchat, WhatsApp, Quora, Tumblr, and Reddit. *Careers in Social Media* comprises twenty-four lengthy chapters on a broad range of occupations including jobs such as Journalist, Advertising and Marketing Manager, Software Developer, Copywriter, Writer, and Photographer. Job titles in social media are constantly evolving, so in this book, we've looked at the ways that social media jobs relate to three specific areas: Advertising and Marketing (which includes business management and development, market analysis, and fundraising); Communications (which includes writing, photography, videography, editing, and more), and Technology (which includes software and computer programming, project management, and more). This excellent reference presents possible career paths and occupations within high-growth and emerging fields in this industry.

Careers in Social Media is enhanced with numerous charts and tables, including projections from the US Bureau of Labor Statistics, and median annual salaries or wages for those occupations profiled. Each chapter also notes those skills that can be applied across broad occupation categories. Interesting enhancements, like **Fun Facts**, **Famous Firsts**, and dozens of photos, add depth to the discussion. Additional highlights in the book include **Conversation With**—a two-page interview with a professional working in a related job—and also **Conversations About**, which offer insight into specific areas of social media work, such as podcasts, customer service, and "viral" posts. The respondents share their personal career paths, detail the potential for career advancement, offer advice for students, and include a "try this" for those interested in embarking on a career in their profession.

Essay Length and Format

Each chapter ranges in length from 3,500 to 4,500 words and begins with a Snapshot of the occupation that includes career clusters, interests, earnings, and employment outlook. This is followed by these major categories:

- **Overview** includes detailed discussions on: Sphere of Work; Work Environment; Occupation Interest; A Day in the Life. Also included here is a Profile that outlines working conditions, educational needs, and physical abilities. You will also find the occupation's Holland Interest Score, which matches up character and personality traits with specific jobs.

- **Occupational Specialties** lists specific jobs that are related in some way, like Landscape Drafter, Urban and Regional Planner, and Architectural Drafter. Duties and Responsibilities are also included.

- **Work Environment** details the physical, human, and technological environment of the occupation profiled.

- **Education, Training, and Advancement** outlines how to prepare for this field while in high school, and what college courses to take, including licenses and certifications needed. A section is devoted to the Adult Job Seeker, and there is a list of skills and abilities needed to succeed in the job profiled.

- **Earnings and Advancements** offers specific salary ranges, and includes a chart of metropolitan areas that have the highest concentration of the profession.

- **Employment and Outlook** discusses employment trends, and projects growth to 2026. This section also lists related occupations.

- **Selected Schools** list those prominent learning institutions that offer specific courses in the profiles occupations.

- **More Information** includes associations that the reader can contact for more information.

Special Features

Several features continue to distinguish this reference series from other career-oriented reference works. The back matter includes:
- Appendix A: Guide to Holland Code. This discusses John Holland's theory that people and work environments can be classified into six different groups: Realistic; Investigative; Artistic; Social; Enterprising; and Conventional. See if the job you want is right for you!
- Appendix B: General Bibliography. This is a collection of suggested readings, organized into major categories.
- Subject Index: Includes people, concepts, technologies, terms, principles, and all specific occupations discussed in the occupational profile chapters.

Acknowledgments

Thanks are due to Allison Blake, who took the lead in developing "Conversations With" and "Conversations About," with help from Vanessa Parks, and to the professionals who communicated their work experience through interview questionnaires. Their frank and honest responses provide immeasurable value to *Careers in Social Media*. The contributions of all are gratefully acknowledged.

EDITOR'S INTRODUCTION

Introduction

Trying to capture the essence of what it means to work in social media is a bit like trying to catch lightening in a bottle. This relatively young industry is still evolving. As soon as one title starts to sound familiar, it is displaced by a newer one. Just a few years ago, the job title "social media manager" didn't exist. Fast forward to today, and almost every company has someone on staff who is responsible for social media. At smaller companies, the person who manages it might be the same person who handles public relations or marketing. At bigger companies, there is usually a dedicated employee.

What Does a Career in Social Media Require?

So, what exactly does a social media manager do? Most people tend to think that social media management means simply answering customer questions on Facebook and Twitter. And while that kind of engagement is a large piece of the puzzle, the job actually goes far beyond answering questions and garnering follows, likes, comments, and shares.

If we take a look at tasks and job functions that go into being a social media professional, whether the moniker used at an individual company is traditional or takes a less "traditional" form —sherpa, guru, maven, swami, czar, or ninja—the work tends to fall into broad categories: manager, coordinator, strategist, analyst, communications worker, editor, producer, researcher, or designer. Your goal might be described as some form of marketing if you use social media to increase awareness or create brand identity and loyalty. You might be engaged with advertising or customer service if your work involves managing customer relations, responding to user questions and comments, or driving sales. You might use social media as a tool in research or as a way to promote a particular political policy, candidate, or campaign. Or, you might be the person who uses the data that social media interactions generate, or the person who develops algorithms and programs to improve user experiences and interactions.

Social media may be all you do, all day, every day, or it might be just one part of your overall job. Your skills in manipulating technology, using software, even writing code or programming, may be the skills you need most. Writing and editing digital content, whether the content is meant to be read, heard, or watched, may be more in your "wheelhouse," or your ability to crunch numbers and read trends in the data might be your ticket to a rewarding career in social media.

Whether you work in entertainment, media, the sports industry, in the sciences, business, finance, non-profits or politics, companies of all sizes have come to depend upon social media as part of their overall strategy. It's the way that companies share information with their clients and customers.

What Does Social Media Mean to a Company?

Hardly anyone escapes some sort of social media exposure at work. Your company might have a profile on LinkedIn or Facebook, or they might have a Twitter feed, an Instagram account, or a presence on other social media networks, including bookmarking networks like Pinterest or Tumblr. They may have their own podcast series to promote the research they are doing or to establish relationships with others in their field. The ability to work with a wide array of social media platforms is the key to rising through the ranks as a social media specialist.

The director of social media is responsible for a company's entire social media strategy, and may well be required to direct and manage the work of other people. As director of social media, you will probably be in charge of posting to social media accounts on several platforms, according to a set schedule. You may or may not be responsible for creating those accounts and that schedule. You may be responsible for creating content or overseeing editors in creating a content calendar. You may also write for or oversee a blog. You might be responsible for creating your company's "voice" and social media personality. You will likely be expected to know more about social media than your supervisor does. Other likely titles for the same job include director or manager of social media marketing; director or manager of social media communication; director or manager of social media relations; or director or manager of social media strategy.

A brand manager or brand ambassador typically posts to a group of social media accounts (with or without a blog), and is directly involved in advertising. An engagement coordinator (or manager) is in charge of the company's social media messaging, as well as taking responsibility for guiding the online behavior of the public. You will be executing (and possibly creating) a marketing strategy that involves getting members of the public to respond to, like, share, or retweet your content (so it goes viral), or provide your company with information it can use later to improve service and drive sales. Other names associated with brand managers and directors include director of community, interactive media associate (or coordinator, or manager), or internet marketing manager.

Scientists in a number of different fields have found that social media is one of the best ways to publish their findings, collaborate, and even conduct research. News organizations rely on social media to attract readers in an increasingly fractured media landscape. Having a story "trend" is one way to make sure that a news organization stays relevant and top-of-mind.

Why Is Content so Important in Social Media?

Content is what makes social media significant. It encompasses anything an individual or brand creates for consumption. Blog posts, photographs, videos, infographics, tweets, GIFs, memes, and SlideShares are all examples of content.

Content marketing is what makes all those consumable pieces of information work for a company or a brand in a cohesive way. It has been defined as:

- a strategic marketing approach focused on creating and distributing valuable, relevant, and consistent content to attract and retain a clearly-defined audience — and to drive profitable customer action.
- creating or curating non-product content and publishing it to contact points with customers to get their attention, to focus on the topic around your solution, and pull them closer to learning more about you.
- anything an individual or an organization creates and/or shares to tell their story.
- the emotional and informational bridge between commerce and consumer. It requires people who love content and what it can do for people.
- advertising that delivers value—rather than just an impression—to its recipient.
- a pull strategy—that is, the marketing of attraction, with content tailor-made to solve the problems of your audience.
- engaging with your community around an idea, instead of a product, by sharing information, ideas, and experiences that benefit others without directly asking for anything in return.

What Do Social Media Workers Have in Common?

- A willingness to engage with others in a digital environment
- A team-based approach to doing work
- An avid interest in technology
- An appreciation of graphics and design
- Curiosity
- Great research skills
- Fascination with statistics and data
- Writing and editing skills

What Is the Role of Technology in Social Media?

Social media, on the scale it exists today, would not be possible without computers, computer programmers, software developers, and network architects. The technicians who create the platforms, write the algorithms that make them work, and develop the systems for capturing and analyzing data are fundamental to any work related to social media.

Digital strategists are responsible for thinking on the macro level about how a company will use technology and social media to achieve their objectives. Network architects, information security specialists, and information project managers all keep the social media engine running by capturing, storing, and analyzing data, as well as making sure that data is kept safe and that both the community members and the company are not put at risk.

How Do You Prepare for an Interview for a Social Media Position?

No matter what the precise job title a company has settled on for a position, social media workers should be able to address a variety of concerns that might affect an organization or company. You should be able to answer these sorts of questions:

What social media platform (or platforms) will be most effective for our company?

This question will reveal what you know or think about the company's "personality" or brand. You might be asked to boil that down to a short phrase. And you will no doubt be assessed to see if you are familiar with the social media presence the company already has on various platforms.

What are the two most important social marketing metrics a company should monitor?

You should be able to talk about engagement in terms of measurable conversation about the company brand and what your goals might be regarding the things people are saying about or doing with your content.

The other important metric is leads, so it is helpful to be able to discuss social campaigns you may have headed up that generated interest, garnered likes, or resulted in leads. You should know the various types of social media advertising and be able to respond quickly to an ongoing "conversation."

How would you differentiate social marketing from social customer service?

Social marketing calls for a conversational approach, one that does not necessarily revolve around sales. You should be able to determine where along the path to a purchase your potential customer is so you can guide them.

Social customer service calls for empathy, patience, and an ability to resolve conflict, as well as knowing when a situation calls for bringing in someone from the management team.

What is the most important aspect of work for a social media manager?

The answer your potential employer is looking for is likely to be monitoring and listening to the audience across all of the brand's social channels, engaging with fans and followers to show that the company is interested in them, cares about their experience, and is actively "engaged" with them.

How would you deal with a social media reputation crisis?

Every individual, celebrity, politician, athlete, or corporation can fall victim to a crisis that affects their reputation. The work of social media experts as it relates to these situations demands that there be a "best practices" approach that has been thought out and put in place *before* a crisis erupts and that mirrors the company's conflict resolution process.

What is your own social media presence? What examples do you have to show?

Employers will want to see your online profile because it demonstrates your abilities with various platforms, including WordPress or other blogging platforms, Facebook, Twitter, even Pinterest. They will want to see if you post regularly to keep material fresh, and whether you have active followers with whom you maintain a conversation.

This is a relatively young career path. Even as recently as ten years ago, it would be hard to find anyone whose title included the term "social media" or who spent their days writing tweets or posting to Facebook or Instagram. The existing job titles and duties in this field are constantly changing to keep up with emerging trends. New tools and technologies, along with as-yet-unknown areas of interest or challenge will keep the field dynamic well into the future, no matter what we may call the professionals who shape the content and communities on the Internet.

Advertising & Marketing Manager

Snapshot

Career Cluster(s): Business, Management & Administration, Hospitality & Tourism, Human Services, Marketing, Sales & Service

Interests: Advertising and marketing, mass media and communications, project management, writing, journalism

Earnings (2016 median pay): $127,560 per year; $61.33 per hour

Employment & Outlook: Average Growth Expected

OVERVIEW

Sphere of Work

Advertising and marketing managers work as employees of marketing and advertising agencies within the communication, information, and business sectors. They serve as the main link or point of contact between clients and the agency, and help to manage the interests of clients within the agency.
Advertising and marketing managers coordinate social media management (including strategies and campaigns), print, television, radio, and multimedia advertising campaigns and projects; in some cases, they may also be responsible for sales and developing new business opportunities.

While advertising and marketing managers contribute to campaign development, they are not technically part of an agency's creative team. Their role is to ensure that campaigns are priced, administered, and executed smoothly and efficiently, and the social media platforms selected align with the client's interests in mind. They ensure that action items and campaign milestones are delivered on time and within budget. Aside from working closely with clients, they coordinate the work activities of personnel such as social media specialists, copywriters, graphic designers, production assistants, art directors, public relations personnel, and market researchers, as well as other project management responsibilities. Advertising and marketing managers are generally supervised by an agency director or client services supervisor.

Work Environment

Advertising and marketing managers work in an office environment within small to large advertising or marketing agencies. Air and car travel may be occasionally required to meet with clients. Evening and weekend work is also often required. Advertising and marketing managers frequently work under pressure and adhere to strict budgets and tight deadlines.

Profile

Interests: Business, Management & Administration, Hospitality & Tourism, Human Services, Marketing, Sales & Service
Working Conditions: Work Inside
Physical Strength: Light Work
Education Needs: Bachelor's Degree
Licensure/Certification: Usually Not Required
Physical Abilities Not Required: Not Climb, Not Kneel
Opportunities for Experience: Internship, Apprenticeship, Volunteer Work
Holland Interest Score*: AES

* See Appendix A

Occupation Interest

Graduates and professionals with a strong interest in social media platforms such as Twitter, Instagram, and Snapchat, advertising and marketing, mass media and communications, and project management are often attracted to the advertising industry. In particular, the role suits people who have an interest in coordinating multiple activities in a fast-paced environment and who are comfortable working closely with others.

Aside from excellent collaborative, communication, and organizational skills, advertising and marketing managers must also possess strong research and analytical skills and high business acumen. They may be expected to formulate and execute budgets, monitor expenses, and assist with financial reporting. In some instances, they will be expected to make sales calls or develop and present new business proposals.

Successful advertising and marketing managers must be able to speak and write fluently, especially in an on-line environment, work with a diverse range of people, adapt to new industries, clients, products and services, and deliver consistent results under pressure. The role also requires considerable tact and diplomacy.

A Day in the Life—Duties and Responsibilities

The typical work day of an advertising and marketing manager includes frequent meetings with staff, clients, and supervisors (generally top-level management or agency owners). The campaign deliverables, which advertising and marketing managers coordinate, are usually subject to tight timeframes and strict deadlines. Therefore, on a daily basis, the role demands excellent organizational and time management skills. Advertising and marketing managers must be adept at multi-tasking, adapting to change, and problem solving.

Advertising and marketing managers generally gain a high level of exposure to different clients, industries, products, and services (although some may specialize in specific industries). The role demands high business (and possibly sales) acumen and the ability to analyze new information quickly and effectively. An advertising and marketing manager is expected to thoroughly research and understand the clients they work with, as well as their client's competitors, and the competitors' competing products and campaigns. This includes developing a deep understanding of the client's industry, customer base, current social media presence, methods and processes, challenges and opportunities, and target markets.

Advertising and marketing managers are expected to have competent computing skills to help them prepare campaign-related and organizational materials, such as financial and marketing reports, client and budget proposals (or "pitches" to acquire new business), and other work-related documents. They may also be expected to develop and manage spreadsheets and databases for project management and accounting purposes.

Duties and Responsibilities

- **Preparing advertising and marketing budgets for clients**
- **Consulting with people in research, creative, and production departments**
- **Overseeing workers in layout, copy, production, and client services**

WORK ENVIRONMENT

Immediate Physical Environment

Office settings predominate. Advertising and marketing managers work for small to large advertising and marketing firms, usually in urban or semi-urban locations. Some travel may be required. Many people work remotely, using collaborative tools and software to work as part of a team.

Job security is sometimes tenuous in the advertising industry. Economic or sector downturns, the loss of client accounts, or reduced client spending can lead to layoffs. This tends to create an atmosphere of intense competition.

Human Environment

Advertising and marketing manager roles demand strong collaborative and team skills. Advertising and marketing managers interact with advertising, business, and creative specialists, such as brand and

Transferable Skills and Abilities

Communication Skills
- Persuading others

Interpersonal/Social Skills
- Asserting oneself
- Being able to work independently
- Cooperating with others
- Having good judgment
- Motivating others
- Working as a member of a team

Organization & Management Skills
- Managing time
- Meeting goals and deadlines
- Paying attention to and handling details

Unclassified Skills
- Keeping a neat appearance

product managers, social media stategists, marketing managers, brand strategists, public relations executives, graphic designers, art directors, multimedia technicians, copywriters, production assistants, and editors. They are likely to work with multiple client contacts, as well as contract or freelance service providers. They usually report to an agency director or owner, or a client services supervisor.

Technological Environment

Advertising and marketing managers use standard business technologies, including telecommunication and social media tools, presentation tools and software, and financial and database software.

EDUCATION, TRAINING, AND ADVANCEMENT

High School/Secondary

High school students can best prepare for a career as an advertising and marketing manager by taking courses in business, math (with an accounting focus), computer literacy, and communications (for example, journalism or business communications). Courses such as social studies, history, and anthropology will also prepare the student for synthesizing research into written materials. The creative aspects of the advertising industry may be explored through art and graphic design. However, it is important to note that advertising and marketing managers work in an administrative, rather than a creative, capacity. In addition, psychology and cultural studies may provide an understanding of group and individual responses to advertising and other forms of communication.

Students should also become involved in extracurricular school activities and projects that develop business and communication skills to gain hands-on experience prior to graduation. Additionally, serving as a club secretary, treasurer, or other office holder will help to develop organizational skills. Participation in student magazines and newsletters will help to build an understanding of print and multimedia communications.

Suggested High School Subjects
- Applied Math
- Arts
- Business Data Processing
- Business Law
- Business Math
- Composition
- Computer Science
- Economics
- English
- Graphic Communications
- Journalism
- Merchandising
- Statistics

Related Career Pathways/Majors

Business, Management & Administration Cluster
- Marketing Pathway

Hospitality & Tourism Cluster
- Lodging Pathway
- Travel & Tourism Pathway

Human Services Cluster
- Consumer Services Pathway

Marketing, Sales & Service Cluster
- E-Marketing Pathway
- Management & Entrepreneurship Pathway

Marketing, Sales & Service Cluster
- Marketing Information Management & Research Pathway

Famous First

The first banner ad was part of AT&T's larger "You Will" campaign, which included a series of television commercials featuring predicted scenes from an internet-enabled future—in many cases quite accurately (for example, self-scanning items at the grocery store). (One failure: AT&T predicted video calling, but not mobile video calling, imagining FaceTime taking place in a phone booth.)

Source: www.theatlantic.com

Postsecondary

At the postsecondary level, students interested in or focused on becoming an advertising and marketing manager should work towards earning an undergraduate degree in communications, advertising, marketing, or business administration, or build a strong liberal arts background. Due to strong competition among candidates, a master's degree is sometimes expected, although practical experience is sometimes more highly regarded than formal qualifications.

A large number of colleges and universities offer advertising, marketing, communications, and business degree programs. Some programs offer internships or work experience with advertising agencies. These experiences may lead to entry-level opportunities. Aspiring advertising and marketing managers can also gain entry into the advertising industry via other roles, such as market research, administration, or sales.

Related College Majors

- Advertising
- Business Administration & Management, General
- Journalism
- Marketing Management & Research
- Public Relations & Organizational Communications

Adult Job Seekers

Adults seeking a career transition into or return to an advertising and marketing manager role will need to highlight qualifications, skills, and experience in areas such as business administration, advertising, and marketing. Necessary skills for a successful transition include account coordination, client liaison, and project management. Marketing and advertising experience with a non-agency corporation is often highly regarded because agency firms value employees who understand the client side of the relationship.

Networking is critical—candidates should not rely solely on job boards and advertised positions to explore work opportunities. As with recent college graduates, adult job seekers may wish to consider entry to the advertising industry via an alternative route, such as market research, administration, or sales.

Professional Certification and Licensure

There are no formal professional certifications or licensing requirements for advertising and marketing managers.

Additional Requirements

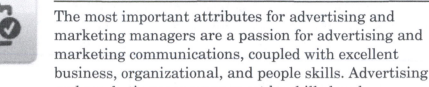

The most important attributes for advertising and marketing managers are a passion for advertising and marketing communications, coupled with excellent business, organizational, and people skills. Advertising and marketing managers must be skilled and diplomatic coordinators, negotiators, and problem solvers. They should be willing to persist under often heavy workloads and with demanding stakeholders.

Fun Fact

Social media use grew rapidly: in 2009, 34 percent of Americans had a social media presence. By 2017, it hit 81 percent.
Source: Statista.com

EARNINGS AND ADVANCEMENT

Earning potential increases as advancement occurs. Advancement may be quick in corporate ranks, partly because turnover can be high as a result of account success or failure. Many firms provide their employees with continuing education opportunities, either in-house or at local colleges and universities, and encourage employee participation in seminars and conferences.

Advertising and marketing managers had median annual earnings of $100,810 in May 2016. The lowest 10 percent earned less than $44,950, and the highest 10 percent earned more than $208,000.

The median annual wage for marketing managers was $131,180 in May 2016. The lowest 10 percent earned less than $67,490, and the highest 10 percent earned more than $208,000.

Advertising and marketing managers may receive paid vacations, holidays, and sick days; life and health insurance; and retirement benefits. These are usually paid by the employer.

EMPLOYMENT AND OUTLOOK

There were approximately 249,600 advertising and marketing managers employed nationally in 2016. Overall employment of advertising, promotions, and marketing managers is projected to grow 10 percent from 2016 to 2026, faster than the average for all occupations. Employment growth will vary by occupation.

Advertising, promotional, and marketing campaigns are expected to continue to be essential as organizations seek to maintain and expand their market share. Advertising and promotions managers will be needed to plan, direct, and coordinate advertising and promotional campaigns, as well as to introduce new products into the marketplace.

However, the newspaper publishing industry, which employs many of these workers, is projected to decline over the next 10 years. The continued rise of electronic media will result in decreasing demand for print newspapers. Despite this decline, advertising and promotions managers are expected to see employment growth in other industries in which they will be needed to manage digital media campaigns that often target customers through the use of websites, social media, or live chats.

Through the Internet, advertising campaigns can reach a target audience across many platforms. This greater reach can increase the scale of the campaigns that advertising and promotions managers oversee. With better advertising management software, advertising and promotions managers can control these campaigns more easily.

Related Occupations
- Advertising Director
- Advertising Sales Agent
- Copywriter
- Electronic Commerce Specialist
- Public Relations Specialist

Conversation With . . .
MICHELE P. DAMBACH

VP Digital Strategy
Watkins McGowan, LLC
Atlanta, Georgia
Marketing, 20 years

1. What was your individual career path in terms of education/training, entry-level job, or other significant opportunity?

I graduated from Stetson University in Florida with a BBA in management and a minor in German and became an international flight attendant for Delta Airlines. Both of my parents are German, and I had the privilege of flying to Germany for dinner with my grandmother once a week. I also earned my MBA in marketing from Mercer University in Atlanta, where I had moved to join Delta.

When I went into marketing, I began as a Sales and Marketing Coordinator, managing campaigns for clients in the CPG (consumer packaged goods) industries. I quickly found that I enjoyed working with clients rather than behind the scenes, so I was promoted to a sales role and managed the East Coast territory. I became a Marketing Services Consultant and held that role for almost 10 years, working with clients such as Gillette, Ocean Spray, and Tyson Foods. The role that best prepared me for where I am today, however, was opening my own digital marketing consultancy after taking a break to raise my children. My traditional print marketing/sales career had naturally led to the transition to digital marketing and sales.

From a business point of view, social media is all about marketing – getting your name out there and driving people to your website. Perhaps the biggest way that businesses and organizations can drive traffic to their sites is by optimizing their SEO (search engine optimization) efforts. Where people like me come in is by harnessing the power of social media for SEO. For instance, I had a client called MedReps.com, a jobs listing site for medical sales representatives. When I first started with them, we didn't always turn up on page one of search engine ranking reports for all of our Tier 1 keywords. We were playing against big members of the marketplace like Glassdoor. We had to think about how people entered queries into a search engine. We did a social media campaign around MedRep's annual salary report and worked with some of our larger, big-name pharma partners. By partnering our social media efforts along with the pharma partner's social media, and having our report linked with a major player's site, our relevancy was increased in the search engine's eyes.

2. What are the most important skills and/or qualities for someone in your profession?

You must be able to multi-task, think quickly, and have a desire to continue learning. You also need to stay abreast of not only technology trends, but trends in whatever industry you are providing the social media to. Your goal is to post relevant content in order to increase engagement by channel, which in turn hopefully generates leads and results in actual revenue once a user enters the sales funnel.

3. What do you wish you had known going into this profession?

I wish I had taken additional writing courses. Writing is a critical component of social media, whether in a management or coordinator role. I've employed several content writers to develop long-form content for blog posts and websites or short-form content such as social media updates. In today's digital marketing environment, analytics is also playing an increasingly important role. Take additional statistics and business analytics courses. Colleges are now offering majors and minors in marketing analytics.

4. Are there many job opportunities in your profession? In what specific areas?

There are always opportunities in the field of digital marketing. Many college graduates choose to start their career with an advertising or PR agency; however, there are also opportunities directly with corporations or non-profits. You can be a specialist or more of a generalist, learning about SEO, social media, marketing analytics, and content marketing.

5. How do you see your profession changing in the next five years, how do you see platforms evolving, and what skills will be required?

Artificial intelligence (AI) is going to change the industry, as will voice. Look at all the things you can do at home with Alexa and similar devices. AI will accelerate the use of chatbots. What we are seeing today is only a fraction of how chatbots and AI can be used to reach end-users.

6. What do you enjoy most about your job? What do you enjoy least about your job?

I like most that my job varies from day to day. My social media role requires that I stay abreast of the latest trends, and what we post on our channels has to be current and thought-provoking. The part I probably enjoy the least is the reporting. It's a critical component of the job, however, because if you aren't measuring what affect your marketing is having on the brand, how do you know if you should keep doing something? I probably put off reporting until the last minute, but it is something that needs to be done at the end of a campaign and/or monthly for longer-term projects.

7. Can you suggest a valuable "try this" for students considering a career in your profession?

Shadow or apply for an internship with an ad agency, which is a wonderful opportunity to learn the various roles available in the digital marketing field and how they work with their clients and what is expected of the agency in terms of deliverables. Second, read industry blogs and publications. I subscribe to several and learn something each time I read them. Several good blogs to follow are by: Seth Godin, Guy Kawasaki, MarketingProfs, and HubSpot.

MORE INFORMATION

Advertising Research Foundation
432 Park Avenue South, 6th Floor
New York, NY 10016-8013
212.751.5656
thearf.org

Advertising Women of New York
25 West 45th Street, Suite 403
New York, NY 10036
212.221.7969
awny@awny.org
www.awny.org

American Advertising Federation
1101 Vermont Avenue, NW
Suite 500
Washington, DC 20005-6306
800.999.2231
aaf@aaf.org
www.aaf.org

National Student Advertising Competition
http://www.aaf.org/default.asp?id=122

Most Promising Minority Students
http://www.aaf.org/default.asp?id=213

American Association of Advertising Agencies
405 Lexington Avenue, 18th Floor
New York, NY 10174-1801
212.682.2500
OBD@aaaa.org
www.aaaa.org

Operation Jumpstart Scholarships
http://www.aaaa.org/careers/scholarships/
Pages/default.aspx

Bill Bernbach Minority Scholarship
http://www.aaaa.org/careers/scholarships/
Pages/scholar_bernbach.aspx

John Mack Carter Scholarship
http://www.aaaa.org/careers/scholarships/
Pages/default.aspx

ANA Multicultural Excellence Scholarship
http://www.aaaa.org/careers/scholarships/
Pages/default.aspx

Advertising Age Media Scholarship
http://www.aaaa.org/careers/scholarships/
Pages/default.aspx

Association for Women in Communications
3337 Duke Street
Alexandria, VA 22314
703.370.7436
btijerina@womcom.org
www.womcom.org

Association of National Advertisers
708 Third Avenue, 33rd Floor
New York, NY 10017-4270
212.697.5950
info@ana.net
www.ana.net

Kylie Grimshaw Hughes/Editor

Advertising Director

Snapshot

Career Cluster(s): Business, Management & Administration, Hospitality & Tourism, Human Services, Marketing, Sales & Service

Interests: Creating social media marketing campaigns, forming budgets, product development

Earnings (2016 median pay): $104,246

Employment & Outlook: Average Growth Expected

OVERVIEW

Sphere of Work

Advertising directors lead teams of promotional and marketing professionals in the conception, creation, and implementation of social media campaigns to generate public interest in goods and services. The position requires a unique combination of skills, including both creative ingenuity and management savvy.

Directors oversee the creative, financial, and clientele aspects of advertising and social media campaigns, ensuring their timely deployment across a variety of social media platforms and quality execution. Directors of advertising work with other executives to identify

marketing strategies, form advertising budgets, and contribute to the conceptualization of the public face of corporations and organizations.

Advertising directors are seasoned professionals with tested management skills who possess several years of experience in the lower tiers of the marketing and promotions field or a closely related discipline, such as public relations or communications development.

Work Environment

Advertising directors work predominantly in professional and office settings. The managerial aspects of the position may require their presence in several different offices and similar professional settings on a daily basis, depending on the realm of industry. Advertising directors work with professionals involved in social media, finance, creative design, and product development. Directors who oversee creative firms, as opposed to marketing departments of single companies, are often required to visit clients at their place of business.

Profile

Interests: Data, People
Working Conditions: Work Inside
Physical Strength: Light Work
Education Needs: Bachelor's Degree
Licensure/Certification: Usually Not Required
Physical Abilities Not Required: Not Climb, Not Kneel
Opportunities for Experience: Internship, Apprenticeship, Volunteer Work
Holland Interest Score*: ESA

* See Appendix A

Occupation Interest

Executive positions in advertising are almost exclusively given to those with at least five to seven years of lower-level experience in marketing and promotions. While specific undergraduate or postgraduate work can prepare students for the position, advertising professionals come from a variety of secondary and postsecondary programs related to marketing and promotions, from communications to graphic design and business management.

A Day in the Life—Duties and Responsibilities

The day-to-day responsibilities of an advertising director consist of monitoring project development, communicating with clients to ensure their continued satisfaction, and recruiting new clients through demonstrations of the firm's capabilities. Monitoring project development is a supervisory duty that entails ensuring all deadlines and timelines are being adhered to by the marketing staff. The ability to complete advertising campaigns in a timely and financially sound manner is a crucial responsibility of advertising directors.

While client representatives may handle the day-to-day interactions with clients, advertising directors also share the responsibility of representing their firm and its work, both to their clientele and to other members of the organization. Such interactions can often include developing appropriate social media messaging for a variety of platforms and communities, soliciting new business with an organization or an advertising firm's sales staff. In such settings, advertising directors must demonstrate how their firm has successfully handled major projects in the past both on time and on budget. This is done through effective interpersonal communication, portfolio presentations, and other visual demonstrations. Professionals with an outgoing personality and an interest in working daily with a variety of different people are often best suited for the networking and team-oriented nature of the position. People who prefer to work alone or in small groups may not be well suited for the large amount of collaboration necessary in the role.

Duties and Responsibilities

- Managing the staff that puts together an advertising package
- Making and maintaining many contacts with clients, freelancers and business people
- Overseeing the visual communication aspects of advertising, such as illustrations, art and photography
- Researching consumer buying trends and the possible market for a specific product
- Deciding which media avenue is best to use for the advertising package
- Developing catchy phrases or jingles and explaining the product and service verbally and in writing

WORK ENVIRONMENT

Immediate Physical Environment

Advertising directors generally work in professional and office settings. They are also often called to meetings off-site, in locations dictated by particular clients.

Transferable Skills and Abilities

Communication Skills
- Speaking effectively
- Writing concisely

Creative/Artistic Skills
- Being skilled in art, music or dance

Interpersonal/Social Skills
- Being able to remain calm
- Being flexible
- Being patient
- Cooperating with others
- Working as a member of a team

Organization & Management Skills
- Handling challenging situations
- Managing time
- Meeting goals and deadlines

Research & Planning Skills
- Solving problems

Human Environment

Strong collaborative and leadership skills are preferable. In addition to positively interacting with clients, advertising directors must also possess the capability to motivate large groups of team members working simultaneously on numerous projects with strict deadlines. Optimum candidates possess the deft public-speaking skills necessary for all positions of leadership.

Technological Environment

Applicable technologies range from telephone, e-mail, and web conferencing to computer software for design, finances, and communications.

EDUCATION, TRAINING, AND ADVANCEMENT

High School/Secondary

High-school students can best prepare for a career in advertising with courses in literature, English composition, foreign languages, dramatic arts, computers, and business management. Participation in student politics can equip students with basic leadership skills that can be utilized in future management positions. Beneficial skills such as communication, teamwork, and problem solving are often garnered through participation in scholastic sports and clubs such as debate, community service, and theatrical arts.

Unpaid or volunteer experience at a marketing or advertising firm can help students learn the entry-level responsibilities of the field and can potentially bolster college applications.

Suggested High School Subjects
- Algebra
- Applied Math
- Arts
- Audio-Visual
- Business
- Composition
- English
- Foreign Languages
- Geometry
- Graphic Communications
- Humanities
- Journalism
- Literature
- Mathematics
- Photography

Related Career Pathways/Majors
Business, Management & Administration Cluster
- Marketing Pathway

Hospitality & Tourism Cluster
- Lodging Pathway
- Travel & Tourism Pathway

Human Services Cluster
- Consumer Services Pathway

Marketing, Sales & Service Cluster
- E-Marketing Pathway
- Management & Entrepreneurship Pathway

Marketing, Sales & Service Cluster
- Marketing Information Management & Research Pathway

Famous First

"Operation Coffeecup" was part of a covert campaign, wherein women were encouraged to write personalized letters to their Senators and Congressmen to "speak out against socialized medicine." "Coffeecup" meets today's criteria for a "viral" marketing campaign: It was designed to appear spontaneous rather than organized and well-funded. It used word-of-mouth communication backed by prepackaged content. And that content was delivered using some of the finest media technology available at the time—full stereophonic sound!

Source: www.huffingtonpost.com

Postsecondary

Advertising directors traditionally have an undergraduate education in advertising itself or a related field, such as public relations, marketing, or graphic design. Undergraduate advertising majors supplement a traditional liberal-arts curriculum with a basic introduction to advertising, including course work in mass communications research, communication theory, new media design, persuasion, and communication law.

Professionals aspiring to careers in advertisement at the managerial level often seek a graduate degree in the field. Graduate studies in advertising allow students to explore an individual project related to a facet of advertising that interests them, in concert with advanced course work in media research, creative strategy development, and communications management. Several institutions offer doctoral-level programs in advertising, though doctorates are primarily sought after by communications researchers, educators, and media analysts, as opposed to professionals seeking a career in the field itself.

Related College Majors
- Advertising
- Business Marketing/Marketing Management
- Mass Communications

Adult Job Seekers

Advertising is a considerably competitive field that requires an intense amount of dedication, particularly in the early part of one's career. Those who achieve management-level positions have often worked tirelessly at developing both their frame of reference and their knowledge of contemporary advertising strategies. They have also embraced positions of leadership and project management throughout their career.

Professional Certification and Licensure

No specific certification is required.

Additional Requirements

Advertising professionals who ascend to managerial positions in the field are effective communicators and proactive problem solvers who can motivate large groups to tackle complex creative problems. Organization, professionalism, and amicability are highly sought-after traits for advertising executives, as is the ability to motivate in an encouraging and proactive manner.

EARNINGS AND ADVANCEMENT

In smaller firms, advancement occurs more slowly than at larger firms. Emphasis is placed on experience, ability, and leadership. Depending on the company, the rank above advertising director may be vice president of the company, executive director over several advertising directors, or president of the company. The median wage for advertising and promotions managers was $100,810 in May 2016. The lowest 10 percent earned less than $44,950, and the highest 10 percent earned more than $208,000.

The median annual wage for marketing managers was $131,180 in May 2016. The lowest 10 percent earned less than $67,490, and the highest 10 percent earned more than $208,000.

Advertising directors may receive paid vacations, holidays, and sick days; life and health insurance; and retirement benefits. These are usually paid by the employer.

EMPLOYMENT AND OUTLOOK

There were approximately 349,600 advertising directors employed nationally in 2016. Overall employment of advertising, promotions, and marketing managers is projected to grow 10 percent from 2016 to 2026, faster than the average for all occupations. Employment growth will vary by occupation.

Advertising, promotional, and marketing campaigns are expected to continue to be essential as organizations seek to maintain and expand their market share. Advertising and promotions managers will be needed to plan, direct, and coordinate advertising and promotional campaigns, as well as to introduce new products into the marketplace.

However, the newspaper publishing industry, which employs many of these workers, is projected to decline over the next 10 years. The continued rise of electronic media will result in decreasing demand for print newspapers. Despite this decline, advertising and promotions managers are expected to see employment growth in other industries in which they will be needed to manage digital media campaigns that often target customers through the use of websites, social media, or live chats.

Through the Internet, advertising campaigns can reach a target audience across many platforms. This greater reach can increase the scale of the campaigns that advertising and promotions managers oversee. With better advertising management software, advertising and promotions managers can control these campaigns more easily.

Related Occupations
- Advertising & Marketing Manager
- Advertising Sales Agent
- Art Director
- Copywriter
- Electronic Commerce Specialist
- Motion Picture/Radio/TV Art Director
- Online Merchant

Conversation With . . .
KIKI L'ITALIEN

CEO and Digital Strategist, Amplified Growth
Host and Podcaster, Association Chat
Alexandria, VA
Digital Marketing field, 13 years

1. What was your individual career path in terms of education/training, entry-level job, or other significant opportunity?

When I was in college, I thought I was going to be a print journalist. I was the editor the school paper at Missouri Southern State University and majored in Mass Communications. I was really fascinated with communicating a story, and I was curious. The advice I'd give to anyone today is, appreciate your curiosity and actively develop it. I've also always been drawn to performance and extemporaneous speaking, and that has helped me in social media and live-streaming.

My first job out of college was working in the marketing department of a local hospital group, then I got a marketing job with the Parenteral Drug Association in Bethesda, MD. I went onto MySpace to see if there was a way the local chapters could communicate across geographical barriers. I then went to work for the American Red Cross national headquarters, the Optical Society of America, and then for a consulting firm called DelCor Technology Solutions, which brought me on because they wanted to try some digital consulting strategies.

I first went out on my own in 2012, full of dreams—but no plan—when a client offered me the same money I was making in my full-time job. You don't think about what happens when that relationship sours, but it went south. I worked for a company called Actify for a year, then left when I had a plan to start my own consulting business. As new clients came in, I really began to appreciate my ability to learn about different aspects of the digital landscape—SEO, SEM, social media advertising, influencer marketing, user experience—and how social media feeds into all of it. My company specializes in social media for non-profits, although I have clients that run the gamut.

I can see the big picture. Some people think social media is all about figuring out how to trick the Facebook algorithm so you can have your live video shown to more people, but the bigger picture is: Why? And then, if somebody sees it, what's the call to action? How do you reverse-engineer so you know what kind of engagement you need so your next social media campaign is effective?

2. **What are the most important skills and/or qualities for someone in your profession?**

Being reliable doesn't sound sexy, but it is absolutely something that will get you hired. You also need to be constantly learning, and resilient.

3. **What do you wish you had known going into this profession?**

I wish I had taken business classes. I also wish I'd better understood project management, because providing the people you work with a sense of security—and the knowledge that you have a plan—lets them know they can rely on you.

4. **Are there many job opportunities in your profession? In what specific areas?**

There are a ton of jobs out there, although the job titles in digital marketing don't mean a whole lot since some titles pull together a number of disciplines. Creative technologists understand the way digital components fit together, but can write copy or are visually creative. If you're just looking for social media generalist jobs, you're cutting yourself short. There are a lot of different jobs if you can create content.

5. **How do you see your profession changing in the next five years, how do you see platforms evolving, and what skills will be required?**

Things have reached peak noise level. People are installing more ad blockers, and even social media people are on digital diets. Where things are headed, it's not enough to do video: you have to understand how to use augmented reality. You're also going to need to truly stand out. The Google algorithm is getting better at sniffing out where people are trying to trick the algorithm by loading up pages with keywords. All our machines are getting very, very good at figuring out what the noise is. It's no longer going to be OK to only turn out articles loaded with keywords. You need to be able to actually produce high-quality content.

6. **What do you enjoy most about your job? What do you enjoy least about your job?**

I most enjoy that I have an excuse to learn about a lot of different things and that I'm able to learn about different types of communities, how they act, and what they're interested in. What I don't like is connected to what I love: things change all the time.

7. **Can you suggest a valuable "try this" for students considering a career in your profession?**

Find a local charity or group you believe in and offer to do their social media for a month. You're going to learn whether you really want to do this or not. It could set your creativity on fire, or you could realize you'd rather do anything besides social media.

MORE INFORMATION

Advertising Research Foundation
432 Park Avenue South, 6th Floor
New York, NY 10016-8013
212.751.5656
thearf.org

Advertising Women of New York
25 West 45th Street, Suite 403
New York, NY 10036
212.221.7969
awny@awny.org
www.awny.org

American Academy of Advertising
831 Fearrington Post
Pittsboro, NC 27312
director@aaasite.org
www.aaasite.org

American Advertising Federation
1101 Vermont Avenue, NW
Suite 500
Washington, DC 20005-6306
800.999.2231
aaf@aaf.org
www.aaf.org

American Association of Advertising Agencies
1065 Avenue of the Americas
16th Floor
New York, NY 10018
212-682-2500
OBD@aaaa.org
www.aaaa.org

Association for Women in Communications
3337 Duke Street
Alexandria, VA 22314
703.370.7436
info@womcom.org
www.womcom.org

Association of National Advertisers
708 Third Avenue, 33rd Floor
New York, NY 10017
212.697.5950
info@ana.net
www.ana.net

John Pritchard/Editor

Advertising Sales Agent

Snapshot

Career Cluster(s): Business, Management & Administration, Marketing, Sales & Service

Interests: Marketing and sales, creating new media, working with clients, analyzing surveys and data

Earnings (2016 median pay): $50,380 per year; $24.22 per hour

Employment & Outlook: Slower than average

OVERVIEW

Sphere of Work

Advertising sales agents plan, develop, and create advertising campaigns for a variety of social media platforms as well as traditional print, television, and radio campaigns to promote client products or services. Their responsibilities include generating sales for and building relationships with current clients, as well as acquiring new clients. Advertising sales agents develop a full understanding of a client's products and services before they plan a campaign.

Campaigns cover a range of advertising types, from ads in print and on radio and television broadcasts to various applications on websites. Advertising sales agents are continually reviewing trends in advertising through consumer surveys and competitive analysis.

Work Environment

Advertising sales agents generally work in busy offices where there is a great deal of pressure to meet advertising campaign deadlines and monthly sales goals. Depending on the size of the agency, advertising sales agents may work independently or with a team; most agents do a combination of both. Although much of their time is spent in meetings, doing research, or making phone calls to current clients, they must also spend a significant amount of time away from the office visiting prospective clients. Advertising is a field that is sensitive to changes in the economy, and prosperous times tend to be extremely busy, requiring agents to work extra hours. Economic downturns, on the other hand, can cause companies to cut advertising budgets, resulting in layoffs at some advertising agencies.

Profile

Interests: Data, People
Working Conditions: Light Work
Physical Strength: Light Work
Education Needs: Bachelor's Degree
Licensure/Certification: Usually Not Required
Physical Abilities Not Required: Not Climb, Not Kneel
Opportunities for Experience: Internship, Apprenticeship, Part Time Work
Holland Interest Score*: ESA

* See Appendix A

Occupation Interest

Advertising sales agents help transform an idea to promote a product or service into a well-developed campaign that generates increased sales for a client. Those attracted to the advertising industry are usually energetic, curious, and creative individuals who understand how to generate persuasive messages. Advertising sales agents tend to be good communicators, both verbally and in writing, and enjoy interaction with a variety of people from a range of industries. They are fast learners and must understand clients' products and wishes before tailoring advertising to meet those needs. Advertising sales agents maintain current knowledge of popular culture and trends in order to understand which themes or images may resonate with consumers and affect spending habits. Using this skill, advertising sales agents can transform an unknown product into one that is widely recognized and purchased.

A Day in the Life—Duties and Responsibilities

Typical daily work tasks of an advertising sales agent revolve around developing a multidimensional media campaign that will generate sales of a client's products or services. Advertising sales agents familiarize themselves with client products and services, review advertising trends, and analyze information from consumer surveys. They present sample advertising work and submit budget estimates to clients for approval before beginning campaigns. Advertising sales agents work with creative teams to develop the strategic messages to be communicated in their campaigns. In addition, advertising sales agents interact with customers, company executives, and sales departments to put together promotional plans that will be transmitted through different media.

Advertising sales agents are also involved in the preparation and use of marketing and advertising brochures, pamphlets, text copy, and graphics for Internet campaigns, and website advertising formats. They evaluate an advertising campaign's success in direct relation to the amount of sales it has generated. Tracking these sales is an important part of an advertising sales agent's job, because the timing of increased sales may indicate that the advertising campaign was effective. Clients periodically re-evaluate their relationship with an advertising agency in terms of overall sales trends. To retain clients over long periods of time, an advertising sales agent must be attentive to short- and long-term sales trends.

When traveling to visit clients, advertising sales agents represent their company; however, they also make an effort to identify with the client's company or organization in order to understand what type of content will best represent the client to consumers. Advertising sales agents often travel to client locations to present campaign recommendations, meet with executives, and discuss the success or failure of previous advertising efforts. Advertising sales agents should be able to communicate to consumers what it is that their client does or sells in the form of persuasive promotional messages that attract attention and increase product or service sales. Often, the persuasive messages used in an advertising campaign are the result of communication between the client and the advertising firm. A client usually knows his or her product or service very well, while the advertising sales agent understands the language, imagery, and consumer behavior patterns that may be beneficial to sales of that particular product.

Duties and Responsibilities
• **Studying the products or services of the client**
• **Reviewing advertising trends and consumer surveys**
• **Organizing facts in order to plan the advertising campaign**
• **Consulting with customers**
• **Budgeting and submitting estimates of costs**
• **Preparing sales contracts**
• **Reviewing and proof-reading layout and copy before printing**
• **Preparing advertising brochures and manuals for publication**

OCCUPATION SPECIALTIES

Outdoor Advertising Leasing Agents

Outdoor Advertising Leasing Agents obtain leases to sites for outdoor advertising, and persuade property owners to lease sites in order to build billboard signs for use in outdoor advertising.

Radio and T.V. Time Sales Representatives

Radio and T.V. Time Sales Representatives contact prospective customers to sell radio and television time for advertising on broadcasting stations or networks.

Signs and Displays Sales Representatives

Signs and Displays Sales Representatives solicit and draw up contracts for signs and displays.

Sales-Promotion Representatives

Sales-Promotion Representatives persuade customers to use sales promotion display items of wholesale commodity distributors.

WORK ENVIRONMENT

Immediate Physical Environment

Advertising sales agents usually work in office environments that are pleasant and comfortable. Unlike many business offices, advertising offices may contain eclectic work rooms or areas meant to inspire creativity and innovative thought in work projects. Advertising sales agents work at computers and have a significant amount of variety in their daily tasks, as they are frequently networking with current and prospective clients or working with creative teams to help build campaigns.

Transferable Skills and Abilities

Communication Skills
- Persuading others
- Speaking effectively
- Writing concisely

Interpersonal/Social Skills
- Being able to work independently
- Cooperating with others
- Working as a member of a team

Organization & Management Skills
- Managing time
- Meeting goals and deadlines

Human Environment

The job of an advertising sales agent involves a great deal of interaction with others. Advertising sales agents work in busy environments where different members of an agency perform different tasks to meet a common goal, often on a tight deadline. Advertising sales agents generally work forty hours per week, but evening or weekend work is not unusual during busy periods. They may travel extensively to client locations both nationally and internationally.

Technological Environment

Advertising sales agents work with computers, the Internet, and word processing, graphic design, and spreadsheet software. They must familiarize themselves with clients' products as needed, which often involves using a new product on a daily basis for a short period of time to evaluate its features.

EDUCATION, TRAINING, AND ADVANCEMENT

High School/Secondary

High school students interested in becoming an advertising sales agent may find it useful to study art, business, communications, English, foreign languages, and applied math. It is beneficial for interested students to take summer jobs with advertising agencies and work on high school publications such as the yearbook and newspaper. Participation in extracurricular organizations geared towards marketing or advertising will give students some familiarity with business situations and formulating marketing solutions.

Suggested High School Subjects
- Applied Math
- Arts
- Business
- College Preparatory
- Composition
- English
- Graphic Communications
- Journalism
- Mathematics
- Merchandising
- Psychology
- Social Studies
- Speech

Related Career Pathways/Majors

Business, Management & Administration Cluster
- Marketing Pathway

Marketing, Sales & Service Cluster
- E-Marketing Pathway
- Marketing Communication & Promotion Pathway
- Professional Sales & Marketing Pathway

Famous First

Before there were social networks or banner ads, there was email advertisement. Gary Thuerk, also known as the father of spam, was a marketing manager at the Digital Equipment Corporation. Although DEC had a strong presence in the East Coast, considering the fact that it was an Massachusetts-based corporation, the email, sent to 400 recipients drawn from the ARPANET directory, was an invitation to West Coast users to a product demonstration of the then-new Decsystem-20 by Digital.

Source: www.adpushup.com

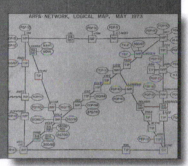

Postsecondary

Postsecondary students interested in pursuing a career as an advertising sales agent will benefit from building a foundation in communications and marketing courses. Other classes should include journalism, advertising, print layout, graphic design, new media, market research, economics, psychology, marketing communications, and advertising history, theory, and ethics. Postsecondary students can gain practical experience through internships at advertising agencies or with any company that has a marketing department or advertises. Entry-level opportunities in advertising or marketing departments give students hands-on experience that can help them learn new skills and make them attractive to future employers.

Related College Majors
- Advertising
- Business & Personal Services Marketing Operations
- Communications, General
- Mass Communications
- Public Relations & Organizational Communications

Adult Job Seekers

Adults interested in working as advertising sales agents can look for entry-level, part-time, or seasonal jobs in the advertising, marketing, or sales fields. It may also be useful to obtain practical experience through a specialized education, volunteer experience, internships, or mentors in professional advertising organizations who can provide guidance about existing career opportunities.

Professional Certification and Licensure

There are no licensing requirements for advertising sales agents. Prominent industry organizations give annual awards to recognize highly successful agency campaigns.

Additional Requirements

Prospective advertising sales agents should have excellent interpersonal skills and be able to work independently and cooperate with others in a team environment. They must be able to influence others, use their knowledge of consumer behavior to influence buying habits, sell their ideas to current and prospective clients, and communicate clearly. Creativity and the desire to stay informed about trends in popular culture are all assets in this occupation.

Fun Fact

Just try to avoid social media while shopping: 91 percent of retail brands use 2 or more social media channels.

Source: Brandwatch.com

EARNINGS AND ADVANCEMENT

Earnings depend on the size and geographic location of the advertising agency, type of accounts handled and gross earnings of the agency. Earnings are also based on the employee's educational background, talent, and experience. The median annual wage for advertising sales agents was $50,380 in May 2016. The lowest 10 percent earned less than $24,320, and the highest 10 percent earned more than $115,430.

Performance-based pay, including bonuses and commissions, can make up a large portion of an advertising sales agent's earnings. Most employers pay some combination of salaries, commissions, and bonuses. Commissions usually are based on individual sales numbers. Bonuses may depend on individual performance, the performance of all sales workers in a group, or the performance of the entire firm.

Advertising sales agents may receive paid vacations, holidays, and sick days; life and health insurance; and retirement benefits. These are usually paid by the employer.

EMPLOYMENT AND OUTLOOK

There were about 149,900 advertising sales agents employed nationally in 2019. Employment of advertising sales agents is projected to decline 4 percent from 2016 to 2026.

Media companies will continue to rely on advertising revenue for profitability. However, employment of advertising sales agents will largely follow broader industry trends, and several of the industries that employ large numbers of these workers are projected to decline. For example, employment in newspaper publishers is expected to decline, although some of this decline may be offset by the sale of digital ads on newspaper websites.

An increasing amount of advertising is expected to be concentrated in digital media, including online video ads, search engine ads, and other digital ads intended for cell phones or tablet-style computers. Digital advertising on the Internet allows companies to directly target potential consumers because websites usually are associated with the types of products that those consumers would like to buy. As a result, employment of advertising sales agents is likely to increase in Internet-focused companies.

Related Occupations
- Advertising & Marketing Manager
- Advertising Director
- Copywriter
- Online Merchant
- Public Relations Specialist
- Real Estate Sales Agent
- Services Sales Representative

MORE INFORMATION

Advertising Age
711 3rd Avenue
New York, NY 10017-4036
212.210.0100
www.adage.com

**Advertising Research
Foundation**
432 Park Avenue South, 6th Floor
New York, NY 10016-8013
212.751.5656
thearf.org

Advertising Women of New York
25 West 45th Street, Suite 403
New York, NY 10036
212.221.7969
awny@awny.org
www.awny.org

**American Advertising
Federation**
1101 Vermont Avenue, NW
Suite 500
Washington, DC 20005-6306
800.999.2231
aaf@aaf.org
www.aaf.org

**American Association of
Advertising Agencies**
405 Lexington Avenue, 18th Floor
New York, NY 10174-1801
212.682.2500
OBD@aaaa.org
www.aaaa.org

**Association for Women in
Communications**
3337 Duke Street
Alexandria, VA 22314
703.370.7436
btijerina@womcom.org
www.womcom.org

**Association of National
Advertisers**
708 Third Avenue, 33rd Floor
New York, NY 10017-4270
212.697.5950
info@ana.net
www.ana.net

**Retail Advertising and
Marketing Association**
325 7th Street NW, Suite 1100
Washington, DC 20004
202.661.3052
www.rama-nrf.org

Susan Williams/Editor

Art Director

Snapshot

Career Cluster(s): Arts, A/V Technology & Communications, Business, Management & Administration

Interests: Advertising trends, art, problem-solving, communicating with others

Earnings (2016 median pay): $89,820

Employment & Outlook: Slower Than Average Growth Expected

OVERVIEW

Sphere of Work

Art directors work in a variety of industries, including advertising, theatre, film, video games, and publishing. While these fields involve different media, the essential task of an art director is the same: an art director oversees the aesthetic direction of a project from its conception to completion. The art director typically does not play an active role in the creation of the various elements of a project, rather he or she works closely with artists and writers to reach a shared goal.

Work Environment

Depending on the industry and the size of the project, an art director can expect to work with varying numbers of artists and writers on a particular project. No matter what the industry, the art director has executive control of the work. All artistic decisions must be made with the art director's consent and approval before being made public. In a large advertising firm, an art director may report to an executive creative director. Art directors usually work during standard business hours. Long hours may be required to meet deadlines.

Profile

Interests: Data, People, Things
Working Conditions: Work Inside
Physical Strength: Light Work
Education Needs: Bachelor's Degree
Licensure/Certification: Usually Not Required
Physical Abilities Not Required: Not Climb, Not Kneel
Opportunities for Experience: Internship, Part Time Work
Holland Interest Score*: AES

* See Appendix A

Occupation Interest

Working as an art director appeals to individuals with creative vision who are able to articulate and carry out that vision in an effective manner. Those drawn to this occupation have a firm grasp of the history of their media, are aware of cultural trends, and have creative minds. They can imagine the final product, whether it's an advertising campaign, a book, a magazine, or a film, and can coordinate the various tasks and elements involved in the creative process. Art directors have strong people skills and work with a team to realize an idea. Those with an undergraduate degree in advertising, art history, or graphic design, or previous experience as a visual artist, actor, or filmmaker would be well suited to the field. Successful art directors should be problem solvers, have strong communication skills, and must be well organized.

A Day in the Life—Duties and Responsibilities

An art director's daily duties vary by industry. Art directors commonly work for film, advertising, and publishing companies.

In large film productions, an art director meets with the prop master and costume and set designers to develop the overall "look" of a movie. He or she reports to the film's production director. The art director is often responsible for scheduling and hiring individuals working in construction, sound, and special effects and ensuring that the set construction and location are ready for filming. The art director also often manages a portion of a film's budget. Art directors for smaller productions may be required to take on more responsibilities and tasks.

In an advertising agency, an art director collaborates with one or more artists, such as graphic designers, illustrators and animators, and copywriters to develop the overall concept for a project. The art director organizes face-to-face or virtual meetings to discuss the relationship between the textual and visual components of an advertisement and any related promotional material. Suggestions may be made from one department to another, with copywriters and artists exchanging ideas about visual and textual aspects of the advertising campaign. During these conversations, the art director acts as facilitator and executive decision maker. Once aesthetic decisions have been made, the art director may supervise the work itself.

An art director working in publishing performs a similar job function to that of an advertising art director. He or she works closely with writers, editors, and designers to establish an aesthetic approach for the layout of a book or magazine. The art director typically has the final say on matters such as the typeface of a book, the visual details of the book interior, and the jacket design that best fits the work.

Duties and Responsibilities

- Working with copywriters, assistants, artists, illustrators, cartoonists, and designers
- Performing duties as graphic designer, illustrator, or artist
- Reviewing portfolios of photographers, illustrators, artists, directors, and producers

WORK ENVIRONMENT

Immediate Physical Environment

Art directors working in advertising or publishing usually work in an office setting. Those working in theatre or film work predominately in offices, but also spend time on the set.

Human Environment

While art directors do not usually hold the top position in any industry, they have considerable control over their specific projects, acting in a guiding, executive role with the various artists, assistants, and writers they supervise.

Transferable Skills and Abilities

Creative/Artistic Skills
- Being skilled in art, music or dance

Organization & Management Skills
- Coordinating tasks
- Managing people/groups

Research & Planning Skills
- Creating ideas

Technological Environment

Art directors interact with clients and colleagues using email, phone, video conferencing, and face-to-face meetings. Computers play a large role in their daily activities. Art directors should have familiarity with graphic and photo-imaging software, as they may make adjustments to a project or need to demonstrate a compositional idea. (Art directors in the film industry may be familiar with even more sophisticated graphic technologies depending on their field.) Experience with web design and computer code can also be valuable as more companies are involved in a broad array of online outreach, including social media, live streaming media, and podcasts.

EDUCATION, TRAINING, AND ADVANCEMENT

High School/Secondary

Students aspiring to become an art director should pursue a rigorous college preparatory program, with an emphasis on coursework in the arts, such as theatre, media arts, computers, drafting, art history, visual art, and English. Students particularly interested in the financial and administrative aspects of art direction may also find advanced courses in economics helpful.

Interested students should research and apply to postsecondary schools that offer a relevant major. Some professional organizations provide career workshops for high school students, as well as scholarships for postsecondary studies in art direction.

Suggested High School Subjects
- Arts
- Audio-Visual
- Business
- Drafting
- English
- Graphic Communications
- Humanities
- Journalism
- Literature
- Mathematics
- Mechanical Drawing
- Photography
- Psychology
- Speech

Related Career Pathways/Majors
Arts, A/V Technology & Communications Cluster
- Visual Arts Pathway

Business, Management & Administration Cluster
- Marketing Pathway

Famous First

Since 2008, The Shorty Awards have honored the best of social media by recognizing the influencers, brands and organizations on Facebook, Twitter, YouTube, Instagram, Snapchat, Musically and more. Past winners include Taylor Swift, Tyler Oakley, Casey Neistat, Hannibal Buress, Malala Yousafzai, Jenna Marbles, J.K. Rowling, Adele, and DJ Khaled. Winners are chosen through a combination of votes from the public and scores given by the Real Time Academy. Source: www.shortyawards.com

Postsecondary

At the university level, students should consider a major in visual art, film studies, art history, English, theatre, art administration, or advertising, depending on their industry of interest. An aspiring art director should major in art administration or pursue summer internships in an industry relevant to their interests.

Some schools are beginning to offer coursework in art direction within their art and/or business departments. Such coursework exposes students to the financial and administrative tasks of art direction. Alternatively, a growing number of institutions offer degrees in art administration.

Related College Majors
• Graphic Design, Commercial Art & Illustration

Adult Job Seekers

Art direction is a highly competitive field; most employers hire those with experience in the industry. Entry-level positions that may lead to a career in art direction are often unpaid or low paying. Young adults may opt for internships to make connections in a particular industry. Artists may easily enter the field and advance to an art director position.

Professional organizations dedicated to art direction, including The Art Director's Guild (ADG) and The Art Director's Club (ADC), offer grants, awards, and networking opportunities. The Art Director's Club maintains a job board of available positions in the United States.

Professional Certification and Licensure

No certifications or licenses are needed to become an art director.

Additional Requirements

Due to the competitive nature of the field, most art directors are extremely motivated, hardworking, efficient, organized, and creative individuals. Successful art directors are excellent communicators and comfortable working collaboratively. Working well under pressure can be a deciding factor for future success, as art directors commonly serve a central role on film productions or advertising campaigns where large financial investments are made. The relative success or failure of a project is often attributed to the art director's work.

EARNINGS AND ADVANCEMENT

The path of advancement most often is receiving a similar job in a larger, more prestigious corporation, agency, or organization. This usually results in increased responsibilities and earnings.

The median annual wage for art directors was $89,820 in May 2016. The lowest 10 percent earned less than $48,660, and the highest 10 percent earned more than $166,400.

Art directors may receive paid vacations, holidays, and sick days; life and health insurance; and retirement benefits. These are usually paid by the employer.

EMPLOYMENT AND OUTLOOK

Art directors held about 90,300 jobs nationally in 2016. Employment of art directors is projected to grow 5 percent from 2016 to 2026, about as fast as the average for all occupations. Art directors will continue to be needed to oversee the work of graphic designers, illustrators, photographers, and others engaged in artwork or layout design.

Employment of art directors is projected to decline in the publishing industry from 2016 to 2026 as traditional print publications lose ground to other media forms. Rather than focusing on the print layout of images and text, art directors for newspapers and magazines will increasingly design for web and mobile platforms.

Employment opportunities may be found in areas such as advertising and public relations agencies, specialized design services, direct marketing agencies, motion picture and video industries, and publishers. Art directors should expect strong competition for available openings.

Related Occupations
- Advertising Director
- Graphic Designer
- Medical & Scientific Illustrator
- Motion Picture/Radio/TV Art Director
- Multimedia Artist & Animator
- Photographer

MORE INFORMATION

The Advertising Club
235 Park Avenue S., 6th Floor
New York, NY 10003-1450
212-533-8080
Fax: 212-533-1929
www.theadvertisingclub.org

The Student Competition and Glenn C.
Smith Scholarship:
www.theadvertisingclub.org/scholarships

Art Directors Club, Inc.
106 West 29th Street
New York, NY 10001
212.643.1440
info@adcglobal.org
www.adcglobal.org

Art Directors Club Awards
www.adcglobal.org/awards

Art Directors Guild
Headquarters Office
11969 Ventura Boulevard, 2nd Floor
Studio City, CA 91604
818.762.9995
www.adg.org

Richard Stiles Scholarship:
www.adg.org/?art=scholarship

**Association for Women in
Communications (AWC)**
National Headquarters
3337 Duke Street
Alexandria, VA 22314
703.370.7436
info@womcom.org
www.womcom.org

Mark Boccard/Editor

Broadcast Technician

Snapshot

Career Cluster(s): Arts, A/V Technology & Communications, Manufacturing, Science, Technology, Engineering & Mathematics

Interests: Broadcast media and technology, audio/visual techniques, film production

Earnings (2016 median pay): $45,550 per year; $20.46 per hour

Employment & Outlook: As fast as average

OVERVIEW

Sphere of Work

Broadcast technicians are responsible for the maintenance and operation of audio or audiovisual equipment that used to create and transmit programming and social media content to viewers and community members. They may control audio equipment, regulating the sound quality and volume level, or monitor the fidelity, brightness, and other visual elements of a video broadcast. As the broadcast environment moves away from traditional television and radio services to on-demand or streaming services, broadcast technicians will need to master the skills necessary to deliver high quality media over unmanaged

IP networks, manage software-defined workflows, accomplish virtualization of content, and employ DC/Cloud technologies within Federal Communications Commission (FCC) regulations. Broadcast technicians at large stations tend to specialize in specific operations, while technicians at smaller stations oversee a number of responsibilities.

Work Environment

Broadcast technicians generally work in media companies of all sorts, as well as traditional radio and television stations. When shows and programs are taped or broadcast from off-site locations, technicians may travel to these locations. They may be required to engage in physical activity during the course of their jobs. Broadcast technicians generally work forty-hour weeks, but since media outlets of all sorts remain on the air during nights, weekends, and holidays, technicians may work erratic shifts.

Profile

Interests: Data, Things
Working Conditions: Work Inside, Work Both Inside and Outside
Physical Strength: Light Work
Education Needs: Junior/Technical/Community College, Bachelor's Degree
Licensure/Certification: Recommended
Physical Abilities Not Required: Not Climb, Not Kneel
Opportunities for Experience: Apprenticeship, Military Service, Volunteer Work, Part Time Work
Holland Interest Score*: RCE

* See Appendix A

Occupation Interest

Broadcast technicians play an integral role in ensuring that broadcasts, whether through social media or traditional outlets such as television or radio, are transmitted properly, making their work a fulfilling career for individuals who thrive in a complex and fast-paced technological environment. The broad range of equipment used in broadcasting includes recording equipment for audio and video, encoding equipment, computers, lights, and transmitters. Broadcast technicians must be able to use a variety of software applications and adapt their work to the needs of various social media platforms.

A Day in the Life—Duties and Responsibilities

Broadcast technicians coordinate with station managers, producers, and directors to ensure that audiovisual systems operate properly during taping and broadcasting. To this end, they monitor the strength and clarity of outgoing and incoming signals, regulate sound and visual effects using sound boards and video monitors, and report any equipment failures or issues. Broadcast technicians repair or disconnect faulty or outdated hardware and install new equipment as needed. Furthermore, they are frequently responsible for maintaining detailed programming logs in accordance with the established policies of the station and the FCC.

In the case of large companies, the work of broadcast technicians is dependent on the specialized field in which they work. For example, lighting technicians spend most of their time ensuring that lights are positioned properly, while transmitter technicians work primarily at the location of the station's transmitter, often in a different building from the main studio. Audio control technicians, meanwhile, work in master control booths and specialize in operating the complex computer-based sound systems used in modern radio and television stations.

In contrast, smaller companies frequently have few or no specialized technicians. Consequently, broadcast technicians working in these environments are often generalists, responsible for lights, sound, transmitters, and all other aspects of the station's technical systems.

Duties and Responsibilities

- Operating equipment that regulates the quality of sound and pictures being recorded or broadcast
- Operating controls that switch broadcasts from one camera or studio to another, from film to live programming or from network to local programs
- Setting up, testing, and operating broadcasting equipment at different locations
- Dismantling and returning equipment to the studio

OCCUPATION SPECIALTIES

Video Operators

Video Operators control video consoles to regulate the transmission of television screens and control the quality, brightness, and contrast of the video output.

Audio Operators

Audio Operators control audio equipment to regulate volume level and sound quality during television broadcasts.

Field Engineers

Field Engineers install and operate portable field transmission equipment to broadcast programs or events originating outside the studio.

Transmitter Operators

Transmitter Operators are responsible for monitoring and logging outgoing signals and for operating the transmitter.

Plant and Maintenance Technicians

Plant and Maintenance Technicians repair, adjust, set up, and service electronic broadcasting equipment. It is their job to determine the cause of signal breakdown and repair it.

Recording Engineers

Recording Engineers operate and maintain video and sound recording equipment. They operate the disk or recording machine to record music, dialogue, or sound effects during recording sessions, radio and television broadcasts or conferences.

WORK ENVIRONMENT

Immediate Physical Environment

Broadcast technicians primarily work in television and radio stations. However, they often work outdoors, either with on-site shooting crews or on outdoor equipment, such as transmitters, located away from the station. Broadcast technicians face some danger of electrocution or other injury when working with high voltages and equipment that is difficult to access.

Transferable Skills and Abilities

Communication Skills
- Speaking effectively
- Writing concisely

Interpersonal/Social Skills
- Working as a member of a team

Organization & Management Skills
- Following instructions
- Paying attention to and handling details

Technical Skills
- Applying the technology to a task
- Performing scientific, mathematical and technical work
- Working with machines, tools or other objects

Human Environment

Depending on their area of work, broadcast technicians may interact with directors, producers, camera and microphone operators, set construction crews, electricians, or on-air personalities. In addition, they may work closely with broadcast technicians specializing in particular tasks.

Technological Environment

The equipment used by broadcast technicians varies based on their responsibilities or specialty and may include sound mixers, cameras, lighting systems and towers, boom microphones, transmitter equipment, master control switchers, oscilloscopes, satellite receivers, and video editors. Technicians may also use video creation, graphic and photo imaging, and office suite computer software.

EDUCATION, TRAINING, AND ADVANCEMENT

High School/Secondary

High school students interested in becoming broadcast technicians should take industrial arts courses related to radio and television repair and electronics. Courses in geometry, trigonometry, and algebra are also highly useful for aspiring technicians. Participation in the school's audiovisual department, as well as theater and other extracurricular activities focused on lighting or sound, is strongly encouraged.

Suggested High School Subjects
- Algebra
- Applied Communication
- Applied Math
- Applied Physics
- College Preparatory
- Electricity & Electronics
- English
- Geometry
- Physics
- Radio & TV Repair
- Theatre & Drama
- Trigonometry

Related Career Pathways/Majors
Arts, A/V Technology & Communications Cluster
- Journalism & Broadcasting Pathway

Manufacturing Cluster
- Maintenance, Installation & Repair Pathway
- Manufacturing Production Process Development Pathway

Science, Technology, Engineering & Mathematics Cluster
- Engineering & Technology Pathway
- Science & Mathematics Pathway

Famous First

The first telecast of a moving object took place in 1925 from a radio station in Washington, DC. It showed a windmill turning. The technology used was called "vision-by-radio." Two years later the first telecast of an image accompanied by sound occurred. It showed Herbert Hoover, then Secretary of Commerce, reading a speech. The picture screen at the receiving end was 2 by 3 inches, a little smaller than those on today's smart phones.
Source: www.earlytelevision.org/

Postsecondary

Following high school, aspiring broadcast technicians frequently complete a technical training program at a vocational school or similar institution. A growing number of broadcast technicians hold associate's or bachelor's degrees, which give those candidates an edge in this highly competitive field and opens up possibilities for career advancement. Some senior-level technicians even hold advanced degrees in engineering.

Related College Majors
- Broadcast Journalism
- Radio & Television Broadcasting
- Radio & Television Broadcasting Technology

Adult Job Seekers

Experienced broadcast technicians are encouraged to apply directly to open positions, while candidates who are new to the field can gain hands-on experience in a variety of areas through internships or entry-level jobs at smaller stations. Unions and trade associations, such as the National Association of Broadcast Employees and Technicians (NABET) and the National Association of Broadcasters (NAB), offer training, resources, and valuable networking opportunities.

Professional Certification and Licensure

No certification is required in order to become a broadcast technician. However, technicians may choose to become certified by the Society of Broadcast Engineers (SBE). As with any voluntary certification process, it is beneficial to consult credible professional associations within the field and follow professional debate as to the relevancy and value of any certification program.

Additional Requirements

Broadcast technicians must have strong mechanical skills, with an ability to quickly analyze often-complex electronic systems and equipment. They must demonstrate both dexterity and monitoring skills, which help identify and correct mechanical issues while under strict time constraints. Some broadcast technicians may be required to lift heavy equipment or climb high structures when necessary, so a degree of physical fitness is helpful.

EARNINGS AND ADVANCEMENT

Earnings of broadcast technicians can vary greatly depending on the size and geographic location of the city or town. Television stations usually pay better than radio stations; commercial broadcasting usually pays more than educational broadcasting; and stations in large markets pay more than those in small ones.

The median annual wage for broadcast and sound engineering technicians was $42,550 in May 2016. The lowest 10 percent earned less than $22,040, and the highest 10 percent earned more than $84,520.

Broadcast technicians may receive paid vacations, holidays, and sick days; life and health insurance; and retirement benefits. These are usually paid by the employer.

EMPLOYMENT AND OUTLOOK

There were approximately 134,300 broadcast technicians employed nationally in 2016. Overall employment of broadcast and sound engineering technicians is projected to grow 8 percent from 2016 to 2026, about as fast as the average for all occupations.

Employment of audio and visual equipment technicians is projected to grow 13 percent from 2016 to 2026, faster than the average for all occupations. More audio and video technicians should be needed to set up new equipment or upgrade and maintain old, complex systems for a variety of organizations.

More companies are increasing their audio and video budgets so they can use video conferencing to reduce travel costs and communicate worldwide with other offices and clients. In addition, an increase in the use of digital signs across a wide variety of industries, such as schools, hospitals, restaurants, hotels, and retail stores should lead to higher demand for audio and video equipment technicians.

Schools and universities are also seeking to improve their audio and video capabilities in order to attract and keep the best students. More audio and visual technicians may be needed to install and maintain interactive whiteboards and wireless projectors so teachers can give multimedia presentations and record lectures.

Employment of broadcast technicians is projected to decline 3 percent from 2016 to 2026. More consumers may choose free over-the-air television programming instead of cable or satellite services, in a practice commonly referred to as "cord-cutting." This may contribute to stronger demand for broadcast television. However, most major networks use a single facility to broadcast to multiple stations, which limits the growth potential for broadcast technicians.

Employment of sound engineering technicians is projected to grow 6 percent from 2016 to 2026, about as fast as the average for all occupations. The television and motion picture industry will continue to need technicians to improve the sound quality of shows and movies.

Related Occupations

- Computer Network Architect
- Computer Support Specialist
- Electrical & Electronics Engineer
- Electronic Engineering Technician
- Motion Picture Projectionist
- Radio Operator

Related Military Occupations

- Audiovisual & Broadcast Technician

Conversation With . . .
ALEX LAUGHLIN

Audio Producer, BuzzFeed News
New York
Podcast producer, 4 years

1. What was your individual career path in terms of education/training, entry-level job, or other significant opportunity?

I graduated from the University of Georgia with a bachelor's degree in women's studies, a minor in English, and an interdisciplinary writing certificate. Even though I didn't major in journalism, I knew I wanted to be a journalist after I graduated, so I was super involved with my student newspaper. I started my freshman year as a general reporter and worked my way into editor roles.

After my freshman year ended, I made a rule for myself: every semester, I would either have an internship, an editor role on the paper, or a leadership role in a student organization. By the time I graduated, I had a nice, full resume, and a wealth of different experiences to inform my post-grad decisions!

Immediately after graduating, I got a job doing social media for a small political magazine in Washington, D.C. I also started producing podcasts while I was there. After about a year, I moved to The Washington Post, where I was a social media editor throughout the 2016 election. Outside of work, I had begun producing a podcast independently to learn more about audio production.

The Post was a super busy and intense job, so once the election was over, I was ready to make a change. In 2017, I moved to BuzzFeed News to produce audio full time.

2. What are the most important skills and/or qualities for someone in your profession?

As a producer, it's hugely important that you learn to anticipate people's needs. At its core, my job is about supporting a team effort to tell a story, so a producer needs to be able to read a situation and identify what they need to do to make it better. Sometimes, that means making a cup of tea for a guest so it's hot and ready when they get to the studio. Sometimes it means ordering food for 12 people the night of a live show so everyone gets a chance to eat before it's time to perform. And sometimes it means reading a whole book before an interview so you can write some really insightful questions!

3. What do you wish you had known going into this profession?

I wish I'd known that even the Greats had a first day on the job. The only way you become one of them is by showing up that first day, and continuing to show up every day after.

4. Are there many job opportunities in your profession? In what specific areas?

Yes! There's so much interest from businesses that want to cash in on the podcast boom. If you're a smart, enterprising audio producer who is willing to work hard, smart, and quickly, then you will have no trouble finding a job.

5. How do you see your profession changing in the next five years? How do you envision platforms evolving? What skills will be required?

I think that smart speaker technology, such as in Google Home and Amazon Echo, will play a much bigger role in how people discover audio content. You won't have to open your smartphone and dig around the podcasts app to find new shows — they'll come right to you.

I also really hope that the industry continues to change and push the boundaries of what podcasts can be. I would love to see more podcasts that are like reality shows, as well as more audio dramas.

6. What do you enjoy most about your job? What do you enjoy least about your job?

I love telling stories that are consumed in such an intimate way. When you listen to a podcast that you really love, you feel like you actually know the hosts. That's so magical! I also love being able to uplift communities' voices that don't traditionally get celebrated in the media. That's a lot of responsibility but it's so important.

7. Can you suggest a valuable "try this" for students considering a career in your profession?

Try recording something yourself. Most smartphones have audio recorders built into them. Next time you go to an exciting event like a birthday party or a parade, try recording some of the sounds (we call it "scene tape"). You'll be surprised at what you start to notice once you're recording! When you're back home and in a quiet place, write out a reflection about the event, and record yourself speaking into the microphone. Bonus points: Upload the audio to your computer and try editing it all together with free software like GarageBand or Audacity.

MORE INFORMATION

Alliance for Women in Media
1760 Old Meadow Road, Suite 500
McLean, VA 22102
703.506.3290
www.allwomeninmedia.org

Broadcast Education Association
1771 N Street, NW
Washington, DC 20036-2891
888.380.7222
beainfo@beaweb.org
www.beaweb.org

**Federal Communications
Commission**
445 12th Street, NW
Washington, DC 20554
888.225.5322
fccinfo@fcc.gov
www.fcc.gov

**International Brotherhood of
Electrical Workers**
900 Seventh Street, NW
Washington, DC 20001
202.833.7000
www.ibew.org

**National Association of
Broadcast Employees and
Technicians**
501 3rd Street, NW
Washington, DC 20001
202.434.1254
mtiglio@cwa-union.org
www.nabetcwa.org

**National Association of
Broadcasters**
1771 N Street NW
Washington, DC 20036
202.429.5300
www.nab.org

**National Cable Television
Association**
Careers in Cable
1724 Massachusetts Avenue, NW
Washington, DC 20036
202.222.2300
webmaster@ncta.com
www.ncta.com

Society of Broadcast Engineers
9102 North Meridian Street
Suite 150
Indianapolis, IN 46260
317.846.9000
www.sbe.org

Michael Auerbach/Editor

Computer & Information Systems Manager

Snapshot

Career Cluster(s): Business, Management & Administration, Information Technology, Science, Technology, Engineering & Mathematics

Interests: Computer systems, analyzing data, solving problems, communicating with others

Earnings (2016 median pay): $135,800 per year; $65.29 per hour

Employment & Outlook: Faster than average

OVERVIEW

Sphere of Work

Computer and information systems managers, also known as information technology (IT) managers, are responsible for organizing, directing, and coordinating operations in a variety of computer-related fields, such as electronic data processing, network security, and systems analysis. They help to establish the IT goals of a company and are in charge of implementing computer systems to successfully meet these goals. IT managers

consult with technology users, vendors, and technicians to help assess a company's IT needs and system requirements that relate to various social media platforms, analytic software, and content management systems.

Work Environment

Computer and information systems managers typically work within an office environment. A majority of managers work directly for computer-systems design and IT services firms. Other managers work for communications companies, financial firms, manufacturing firms, or government offices on a federal, state, or local level. As communications technologies improve, it is not uncommon for computer and information systems managers to telecommute. Most managers work full time during the week. Some overtime may be required.

Profile

Interests: Data, People, Things
Working Conditions: Work Inside
Physical Strength: Light Work
Education Needs: Bachelor's Degree, Master's Degree
Licensure/Certification: Recommended
Physical Abilities Not Required: Not Climb, Not Kneel
Opportunities for Experience: Military Service, Volunteer Work, Part Time Work
Holland Interest Score*: ECI

* See Appendix A

Occupation Interest

The computer and information systems profession normally appeals to people who have strong analytical and problem-solving skills and a solid background in computer systems. New innovations in computer systems mean that an IT manager must stay on top of the latest technologies in order to remain competitive. The profession tends to attract people who enjoy collaborating with others to solve problems. Most managers enter the profession with a computer-science or business degree, but many others come from diverse career backgrounds.

A Day in the Life—Duties and Responsibilities

Computer and information systems managers apply their knowledge and problem-solving skills to improve the computer systems of an organization. This work has become increasingly important as companies expand their online reach to work with business partners and customers across a variety of media and platforms. They must be able to collaborate with employees and others in the IT field. The workday of a computer and information systems manager can vary, depending on the organization's specific field. Meetings with other managers, technology vendors, and IT personnel are common.

Throughout the day, a manager helps plan, organize, and direct the installation and upgrading of the organization's computer hardware and software. They work with others in IT to make sure the organization's network and electronic data are secure. Part of their daily routine usually entails assigning and reviewing the work of others in IT, including systems analysts and programmers. Before a new or modified computer system or program is implemented, a manager must review and approve it. During all of these activities, managers adhere to their organization's operational budget; in order to maintain this budget, they need to negotiate with technology vendors.

It is rare for one manager to perform all of these duties. Most managers have a specialty position and work in a specific IT team of an organization. For example, a chief technology officer (CTO) will assess new technologies and determine if they will be a benefit to an organization, while a chief information officer (CIO) is in charge of directing the organization's overall technology strategy. If an organization does not have a CIO, then the CTO typically handles those responsibilities.

Duties and Responsibilities

- Managing all organizational computing systems
- Meeting with management team, department heads and vendors to jointly cooperate and solve problems
- Consulting with management and other organization members to determine computing needs
- Reviewing and coordinating project schedule
- Providing organization members with technical support
- Developing information resources that deal with issues in data security and disaster recovery
- Creating and understanding organization goals and procedures
- Training and supervising technical staff
- Staying up to date with the latest technology

OCCUPATION SPECIALTIES

Chief Technology Officers

Chief Technology Officers evaluate the newest and most innovative technologies and determine how these can help their organization.

Information Technology Directors

Information Technology Directors manage the computer resources for their organization.

Project Managers

Project Managers develop requirements, budgets, and schedules for their organization's information technology projects.

WORK ENVIRONMENT

Transferable Skills and Abilities

Research & Planning Skills
- Identifying problems
- Solving problems

Technical Skills
- Performing scientific, mathematical and technical work
- Using technology to process information
- Understanding which technology is appropriate for a task
- Applying the technology to a task
- Maintaining and repairing technology
- Working with machines, tools or other objects

Immediate Physical Environment

Computer and information systems managers spend the majority of their workday in well-lit office environments. The specifics of the environment vary depending on the organization that employs them.

Human Environment

Collaboration and communication are essential to the job of a computer and information systems

Communication Skills
- Speaking effectively
- Writing concisely
- Listening attentively
- Reading well

Interpersonal/Social Skills
- Motivating others
- Cooperating with others
- Asserting oneself
- Being able to work independently

Organization & Management Skills
- Paying attention to and handling details
- Performing duties which change frequently
- Managing people/groups
- Managing time
- Managing equipment
- Demonstrating leadership
- Making decisions
- Meeting goals and deadlines
- Working quickly when necessary

Research & Planning Skills
- Analyzing information
- Developing evaluation strategies
- Using logical reasoning
- Setting goals and deadlines
- Defining needs

manager. In order to accurately assess the needs and goals of an organization's system, a manager has to collaborate with IT personnel, systems analysts, and technology vendors. Managers usually have to negotiate prices with technology vendors.

Technological Environment

Computer and information systems managers work with a large assortment of computer systems, hardware, and software. Each system is different, depending on the organization's field. If a manager is telecommuting, a variety of communication technologies can be used, including a laptop or smartphone.

EDUCATION, TRAINING, AND ADVANCEMENT

High School/Secondary

Employers typically require applicants to have at least a high school diploma or an equivalent degree, although most positions in the field require a bachelor's degree or higher. High schools normally offer an assortment of classes that an individual interested in the profession could benefit from. Any courses in computer science, mathematics, and business management would help an aspiring IT manager develop a good background for the profession. Some high schools even offer extracurricular computer clubs, where the fundamentals of computer systems can be learned.

Suggested High School Subjects
- Algebra
- Applied Communication
- Applied Math
- Business & Computer Technology
- Business Data Processing
- Calculus
- College Preparatory
- Computer Programming
- Computer Science
- English
- Geometry
- Keyboarding
- Mathematics
- Statistics
- Trigonometry

Related Career Pathways/Majors

Business, Management & Administration Cluster
- Management Pathway

Information Technology Cluster
- Programming & Software Development Pathway

Science, Technology, Engineering & Mathematics Cluster
- Engineering & Technology Pathway

Famous First

Charles Babbage (1791–1871) was an English polymath (a mathematician, philosopher, inventor and mechanical engineer) who originated the concept of a digital programmable computer and is thus considered by some to be a "father of the computer." Babbage is credited with inventing the first mechanical computer that eventually led to more complex electronic designs, though all the essential ideas of modern computers are to be found in Babbage's analytical engine.

Source: www.computer.org

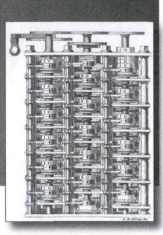

Postsecondary

Typically, a computer and information systems manager must have at least a bachelor's degree. While managers enter the field from a variety of different educational backgrounds, the majority of them have degrees in computer science, information science, or a related field. Most managers have taken courses in computer programming, advanced mathematics, and software development. Because of the various business aspects of the profession, many managers also have completed business-related courses.

Some employers require that a manager have a graduate degree. A common graduate degree for a manager is a master of business administration (MBA), which typically takes two years to complete. It is common for people pursuing their MBAs to take these classes in the evenings, after work, thereby gaining work experience while also completing their graduate studies.

Most technical schools offer computer-science or programming programs. Usually these programs last from six months to a year. Students are given formal classroom instruction as well as hands-on training. Technical schools are a great place for an individual to network with more experienced people in the field. Many of these schools also offer job-placement programs.

Because new developments in computer technology are occurring regularly, managers should be willing to pursue professional-development courses throughout their career in order to stay competitive and relevant.

Related College Majors
- Computer Programming
- Computer Science
- Information Sciences & Systems
- Management Information Systems & Business Data Processing

Adult Job Seekers

Anyone interested in a career as a computer and information systems manager should be aware that it takes years of experience and training in order to attain a managerial position. For instance, CTOs may need up ten to fifteen years of IT experience before being considered for the position. A strong background in computer and information systems is required, so an individual entering the field should be sure he or she has the necessary experience. If an individual has no experience in the field, he or she should consider enrolling in a college or technical school that offers a relevant program.

Professional Certification and Licensure

Although it is usually not required, a manager can choose to become certified as a specialist in a number of different IT applications. Managers with professional certification are more likely to advance into higher-paying positions. Professional certification is a way for an individual to demonstrate his or her skill and expertise in the profession. Managers can attain certification through independent certifying agencies or technology vendors.

Additional Requirements

Computer and information systems management demands great collaborative and communication skills. Managers must also be good at solving problems and managing budgets and be able to think independently and creatively. The job requires strong analytical skills in order to assess the best way to solve an IT-related problem.

EARNINGS AND ADVANCEMENT

Earnings depend on level of responsibility and specialty. Median annual earnings of computer and information systems managers was $135,800 in May 2016. The lowest 10 percent earned less than $82,360, and the highest 10 percent earned more than $208,000.

Computer and information systems managers may receive paid vacations, holidays and sick days; life and health insurance; and retirement benefits. These are usually paid for by the employer. At higher levels of management, they can also receive benefits such as expense accounts, stock options, and bonuses.

EMPLOYMENT AND OUTLOOK

Computer and information systems managers held about 367,600 jobs nationally in 2016. Employment of computer and information systems managers is projected to grow 12 percent from 2016 to 2026, faster than the average for all occupations.

Demand for computer and information systems managers will grow as firms increasingly expand their operations to digital platforms. Computer and information systems managers will be responsible for implementing these goals.

Employment growth will result from the need to bolster cybersecurity in computer and information systems used by businesses. Industries such as retail trade will need to implement more robust security policies as cyber threats increase.

An increase in the popularity of cloud computing may result in firms outsourcing services from in-house IT departments to cloud-computing companies. This will shift IT services from IT departments in noncomputer industries, such as financial firms or schools, to firms engaged in computer systems design and related services and those in data processing, hosting, and related services.

Related Occupations
- Computer Engineer
- Computer Network Architect
- Computer Programmer
- Computer Support Specialist
- Computer Systems Analyst
- Database Administrator
- General Manager & Top Executive
- Information Security Analyst
- Information Technology Project Manager
- Librarian
- Medical Records Administrator
- Network & Computer Systems Administrator
- Operations Research Analyst
- Software Developer
- Web Administrator
- Web Developer

Related Military Occupations
- Computer Programmer
- Computer Systems Officer
- Computer Systems Specialist

Conversation With . . .
JASON TOWNSEND

Deputy Social Media Manager
National Aeronautics and Space Administration (NASA)
Washington, D.C.
Social media professional, 15 years

1. What was your individual career path in terms of education/training, entry-level job, or other significant opportunity?

I have more than 15 years of professional and freelance experience communicating online, starting in 1999 as a freelance web designer for small businesses and for student organizations at colleges and universities. I was a full-time summer intern at NASA's Goddard Space Flight Center, building webpages and doing other work for their public affairs office. That internship grew into a year-round part-time job, and full-time during school breaks, for the remainder of my undergraduate years.

Upon graduation, NASA wasn't hiring in my field, so I took a job working on technology projects for a grant program that lasted a year. At the end of the grant, I moved to a job as webmaster at a think tank here in Washington and continued to hone my skills before returning to NASA as a contract editor and producer for the Webby Award-winning NASA.gov website. I was also involved in supporting the growing presence NASA had on social media.

After a few years, I took a position as webmaster at the National Oceanic and Atmospheric Administration (NOAA), specializing in the creation, development, and operations of online communications for NOAA.gov and NOAA's social media accounts.

And that leads me to my current job at NASA, where I serve as the Deputy Social Media Manager, overseeing and coordinating NASA's expansive social media footprint across multiple platforms and accounts that represent NASA's work pioneering the future in space exploration, scientific discovery, and aeronautics research.

2. What are the most important skills and/or qualities for someone in your profession?

There are no set requirements or skill sets for our social media team, which results in a huge range of folks. We have people who are IT specialists and people who are scientists posting on social media, but most of the people who oversee social media here are communications specialists who don't have science backgrounds. And that's a good thing when you're communicating highly scientific or technical information to the public. You can easily put yourself in their shoes to ask, "What would I want to know about this?" You do need to strive for accuracy when working in this field.

3. What do you wish you had known going into this profession?

Change is the only constant. Social media moves fast and what worked yesterday isn't necessarily what works today and most certainly isn't what you'll be doing tomorrow. You have to look at trends and keep your skill set sharp to stay on top of the platforms and where social media is going.

4. Are there many job opportunities in your profession? In what specific areas?

In social media, there are two types of teams you find and both are advantageous to sharpening your skills. Joining a smaller team, you tend to learn to do it all—make GIFs, edit video, write social media posts, take snaps for your stories, and more. But on a larger team, you tend to specialize in one of the content types or platforms. Everyone approaches the work differently, and you get to learn and see the plethora of ideas and processes different people bring to the table to create the best products possible.

5. How do you see your profession changing in the next five years? How do you envision platforms evolving? What skills will be required?

I expect to see more experiential media-rich content on social media. With more augmented reality and virtual reality technology getting into the hands of audiences, I expect to see content that takes advantage of this and allows people to be embedded in ways that can "transport" them to everything from galaxies "far, far away" to a newsworthy location where the action is happening. I suspect that social media platforms will allow for the wider spread of this content and also bring together audiences of like-minded fans.

6. What do you enjoy most about your job? What do you enjoy least about your job?

I love that no two days are ever totally alike. We coordinate a lot of different content, so some days may have tons of science news and we end up working with mission staff and science colleagues to share the latest in cutting-edge research and discoveries. They are sometimes literally rewriting science textbooks. Other days, we'll be doing live coverage on exciting events like spacewalks or satellite launches. On days without big mission activities, we coordinate upcoming content with our team, discuss best practices, or look at ways to optimize our content for different platforms.

We're lucky we have so much compelling content to post, but sometimes we'll have ten to twelve stories to tell on the same day that are all equally deserving of the spotlight. Spacing them out enough so they're not stealing the attention from one another can be a challenge. To help alleviate that pressure, we now share content on weekends.

7. Can you suggest a valuable "try this" for students considering a career in your profession?

One of the biggest pieces of advice I give students is to get an internship. You gain experience that can be essential in landing your first full-time job out of school. My internship at NASA Goddard was invaluable at building a network of contacts and a body of experience that continues to propel me throughout my career.

MORE INFORMATION

Association for Computing Machinery
2 Penn Plaza, Suite 701
New York, NY 10121-0701
800.342.6626
acmhelp@acm.org
www.acm.org

Association of Information Technology Professionals
401 North Michigan Avenue
Suite 2400
Chicago, IL 60611
800.224.9371
aitp_hq@aitp.org
www.aitp.org

Computing Research Association
1828 L Street NW, Suite 800
Washington, DC 20036
202.234.2111
info@cra.org
www.cra.org

Institute for the Certification of Computer Professionals
2400 East Devon Avenue, Suite 281
Des Plaines, IL 60018
800.843.8227
office2@iccp.org
www.iccp.org

Institute of Electrical and Electronics Engineers Computer Society
2001 L Street NW, Suite 700
Washington, DC 20036-4928
202.371.0101
help@computer.org
www.computer.org

Patrick Cooper/Editor

Computer Network Architect

Snapshot

Career Cluster(s): Information Technology, Science, Technology, Engineering & Mathematics
Interests: Computer Science, engineering, analyzing data, solving problems
Earnings (2016 median pay): $101,210 per year; $48.66 per hour
Employment & Outlook: Average Growth Expected

OVERVIEW

Sphere of Work

Computer network architects, also known as data communications analysts, or network analysts, conceptualize, build, and maintain computer information networks for businesses and organizations. Network architects may be employed as part of an organization's computing staff or by companies who specialize in assisting businesses with setting up, monitoring, and maintaining their computer networks. They work closely with other senior members of a company's computing staff, including network security personnel and systems administrators.

Work Environment

Network architects work almost exclusively in administrative and office settings. Some projects, however, may require off-site work. The majority of network architects are employed by computer companies, educational organizations, governments, and finance companies. They are also employed in manufacturing and telecommunications.

Profile

Interests: Data, Things
Working Conditions: Work Inside
Physical Strength: Light Work
Education Needs: Bachelor's Degree
Licensure/Certification:
Recommended
Physical Abilities Not Required: Not Climb, Not Kneel
Opportunities for Experience: Military Service, Volunteer Work, Part Time Work
Holland Interest Score*: ICR

* See Appendix A

Occupation Interest

Network architects have a passion and commitment to computing. The field attracts technologically skilled individuals who enjoy analyzing, dissecting, and developing solutions for complex problems. In addition to significant experience with computers and electronics, most network architects are also well versed in fields such as engineering technology, mathematics, and telecommunications.

A Day in the Life—Duties and Responsibilities

Network systems and data communication analysts traditionally work regular business hours, with some exceptions and lengthier hours required during emergencies or for the completion of large-scale projects.

Network architects are responsible for a diverse workload that can require involvement in different tasks and projects simultaneously. Those who are employed by a singular entity are able to focus on modifications and maintenance of one system; conversely, network architects who are employed by computer firms that work with several business clients often work on multiple systems simultaneously.

Computer network architects who are employed by a singular organization, government agency, or business spend their days making adjustments to network technologies to ensure they meet the organization's necessary capacity or traffic volumes. They also address any errors that arise within network systems and repair them quickly to avoid lapses in productivity or communication.

Network architects employed by telecommunications and computer companies specialize in designing, installing, and maintaining networks that are custom-made for the needs of a specific business or organization. The planning process involves extensive collaboration with administrators and staff members. Insight into a particular company's or organization's production process helps network architects determine the type of system and related technical apparatus that can best suit any data communications needs. Network architects also custom-design systems to cater to the needs of business customers, a task that is particular common in industries such as e-commerce, education, media, and publishing.

Duties and Responsibilities

- Designing, implementing, maintaining and modifying all aspects of network and data communications systems
- Monitoring the performance of network and data communications systems and troubleshooting when required
- Maintaining and creating backups of files on the network server to ensure their safety if network problems occur
- Determining when hardware, software and equipment upgrades are necessary
- Diagnosing and solving data communications problems
- Creating procedures for installing and troubleshooting network and data communications hardware and software
- Performing regular tests to ensure that all security measures are functioning properly
- Training users in the proper application of equipment

WORK ENVIRONMENT

Transferable Skills and Abilities

Communication Skills
- Speaking effectively
- Writing concisely
- Listening attentively
- Reading well

Interpersonal/Social Skills
- Being able to work independently

Organization & Management Skills
- Paying attention to and handling details
- Performing duties which change frequently
- Managing time
- Managing equipment/materials
- Coordinating tasks
- Making decisions
- Handling challenging situations

Research & Planning Skills
- Identifying problems
- Determining alternatives
- Gathering information
- Solving problems
- Defining needs
- Analyzing information
- Developing evaluation strategies

Technical Skills
- Performing scientific, mathematical and technical work
- Working with machines, tools or other objects
- Using technology to process information
- Understanding which technology is appropriate for a task
- Applying the technology to a task
- Maintaining and repairing technology

Immediate Physical Environment

Computer network architects work primarily in administrative and office settings.

Human Environment

Much of tasks inherent in the work of a network architect require strong collaboration skills. Network architects are also required to solicit information from coworkers and explain complex processes to colleagues and fellow professionals on a daily basis.

Technological Environment

Data architects traditionally have expert-level knowledge of numerous technological tools and software applications ranging from network management, administration, and transaction security software. They are also experts in computer server systems, network switches, programming languages, and connectivity technologies.

EDUCATION, TRAINING, AND ADVANCEMENT

High School/Secondary

High school students can best prepare for a career in network architecture and data communication analysis by completing courses in algebra, calculus, geometry, trigonometry, desktop publishing, programming, and computer science. Advanced placement classes in mathematics and computer-related subjects are also recommended.

Many high school students take advantage of summer internships and volunteer programs offered by local companies to gain a better understanding of computers and computer networks in everyday applications in the professional world.

Suggested High School Subjects
- Algebra
- Applied Communication
- Applied Math
- Business & Computer Technology
- Business Data Processing
- Calculus
- College Preparatory
- Computer Programming
- Computer Science
- English
- Geometry
- Keyboarding
- Mathematics
- Statistics
- Trigonometry

Related Career Pathways/Majors
Information Technology Cluster
- Network Systems Pathway

Science, Technology, Engineering & Mathematics Cluster
- Engineering & Technology Pathway

Famous First

On October 29th 1969, two computers connected to form the ARPANET and launch the world's first successful packet-switched wide area computer network. This first connection, in the form of a logon request, was sent to SRI International (then known as Stanford Research Institute) from the University of California, Los Angeles (UCLA). This remote access initiated a new, flexibly formed network structure for computer resource sharing. While not yet an internet, it did lay critical groundwork for the subsequent Internet and the dramatic changes in how we conduct business, communicate, socialize, learn, distribute knowledge, and travel.

Source: www.computinghistory.org.uk

Postsecondary

Possession of a bachelor's degree in a computer technology-related field is a commonplace requirement for nearly all employment vacancies in network architecture, particularly those at the entry level. While professionals reach the career path of networks system and data communications architect from numerous academic and professional experiences, network architecture is a distinct field of study at many colleges and universities throughout the United States.

Students enrolled in degree paths related to network design and administration complete coursework in programming, network security, systems analysis and design, technical writing, advanced mathematics, and project management.

Related College Majors
- Computer Engineering
- Computer Engineering Technology
- Computer Maintenance Technology
- Computer Programming
- Computer Science
- Data Processing Technology
- Information Sciences & Systems
- Management Information Systems & Business Data Processing

Adult Job Seekers

Individuals with no background in a related field should enroll in a college or a technical or vocational school that offers a program in network systems data. Technical schools are also a great place for job seekers to network. Communication technologies and standards are always changing, so those making a career transition into the network systems field should be willing to continue learning throughout their career.

Given the amount of technical aptitude required of the position, data communications is not traditionally a field that people seek out when changing careers. Individuals with previous professional experience or academic training in a technological field might find the transition possible.

Professional Certification and Licensure

Dozens of networking certifications are available for professionals in the data communications industry. Network certifications are tailored to specific industries and network communications needs and are available from myriad vendors, associations, and professional organizations that are recognized by professionals in the network communications industry. Additionally, the accumulation of certificates is a common way of illustrating expertise throughout the industry.

Additional Requirements

In addition to excellent technological and computer skills, network architects must possess the patience and resolve to work on complex problems for long periods until the most effective and efficient solution is uncovered. Network professionals must also be willing team players who can work in concert with other computing professionals in a productive manner.

Fun Fact

The first recognizable social media site was created in 1997 and was called Six Degrees. Blogging sites started becoming popular two years later.
Source: Smallbiztrends.com

EARNINGS AND ADVANCEMENT

The median annual wage for computer network architects was $101,210 in May 2016. The lowest 10 percent earned less than $55,610, and the highest 10 percent earned more than $158,590.

Computer network architects may receive paid vacations, holidays, and sick days; life and health insurance and retirement benefits. These are usually paid by the employer.

EMPLOYMENT AND OUTLOOK

Information security analysts, web developers, and computer network architects as a group held about 320,000 jobs nationally in 2016. Employment of computer network architects is projected to grow 6 percent from 2016 to 2026, about as fast as the average for all occupations.

Demand for computer network architects will increase as firms continue to expand their information technology (IT) networks. Designing and building these new networks, as well as upgrading existing ones, will create opportunities for computer network architects. The expansion of healthcare information technology will also contribute to employment growth.

Adoption of cloud computing, which allows users to access storage, software, and other computer services over the Internet, is likely to dampen the demand for computer network architects. Organizations will no longer have to design and build networks in-house; instead, firms that provide cloud services will do this. Smaller firms with minimal IT requirements will find it more cost effective to contract services from cloud service providers. However, because architects at cloud providers can work on more than one organization's network, these providers will not have to employ as many architects as individual organizations do for the same amount of work.

Related Occupations

- Broadcast Technician
- Computer & Information Systems Manager
- Computer Engineer
- Computer Programmer
- Computer Service Technician
- Computer Support Specialist
- Computer Systems Analyst
- Database Administrator
- Electronic Equipment Repairer
- Information Security Analyst
- Information Technology Project Manager
- Network & Computer Systems Administrator
- Software Developer
- Web Administrator
- Web Developer

Related Military Occupations

- Computer Programmer
- Computer Systems Officer
- Computer Systems Specialist

Conversation About . . .
PRIVACY AND SOCIAL MEDIA
Hayley Kaplan

Owner of What is Privacy?
Los Angeles, California

1. How much privacy do Americans have in the online arena?

Most people have no clue how little privacy we have. Everything we do online is tracked, unless we take steps to hide our browsing history. Our spending habits help businesses know how and what to market to us.

With a few clicks and without spending a dime, anyone can access all sorts of personal information from data broker sites. For a small fee, they can get a detailed background report with even more invasive information.

Procedures and regulations differ from state to state and some states make it remarkably easy to access official public records online. I've worked with victims of rape, assault and also victims of stalking. Online public records can make citizens vulnerable, especially if their home address is online, as in the case of an assault victim. If you make a political donation, it's online because campaigns have to be transparent. I try to educate people that every action has a consequence and we need to consciously think about that before we act.

2. What are some examples of people not thinking through the consequences of online actions?

Every Facebook profile picture is public. I know a police officer whose profile picture was a photo of her and her daughter. She thought she was doing a good job because she's monitoring her kid's account on Instagram, but her profile photo put her daughter in jeopardy.

A high school student went to a gay pride parade wearing a t-shirt with a graphic image and a crude saying on it. Years later the picture surfaced and he was ousted from his professional golfing career.

My mantra is "Anything I put online should be OK for anyone to see." People need to learn how to interact with each other without having to put it online. Just enjoy a moment. If you find yourself thinking that you must get a photo or video of everything you do to post online rather than enjoying and experiencing what you're doing, it's time to rethink things.

3. It sounds like you also have to worry about what other people post.

Absolutely. It's not hard to ruin a person's reputation nowadays. People constantly go out of their way to post bad reviews and malicious content. There are plenty of sites that welcome negative information. Also, someone can easily post a photo that you'd rather not have online, even if there is no malice intended. Sexting is very dangerous because a risqué private photo can end up being very public.

4. What challenges do businesses face in the realm of privacy?

A business that doesn't protect employee and customer data can face large fines. Businesses must take steps to prevent themselves from being hacked, and know how to recover and have the least amount of damage if they do get hacked. The rules under the General Data Protection Regulation in the EU are strict. We don't have comparable regulations—I hope we do eventually—but any company in the U.S. that markets to the EU or any international business needs to comply and know how to protect their customers' data. Marketing data that businesses collect is valuable but must be protected. It's a balancing act.

5. Any other downsides to social media and the internet that students should think about?

Cyber bullying is a horrible byproduct of the internet.

Over-posting of personal or inappropriate information can come back to haunt a person in terms of college and job acceptances.

We'll need the equivalent of AA, Alcoholics Anonymous (SMA - Social Media Anonymous?) for people addicted to social media who suffer serious repercussions as a result. Posture is awful from computers and hands are suffering from typing. Concentration and attention spans are limited as we multitask from one thing to another instead of focusing on a single activity. The ability to communicate in live situations has decreased and panic sets in when we realize we don't have our phones nearby.

One thing is for sure, the Internet will continue to give rise to negative side effects, and this will open up new careers along the way for those who foresee the problems and come up with solutions.

MORE INFORMATION

Association for Computing Machinery
2 Penn Plaza, Suite 701
New York, NY 10121-0701
800.342.6626
acmhelp@acm.org
www.acm.org

Computing Technology Industry Association
1815 S. Meyers Road, Suite 300
Oakbrook Terrace, IL 60181-5228
630.678.8300
www.comptia.org

IEEE Computer Society
2001 L Street, NW, Suite 700
Washington, DC 20036-4928
202.371.0101
help@computer.org
www.computer.org

National Workforce Center for Emerging Technologies
Bellevue College
3000 Landerholm Circle SE, N258
Bellevue, WA 98007-6484
425.564.4229
mmajury@bellevuecollege.edu
www.nwcet.org

Network Professional Association
1401 Hermes Lane
San Diego, CA 92154
888.672.6720
www.npa.org

John Pritchard/Editor

Computer Programmer

Snapshot

Career Cluster(s): Architecture & Construction, Finance, Information Technology, Science, Technology, Engineering & Mathematics

Interests: Computer science, computer technology, solving problems, working alone, working with a team

Earnings (2016 median pay): $79,840 per year; $38.39 per hour

Employment & Outlook: Slower than average

OVERVIEW

Sphere of Work

Computer programmers are part of the larger information technology (IT) industry. Programmers specialize in creating computer applications and programs. Training for this occupation involves specialized instruction in one or more programming languages, which are sets of codes that instruct computers to perform various functions. Most computer programmers specialize in one or a few programming languages, each of which is used for various types of specialized functions. For instance, there are specific languages used to program 3-D and moving graphics, while other types of languages are typically used for basic web design and database construction.

Work Environment

Computer programmers work in office environments and typically do most of their work at a desk in front of a computer terminal. Though many programmers work in company offices, some programmers may complete a portion of their work off-site and may work from home, depending on their access to appropriate equipment and networks. Many computer programmers work during regular business hours, though the nature of the work is such that programming may be completed at any time, and many programmers may choose to work irregular hours.

Though some computer programmers work independently, programmers often coordinate with other IT professionals, including project managers, designers, and computer operators. Therefore, computer programmers benefit from skill in both customer service and interpersonal communication. Those who can work well as part of a team will have an advantage finding and maintaining employment in the field.

Computer programmers may work in a variety of organizations, from corporate offices to research facilities. Programmers who work as independent contractors may be hired by a variety of clients, from companies producing web content to film and production studios. Computer programming is at the forefront of technological development and has rapidly become an important facet of commerce, marketing, and communication for hundreds of modern industries.

Profile

Interests: Data
Working Conditions: Work Inside
Physical Strength: Light Work
Education Needs: Junior/Technical/Community College, Bachelor's Degree
Licensure/Certification: Recommended
Physical Abilities Not Required: Not Climb, Not Kneel, Not Hear and/or Talk
Opportunities for Experience: Internship, Military Service, Part Time Work
Holland Interest Score*: IRE

* See Appendix A

Occupation Interest

Those seeking a career in computer programming should be self-motivated and comfortable with tight schedules and deadlines. In addition, programmers must stay abreast of developments in the field and must be comfortable engaging in continuing education to stay informed about the latest evolutions in programming. Those seeking to work as independent contractors will also benefit from learning how to market their services to potential clients and must be motivated enough to pursue work and compete for projects.

A Day in the Life—Duties and Responsibilities

Most computer programmers spend their work hours in either home or work office environments and do most of their work at a desk in front of either a laptop or desktop computer terminal. While a specific project may have a strict deadline, programming work in general can be done at any time of day and can be broken up into numerous separate work periods.

During a typical day on the job, a programmer may write and test code for a certain application and may spend hours refining ongoing projects. In addition, programmers generally work alongside a number of other IT professionals to complete certain projects. A certain amount of time must be dedicated to communicating with colleagues and customers. Part of a workday may also be spent in meetings with designers, project managers, or customers.

Computer programmers working in corporate environments may need to devote more of their time to working with members of a production team, while those working independently may be more able to organize their schedules according to personal preference. In addition, independent contractors must often spend time marketing their work and looking for new jobs. This process may involve sending out queries and applications as well as producing and maintaining a portfolio of work to show potential clients.

Duties and Responsibilities

- Studying problems and determining the steps necessary to solve them
- Documenting the steps involved to create the program
- Testing to make sure the instructions are correct and will produce the desired results
- Rewriting programs if desired results are not produced
- Modifying existing programs to meet new requirements
- Preparing an instruction sheet for use of the program

OCCUPATION SPECIALTIES

Engineering and Scientific Programmers

Engineering and Scientific Programmers write programs to solve engineering or scientific problems by applying a knowledge of advanced mathematics and an understanding of the computer.

WORK ENVIRONMENT

Immediate Physical Environment

Computer programmers tend to work in office environments, using a computer terminal to do their work. In large companies with multiple programmers, each programmer may occupy a cubicle, or they may work in shared or private offices, depending on the company. In many cases, programmers are able to complete work on variable schedules, and some may choose to work on certain projects outside of regular business hours. Independent contractors may work from home or from an independent office.

Human Environment

The human environment for a computer programmer can vary considerably according to the industry of employment and whether the individual works as an employee or an independent contractor. In corporate environments, programmers often work alongside designers, technicians, and project managers and function as part of an overall IT team that cooperates to complete projects. Independent contractors work alone most of the time and often work from home.

Whether working as an employee or an independent contractor, computer programmers benefit from strong interpersonal communication skills. Programmers often work to translate ideas produced by designers, project managers, and clients into functional programs. They benefit from strong communication skills and the ability to work with clients, customers, and colleagues.

Transferable Skills and Abilities

Communication Skills
- Speaking effectively
- Writing concisely

Organization & Management Skills
- Following instructions
- Organizing information or materials
- Paying attention to and handling details
- Performing routine work

Research & Planning Skills
- Solving problems
- Using logical reasoning

Technical Skills
- Working with data or numbers

Technological Environment

Computer programming is a rapidly developing field at the forefront of information technology, and programmers must be able to stay abreast of new developments. While the core languages used by programmers may change little from month to month, developers producing software and tools for programmers frequently introduce new products.

In addition, computer programmers must endeavor to remain at the forefront of hardware technology. Computer manufacturing companies frequently introduce new models and new components that provide advancements in speed and processing capability. Computer programmers also benefit from knowledge of computer maintenance and repair, which helps them to prevent hardware and equipment conflicts that can hinder their work.

EDUCATION, TRAINING, AND ADVANCEMENT

High School/Secondary

High school students can prepare for a career in computer programming by taking classes in basic computer science. Some high schools may offer more specific classes in subjects such as web navigation and design, graphic arts, and even basic programming.

Students are advised to explore any computer classes offered in order to gain additional experience in basic computer literacy and operation.

Suggested High School Subjects
- Accounting
- Algebra
- Applied Communication
- Applied Math
- Bookkeeping
- Business & Computer Technology
- Business Data Processing
- Calculus
- College Preparatory
- Computer Programming
- Computer Science
- English
- Geometry
- Keyboarding
- Mathematics
- Statistics
- Trigonometry

Related Career Pathways/Majors

Architecture & Construction Cluster
- Design/Pre-Construction Pathway

Finance Cluster
- Banking & Related Services Pathway

Information Technology Cluster
- Programming & Software Development Pathway

Science, Technology, Engineering & Mathematics Cluster
- Science & Mathematics Pathway

Famous First

Ada Lovelace best understood the promise of Charles Babbage's Analytical Engine, and the potential that computers would one day fulfill. The daughter of Romantic poet Lord Byron, Lovelace was a gifted mathematician and intellectual who translated an Italian article on the Analytical Engine and supplemented it with extensive notes on the machine's capabilities. In these notes she not only explained the engine more clearly than Babbage, but also described an algorithm it could carry out that is often considered to be the world's first computer program.

Source: www.pcreview.co.uk

Postsecondary

Computer programming is a burgeoning field, and most colleges, universities, and technical schools now offer specialized degree and certificate programs in different areas of computer science. Many community colleges and four-year institutions offer classes in computer programming, which generally include one or more separate classes on each programming language.

Postsecondary students can pursue computer programming as a degree focus or as a secondary educational focus. In addition to undergraduate-level programs, several institutions offer graduate-level programs in computer programming for those holding degrees in computer science. Students pursuing degree or certification programs will typically complete assignments that can form the basis of their professional portfolios and can be shown to potential employers. Employers often evaluate potential employees based on the strength of their professional or personal portfolios.

Related College Majors

- Computer Engineering
- Computer Maintenance Technology
- Computer Programming
- Computer Science
- Information Sciences & Systems
- Management Information Systems & Business Data Processing

Adult Job Seekers

Adults seeking to enter the computer programming field are advised to seek out continuing education classes through a community college or technical school. Many institutions offer night and evening classes and online courses, which may or may not be part of a certification program. Adults can also audit classes at universities or community colleges to better assess whether computer programming is of interest as a career path.

Professional Certification and Licensure

There are no certification or licensing standards for computer programmers; however, some individuals may pursue voluntary certification. Such certification programs offer professional proof that a student has completed a certain number of hours working with a specific type of programming or programming language. Computer programmers should consult credible professional associations within the field and follow professional debate as to the relevance and value of any certification program.

Additional Requirements

Computer programmers must be highly self-motivated and detail oriented. Small errors in a program's code can lead to major problems in the final product, and programmers must therefore be capable of carefully checking and rechecking their work to ensure accuracy at every stage of the process.

EARNINGS AND ADVANCEMENT

Earnings of computer programmers depend on the complexity of the work they do and to some extent on the area of the country in which they work. Earnings tend to be slightly higher in large urban areas. Median annual earnings of computer programmers were $79,840 in 2016. The lowest 10 percent earned less than $45,570, and the highest 10 percent earned more than $130,360.

Computer programmers may receive paid vacations, holidays, and sick days; life and health insurance; and retirement benefits. These are usually paid by the employer.

EMPLOYMENT AND OUTLOOK

Computer programmers held about 294,900 jobs nationally in 2016. Employment of computer programmers is projected to decline 7 percent from 2016 to 2026. Computer programming can be done from anywhere in the world, so companies sometimes hire programmers in countries where wages are lower. This ongoing trend is projected to limit employment growth for computer programmers in the United States. However, the high costs associated with managing projects given to overseas programmers sometimes offsets the savings from the lower wages, causing some companies to bring back or keep programming jobs in the United States.

Related Occupations
* Computer & Information Systems Manager
* Computer Engineer
* Computer Network Architect
* Computer Operator
* Computer Support Specialist

- Computer Systems Analyst
- Computer-Control Tool Programmer
- Database Administrator
- Information Security Analyst
- Mathematician
- Network & Computer Systems Administrator
- Operations Research Analyst
- Software Developer
- Web Administrator
- Web Developer

Related Military Occupations
- Computer Programmer
- Computer Systems Specialist

MORE INFORMATION

Association for Computing Machinery
2 Penn Plaza, Suite 701
New York, NY 10121-0701
800.342.6626
acmhelp@acm.org
www.acm.org

Association of Information Technology Professionals
401 N. Michigan Avenue, Suite 2400
Chicago, IL 60611-4267
800.224.9371
aitp_hq@aitp.org
www.aitp.org

IEEE Computer Society
2001 L Street NW, Suite 700
Washington, DC 20036-4928
202.371.0101
help@computer.org
www.computer.org

Institute for the Certification of Computer Professionals
2400 East Devon Avenue, Suite 281
Des Plaines, IL 60018-4610
800.843.8227
office@iccp.org
www.iccp.org

National Association of Programmers
P.O. Box 529
Prairieville, LA 70769
info@napusa.org
www.napusa.org

Micah Issitt/Editor

Copywriter

Snapshot

Career Cluster(s): Arts, A/V Technology & Communications, Business, Management & Administration

Interests: Writing, being creative, current events, research, analyzing data, communicating with others

Earnings (2016 median pay): $61,240 per year; $29.44 per hour

Employment & Outlook: Average Growth Expected

OVERVIEW

Sphere of Work

Copywriters work within the communication and information sectors. They research and prepare the written words that accompany advertising, promotional, and marketing materials. These include brochures, print advertising, press releases, scripts for television and radio commercials, websites, direct mail pieces, and any other communications that call for an ability to write engaging and persuasive content.

Copywriters are often employed by marketing and advertising agencies, but they may also work as independent freelancers. Copywriting is a highly

collaborative role, which usually demands working with a team of creative colleagues and supervisors. Copywriters interact with other communication specialists, such as marketers, brand strategists, advertising executives, public relations executives, graphic designers, art directors, multimedia technicians, and editors. They are also likely to work with clients and business specialists across a broad range of industries, topics, products, and services.

Work Environment

Copywriters work in an office environment, although the role is sufficiently flexible to accommodate working from any place where computer and telecommunication technologies are readily available. Freelance copywriters may work remotely, from a home office or other setting.

Full-time copywriters generally work for marketing and advertising agencies or within other communication outlets. A full-time employee may expect to work forty hours per week during normal office hours. They may be required to work longer hours, as needed.

Profile

Interests: Data
Working Conditions: Work Inside
Physical Strength: Light Work
Education Needs: Bachelor's Degree
Licensure/Certification: Usually Not
  Required
Physical Abilities Not Required: Not
  Climb, Not Kneel, Not Hear and/or Talk
Opportunities for Experience:
  Internship, Volunteer Work, Part Time
  Work
Holland Interest Score*: ASI

* See Appendix A

Occupation Interest

Copywriting attracts graduates and professionals who have a strong grounding in written communications. This occupation suits people with an interest in writing and a flair for creative expression and engaging an audience. Copywriters must be able to write fluently on a broad range of topics and to manage multiple projects concurrently. They usually have a strong interest in trends and markets.

In addition to having excellent writing skills, copywriters must possess strong research and analytical abilities. They must have advanced oral communication and collaboration skills and the ability to produce creative work under pressure. Copywriting demands good organizational, prioritization, and time management skills.

Copywriters must also be able to respond positively to constructive criticism and feedback about the work they produce.

A Day in the Life—Duties and Responsibilities

The copywriter's day is characterized by periods of independent and collaborative work. As a member of a creative team, copywriters meet with their colleagues, supervisors, and clients on a daily basis to brainstorm and present ideas as well as develop, analyze, and critique creative strategies and solve problems. Copywriters spend solitary time researching, draft advertising and promotional materials, and revising content as needed. Research may entail activities like referring to consumer surveys or conducting interviews. The solitary aspects of the occupation demand high levels of self-discipline and self-motivation. This is especially important for freelance copywriters who spend much of their time working alone and managing their own workloads.

The copywriter's daily output includes written content and concepts for brochures, print advertising, billboards, press releases, scripts for television and radio commercials, websites, direct mail pieces, and other marketing materials. The copywriter may find that the projects and assignments they work on are subject to tight timeframes and strict deadlines. It is a daily challenge for copywriters to produce high quality creative work under pressure.

Copywriters may be expected to contribute within their workplaces more widely. This may include some administrative duties, such as tracking project hours.

Duties and Responsibilities

- Coming up with creative concepts that will sell a product or idea
- Developing a central theme for a campaign
- Promoting your work to agencies, clients or upper management

WORK ENVIRONMENT

Immediate Physical Environment

Office settings predominate. Copywriters in full-time employment generally work for small to large marketing and advertising firms or in other corporate contexts. Freelance copywriters often work from home.

Transferable Skills and Abilities

Communication Skills
- Expressing thoughts and ideas
- Persuading others
- Writing concisely

Interpersonal/Social Skills
- Being able to remain calm
- Being able to work independently
- Respecting others' opinions

Organization & Management Skills
- Managing time
- Meeting goals and deadlines

Research & Planning Skills
- Creating ideas

Human Environment

Copywriting demands strong collaborative skills. Copywriters interact with other communication and creative specialists, such as marketers, brand strategists, advertising executives, public relations executives, graphic designers, art directors, multimedia technicians, and editors. They are also likely to work with clients and business specialists across a broad range of industries.

Technological Environment

Copywriters use technologies that range from telephone, email, and the Internet to word processing software. Copywriters may also be expected to work with web content management systems and blogging software. Advanced computing skills and an understanding of multimedia, social media, and emerging media technologies are considered an advantage.

EDUCATION, TRAINING, AND ADVANCEMENT

High School/Secondary

High school students can best prepare for a career in copywriting by taking courses in English literature, language and composition, social studies, journalism, and business communications. The creative nature of copywriting may be explored through art and graphic design; the business aspects through business studies, accounting and entrepreneurship; and the technology aspects through computer literacy. Courses such as history and anthropology can also prepare the student for synthesizing research into written materials. Psychology and cultural studies may provide an understanding of group and individual responses to written and visual messaging. Extracurricular school activities that involve writing can also provide students with an opportunity to develop their writing skills and learn from others prior to graduation. Such activities might include entering writing competitions and writing for school newspapers or club newsletters.

Suggested High School Subjects
- Applied Communication
- Composition
- English
- Foreign Languages
- Journalism
- Literature
- Psychology

Related Career Pathways/Majors
Arts, A/V Technology & Communications Cluster
- Journalism & Broadcasting Pathway

Business, Management & Administration Cluster
- Marketing Pathway

Famous First

The Wall Street Journal's famous "Two Young Men" letter is often cited as a "first" in copywriting. The two-page letter tells the story of two men, reunited at their 25th college reunion. Both were well-off, married, and had worked for the same company since college. One of them was a small departmental manager. The other was the company's president. The copy asks the rhetorical question of what separated these two men, then goes on to pitch the Wall Street Journal.

Source: contentequalsmoney.com/history-of-copywriting/

Postsecondary

Graduates from a diverse range of disciplines can become copywriters. The most common pathway to copywriting is by obtaining an undergraduate degree in communications, advertising, marketing, or journalism. Coursework in the social sciences can also be helpful preparation for writing persuasive content. A large number of colleges and universities offer courses in copywriting. There are also an increasing number of certified and non-certified copywriting programs, seminars, and workshops offered by private companies, academies, and professional associations.

Postsecondary students interested in a career in copywriting are also encouraged to become involved in extracurricular, club, or volunteer roles where they can develop their writing skills and begin to build a writing portfolio.

Related College Majors
- Advertising
- Communications, General
- English Language & Literature, General
- Liberal Arts & Sciences/Liberal Studies
- Marketing Management & Research
- Public Relations & Organizational Communications

Adult Job Seekers

Adults seeking a career transition into copywriting are advised to develop copywriting experience and a portfolio through part-time or volunteer work for a charity, non-profit organization, local club, or association. Writing a personal blog is another way to build a portfolio while also developing the daily discipline of writing.

An increasing number of copywriting opportunities are advertised on non-traditional job sites. The proliferation of web-based freelance writing sites allows people with little or no previous copywriting experience to upload their own articles for sale or bid for writing projects.

Taking writing courses may assist with networking and portfolio development. Self-guided learners may also benefit from reading "how to" books about copywriting or by undertaking short courses, seminars, or workshops.

Professional Certification and Licensure

There are no required professional certifications or licenses for copywriting. Practical experience generally outweighs formal qualifications in this occupation. Some professional associations provide certifications in the field. The American Marketing Association offers the Professional Certified Marketer (PCM) certification, which requires association membership and completion of a written exam. Consult credible professional associations within the field and follow professional debate as to the relevancy and value of any certification program.

Additional Requirements

The most important attribute for prospective copywriters is a love of writing combined with interest in a broad range of topics. In addition to advanced writing skills, copywriters must possess strong social and cultural awareness, an understanding of trends and markets, and the ability to write about products and services in emotionally engaging terms. A portfolio of writing samples is essential.

EARNINGS AND ADVANCEMENT

Copywriters can become copy supervisors or creative supervisors within an organization. Earnings for copywriters vary greatly depending on the specific job and the size, prestige and location of the company. Copywriters working in large organizations in urban areas can demand higher annual earnings. Median annual earnings of copywriters were $48,197 in 2018.

Copywriters may receive paid vacations, holidays, and sick days; life and health insurance; and retirement benefits. These are usually paid by the employer.

EMPLOYMENT AND OUTLOOK

Writers, of which copywriters are a specialty, held about 146,000 jobs nationally in 2016. About one-half of salaried writers worked in the information sector, which includes advertising; newspaper, periodical, book, and directory publishers; radio and television broadcasting; software publishers; motion picture and sound recording industries; Internet service providers, web search portals, and data processing services; and Internet publishing and broadcasting.

Employment is expected to grow slower than the average for all occupations through the year 2020, which means employment is projected to increase 3 percent to 9 percent. Turnover is relatively high in this occupation. Freelancers often leave the field because they cannot earn enough money.

Related Occupations

- Advertising & Marketing Manager
- Advertising Director
- Advertising Sales Agent
- Electronic Commerce Specialist
- Journalist
- Public Relations Specialist
- Radio/TV Announcer and Newscaster
- Technical Writer
- Writer & Editor

Conversation About . . .
SOCIAL MEDIA SPECIALISTS
Lanae Spruce

Social Media Specialist, Smithsonian Institution
Washington, D.C.

Lanae Spruce stays on top of the latest trends. And whether posting, tagging, or tweeting, she always shows she's in the know.

Lanae is a social media specialist for the Smithsonian Institution's new National Museum of African American History and Culture in Washington, D.C. She uses social media to promote the museum's mission and vision. Like others in her field, Lanae links the subject of her work with current events. "There's always something going on in real time," she says, "and we try to enhance the conversation through the perspective of our museum."

1. What do social media specialists do?

Social media specialists communicate with the public through platforms that allow users to create and share content online. They run their employers' social media accounts, working to build a brand's reputation.

We post content—such as images, text, or videos—to spark interest in a topic that relates to the brand as a whole. For example, I might share photos from the museum's exhibit of music to make sure all of our social platforms are telling stories about our museum that people can relate to.

In addition, social media specialists follow conversations and interact with the public online. You never know what to expect, especially when dealing with online content. A fun hashtag might pop up and, if appropriate, we find ways to respond and share our content.

We sometimes collaborate with others to promote their employer's cause. For example, we might work on a team with marketing consultants to publicize an event.

To track the effectiveness of their communication strategies, social media specialists set goals and then measure success against those goals. For example, I might aim for a social media campaign post to be shared 40 times and then use an online tool to analyze the results.

2. How do you become a social media specialist?

To work as a social media specialist, you'll need certain skills, education, and other qualifications.

At a minimum, you must be familiar with social media platforms. You should also be comfortable using networking tools, such as ones designed to post across several social media accounts.

Equally important is the ability to understand your audience and its interests. It goes back to seeing what fans are talking about and knowing your audience and what it expects from you. If your audience is concerned about an issue that you don't address, for example, you're not being effective.

Creativity and communication skills are also key for presenting familiar content in interesting ways. We may have told the story a million times before, but we're always looking for a new angle, a new way to keep people engaged.

And you should be able to make judgment calls quickly, particularly when handling sensitive topics. You have to always be aware of what's going on. If there's a natural disaster, you don't want to be tweeting about what was on TV last night.

To become a social media specialist, you typically need a bachelor's degree. You should expect to study subjects such as public relations, communications, and business. I earned my bachelor's degree in journalism and my master's degree in Internet marketing, which gives me a solid foundation for both the writing and promoting I do in my job.

While in school, you may consider pursuing an internship or activities that show your leadership, writing, or social media expertise. Touting those accomplishments may make you more attractive to future employers—especially for your first job after graduating.

Employers often prefer to hire workers who have worked in social media, public affairs, or a related field. I gained experience after college by working for an online business, using social media to respond to customers.

You might learn about social media use on your own, supplementing what you already know with what you read online. Taking classes or earning certifications may boost your credentials even more.

3. What should you expect as a social media specialist?

Managing an employer's social media accounts is often more challenging than managing personal accounts. But there's plenty to enjoy about the work.

As a social media specialist, you'll interact with the public in lots of different ways. One minute, you might be fielding criticism; the next, you'll respond to positive feedback.

Throughout it all, you must maintain a professional tone and keep your employer's best interests in mind. You have to make sure that whatever you're posting reflects the brand's mission and goals, and you have to have a strategy.

Constantly monitoring the brand's reputation and keeping up with current events may be all-consuming. That can be both bad and good. It can be a challenge for your personal life. But the real-time piece that makes my job hard also makes it fun.

The U.S. Bureau of Labor Statistics (BLS) groups social media specialists with other types of public relations specialists. These workers might go by a various job titles, including digital engagement specialist, social media strategist, and online community manager.

In May 2015, there were about 218,910 public relations specialists working in wage and salary jobs, according to BLS. Their median annual wage was $56,770, higher than the $36,200 median for all workers. These data do not include employment and wages of self-employed workers.

Increased use of social media as a way for businesses to communicate with the public may mean that you'll find ample opportunities for work. But because of social media's popularity, you may encounter competition for those jobs.

I suggest staying up to date on social platforms and trends. Follow some of your favorite brands and watch what they do. As social media evolves and grows, you need to constantly look for ways to be better.

Elka Torpey. "Social media specialist," *Career Outlook*,
U.S. Bureau of Labor Statistics, November 2016.

Digital Analytics Association
401 Edgewater Pl # 600
Wakefield, MA 01880
(781) 876-8933
digitalanalyticsassociation.com

Interactive Advertising Bureau
116 East 27th Street
6th floor
New York, NY 10016
(212) 380-4700
www.iab.com

International Bloggers Association
PO BOX 193
Elizabethtown, KY 42702
internationalbloggersassociation.com

International Digital Media and Arts
Association (iDMAa)
c/o School of Media Arts
Columbia College Chicago
33 E. Congress, Rm 600B
Chicago, IL 6060
www.idmaa.org

Professional Travel Bloggers Association
contact@travelbloggersassociation.com
travelbloggersassociation.com/
Social Media Association
Atlanta, GA
socialmediaassoc.com

Social Media Managers Association
Chichester, West Sussex
UK
01243-601236
socialmediamanagersassociation.com

Conversation About . . .
SEO AND SOCIAL MEDIA
Michele Dambach

VP Digital Strategy, Watkins McGowan, LLC,
Atlanta, GA

1. What is SEO?

Search Engine Optimization (SEO) is making sure you are utilizing the right keywords to drive people to your site when they search for a topic. The goal is to have your top tier keywords display content on page one of a search engine's results. There are some things you can do in the code or backend of your website that help optimize those efforts. Search engines continuously update their algorithms, making SEO a key tool for marketers.

2. How is SEO adapted to social media?

Say somebody sees an article that you shared on Twitter in order to drive traffic, and that person lands on your website. If they spend an average of two to four minutes, that's going to help you in your rankings from SEO. That person came in from social media, liked what they saw, and stuck around. But if someone clicks on an article link, comes to your site, lands on a page that has nothing to do with what they were looking for and they bounce, that can hurt you.

3. How does that impact SEO rankings?

The length of stay and depth of the search on your own site has a direct impact on your ranking. (Page depth means that your social media post contained keywords a person was looking for, so they stayed on your site and spent more time there.)

4. What is the value of SEO?

Say someone is looking on a search engine and types in a query for, "How do I write a resume?" If the search results return your website and they click on it, you need to take them to a landing page that talks about writing a resume. If not, they will more than likely get frustrated and leave your site quickly. Search engines don't like that. This is the keywords optimization part of SEO, which is just one of the ranking factors search engines take into consideration.

5. How does that impact advertising?

To me, programmatic advertising is really evolving into a one-to-one personalization experience. I know more about you, and hopefully I can reach you at the time you're making that critical decision on what to purchase.

6. What does that mean for personal privacy?

When you're using the internet, you know you're being tracked with cookies and consumers should keep that in mind. If you have a problem with that as a consumer, you can disable the cookies. On the flip side, maybe you could be saving some money. It's a tradeoff.

But, for instance, insurance companies may be using this information to measure credit-worthiness. There have been studies done and there is a fine line on what's "Big Brother" and what's not.

MORE INFORMATION

Advertising Research Foundation
432 Park Avenue South, 6th Floor
New York, NY 10016-8013
212.751.5656
thearf.org

Advertising Women of New York
25 West 45th Street, Suite 403
New York, NY 10036
212.221.7969
awny@awny.org
www.awny.org

American Advertising Federation
1101 Vermont Avenue, NW
Suite 500
Washington, DC 20005-6306
800.999.2231
aaf@aaf.org
www.aaf.org

American Advertising Federation
1101 Vermont Avenue NW, Suite 500
Washington, DC 20005-6306
202.898.0089
aaf@aaf.org
www.aaf.org

National Student Advertising Competition
www.aaf.org/default.asp?id=122

Most Promising Minority Students
www.aaf.org/default.asp?id=213

American Association of Advertising Agencies
405 Lexington Avenue, 18th Floor
New York, NY 10174-1801
212.682.2500
www.aaaa.org

American Association of Advertising Agencies Scholarships Programs:
www.aaaa.org/careers/scholarships/Pages/default.aspx
American Association of Advertising Agencies Internships:
www.aaaa.org/careers/internships/Pages/default.aspx

American Marketing Association
311 South Wacker Drive, Suite 5800
Chicago, IL 60606
800.262.1150
info@ama.org
www.marketingpower.com

American Society of Magazine Editors
810 Seventh Avenue, 24th Floor
New York, NY 10019
212.872.3700
asme@magazine.org
www.magazine.org/editorial/asme

Association for Women in Communications
3337 Duke Street
Alexandria, VA 22314
703.370.7436
info@womcom.org
www.womcom.org

Association of National Advertisers
708 3rd Avenue, 33rd Floor
New York, NY 10017
212.697.5950
www.ana.net

Barbara Bacci Mirque Scholarship Fund
for family-friendly content:
www.ana.net/content/show/id/afe-
scholarships

Dow Jones Newspaper Fund, Inc.
P.O. Box 300
Princeton, NJ 08543-0300
609.452.2820
djnf@dowjones.com
www.newsfund.org

International Association of Business Communicators
601 Montgomery Street, Suite 1900
San Francisco, CA 94111
800.776.4222
service_centre@iabc.com
www.iabc.com

Public Relations Society of America
33 Maiden Lane, 11th Floor
New York, NY 10038-5150
212.460.1400
membership@prsa.org
www.prsa.org

Society for Technical Communication
9401 Lee Highway, Suite 300
Fairfax, VA 22031
703.522.4114
www.stc.org

Kylie Hughes/Editor

Customer Service Representative

Snapshot

Career Cluster(s): Business, Management & Administration, Finance, Health Science, Human Services, Marketing, Sales & Service, Transportation, Distribution & Logistics

Interests: Talking on the telephone, interacting with people, handling conflict

Earnings (2016 median pay): $32,300 per year; $15.53 per hour

Employment & Outlook: Average Growth Expected

OVERVIEW

Sphere of Work

Customer service representatives provide a wide range of support to customers and serve as the primary point of contact between a company and its customer base. They spend the work day responding accurately to customer questions and inquiries, many of which arrive via social media, solving customer problems, and handling customer complaints. Customer service representatives are found in a very broad range of industries and in any context where an organization provides

product or service support to its customers. For this reason, customer service representatives are usually well-trained in their company's products and services and policies and procedures. Many also perform administrative tasks such as placing orders and processing invoices and returns.

Work Environment

Customer service representatives generally work in office environments. Most work in call centers, but many will also work in retail and other commercial environments. Customer service representatives interact constantly with customers. In many cases, this involves responding to comments or questions that arrive through social media such as Facebook or Twitter feeds. It may also involve writing or assisting customers in person. This may include other customer service representatives and supervisors, as well as people from other departments. Customer service representatives engaged in full-time work may expect to work approximately forty hours per week, but work hours may vary significantly depending on the employer and industry. Extended customer service hours usually mean that a customer service representative will work some evening or weekend shifts. Part-time roles are also available.

Profile

Interests: Data, People
Working Conditions: Work Inside
Physical Strength: Light Work
Education Needs: On-The-Job Training, High School Diploma or G.E.D
Licensure/Certification: Usually Not Required
Physical Abilities Not Required: Not Climb, Not Kneel, Part Time Work
Holland Interest Score*: CES

* See Appendix A

Occupation Interest

This occupation suits people who enjoy interacting with other people on a daily basis. Those attracted to customer service roles generally have good communication skills and find satisfaction in interacting with people. They should be able to demonstrate patience and empathy when dealing with customer complaints or questions. In some cases, customer service representatives may also be required to be highly proficient or knowledgeable in a certain technical field (for example, customer service representatives who provide computing helpdesk support).

A Day in the Life—Duties and Responsibilities

A customer service representative's work involves assisting and supporting customers with their inquiries. This may include answering questions, providing technical help and advice, processing orders, taking payment information, responding to complaints, forwarding customers to supervisors for difficult inquiries, and performing other tasks as needed.

This is a role which requires patience, empathy, and tact, especially when dealing with customer complaints. It also requires the ability to solve problems. In many instances, customer service representatives must be able to deal with a large volume of customer inquiries, especially if they are employed in call centers or similar environments.

Customer interactions may occur on the internet though the company website or social media sites, on the telephone, and/or via email and instant messaging (chats). In the course of resolving customer inquiries they may be searching for and entering information into databases, preparing letters and emails, and using the Internet.

Customer service representatives may expect to communicate and collaborate with a variety of colleagues and/or third party vendors. Interorganizational coordination may be required among a variety of departments and the customer service representative may be required to attend meetings or regularly liaise with other individuals and groups. They may have to attend periodic training to familiarize themselves with new company products and policies.

Duties and Responsibilities

- Demonstrating company goodwill
- Tracing through complicated billing or shipping problems
- Investigating service difficulties and providing solutions
- Solving customer problems

WORK ENVIRONMENT

Immediate Physical Environment

Office settings predominate. Many industries employ customer service representatives, and the specific physical environment will be influenced by the size and type of employer. There is a trend among some national and global companies to consolidate their customer support services at a single location. These work environments are often call centers.

Human Environment

Customer service representative roles demand strong communication skills. This job involves almost constant interaction with people, so patience, courtesy, and attention to detail are highly regarded. Some customer service representative roles include face-to-face contact with customers while others may involve only telephone or Internet-mediated contact.

Transferable Skills and Abilities

Communication Skills
- Listening attentively
- Speaking effectively

Interpersonal/Social Skills
- Being able to work independently
- Cooperating with others
- Working as a member of a team

Organization & Management Skills
- Managing conflict

Technological Environment

Daily operations will demand the use of standard office technologies, including telephone, e-mail, photocopiers, and Internet. Customer service representatives are usually also required to use computers and software, including word processing programs, spreadsheets, and specialist databases. Keyboarding skills are an advantage.

EDUCATION, TRAINING, AND ADVANCEMENT

High School/Secondary

High school students can best prepare for a career as a customer service representative by taking courses in business and communications. Foreign languages may be advantageous as an increasing number of employers work in cross-cultural contexts and extend into global markets. Studies in mathematics and accounting provide a foundation for the numerical requirements of the role. Likewise, computing and keyboarding would be beneficial. Psychology and cultural studies may help candidates to develop empathetic relationship skills and to gain insight into creative problem solving. Becoming involved in part-time customer service work while still in high school (e.g. afterschool or weekend work in administration, hospitality, or retail) is an excellent way to gain entry-level experience into the customer service profession.

Suggested High School Subjects
- Business & Computer Technology
- English
- Foreign Languages
- Keyboarding
- Mathematics
- Psychology
- Speech

Related Career Pathways/Majors
Business, Management & Administration Cluster
- Administrative & Information Support Pathway

Business, Management & Administration Cluster
- Business Financial Management & Accounting Pathway

Business, Management & Administration Cluster
- Marketing Pathway

Finance Cluster
- Banking & Related Services Pathway

Finance Cluster
- Insurance Services Pathway

Health Science Cluster
- Health Informatics Pathway

Human Services Cluster
- Consumer Services Pathway

Marketing, Sales & Service Cluster
- Buying & Merchandising Pathway

Transportation, Distribution & Logistics Cluster
- Sales & Service Pathway

Famous First

In 1876, the telephone was invented and started changing the way businesses handled customer service. Now, customers could call a company and set everything up over the phone. In 1894, customer service took another leap forward with the invention of the switchboard. Customers could call stores and businesses directly across the entire country through a simple connection. This made it much easier to get help and ask questions without leaving home.

Source: serversitters.com

Postsecondary

The customer service representative profession generally requires no formal postsecondary educational qualifications, although an associate's or bachelor's degree in psychology, communications, or a related discipline may be attractive to employers. On-the-job experience in customer service support and delivery is usually considered more important than formal qualifications. Many employers will provide extensive induction and on-the-job training to ensure that their customer service representatives become experts in the products and services they represent.

Related College Majors
- Administrative Assistant/Secretarial Science, General
- General Retailing & Wholesaling Operations & Skills
- General Selling Skills & Sales Operations
- Receptionist Training

Adult Job Seekers

Adults seeking a career transition into or return to a customer service representative position are advised to refresh their skills and update their resume. Entry-level opportunities may exist as part-time, full-time, after-hours or weekend roles, as well as temporary or contract jobs. Aspiring customer service representatives may first obtain experience in the same company at a lower level and then progress to the customer service representative position. Opportunities for career advancement will depend largely on the size and type of organization in which the candidate works and their breadth of experience. Larger organizations may provide a tiered promotional system which ties the customer service representative's position title and wages to their level of experience and/or length of service. Customer service representatives seeking promotion may consider opportunities in supervisory or management roles.

Professional Certification and Licensure

There is no professional certification or licensure required for customer service representatives.

Additional Requirements

High quality customer service is increasingly recognized by business leaders and managers as a major driver of business success, since it helps consumers distinguish between organizations that provide similar goods and services. This is slowly helping to transition the perception of customer service from a basic business support role to a more highly valued profession and career. Those individuals who achieve proficiency in a foreign language may have an advantage over other candidates. Customer service representatives should be skilled at remaining courteous even when conversing with rude customers. Effective, professional conflict resolution is extremely valuable in this position.

Fun Fact

If you do social media work for a brand, you'd better be quick on your feet because 78 percent of people who complain to a brand via Twitter expect a response within an hour.
Source: Brandwatch.com

EARNINGS AND ADVANCEMENT

Advancement may mean becoming head of customer service or, in a small to medium sized firm, becoming an office manager. Median annual earnings of customer service representatives were $32,300 in 2016. The lowest ten percent earned less than $20,810, and the highest ten percent earned more than $53,730.

Customer service representatives may receive paid vacations, holidays, and sick days; life and health insurance; and retirement benefits. These are usually paid by the employer.

EMPLOYMENT AND OUTLOOK

Customer service representatives held about 2.8 million jobs nationally in 2016. Employment of customer service representatives is projected to grow 5 percent from 2016 to 2026, about as fast as the average for all occupations.

Overall employment growth should result from growth in industries that specialize in handling customer service. Specifically, telephone call centers, also known as customer contact centers, are expected to add the most new jobs for customer service representatives. Employment of representatives in these centers is projected to grow 36 percent from 2016 to 2026. Some businesses are increasingly contracting out their customer service operations to telephone call centers because the call centers provide consolidated sales and customer service functions.

Employment growth of customer service representatives in all other industries will be driven by growth of those industries, as well as consumers' demand for products and services that require customer support. Some companies will continue to use in-house service centers to differentiate themselves from competitors, particularly for inquiries that are more complex, such as refunding accounts or confirming insurance coverage.

However, some companies are increasingly using Internet self-service or interactive voice-response systems that enable customers to perform simple tasks, such as changing addresses or reviewing account billing, without speaking to a representative. Improvements in technology will gradually allow these automated systems to perform more advanced tasks

Related Occupations
- Administrative Assistant
- Computer Support Specialist
- Online Merchant
- Receptionist & Information Clerk
- Retail Salesperson
- Secretary

Conversation About . . .
SOCIAL MEDIA IN CUSTOMER SERVICE
Aaron Maass
Founder & CEO
MaassMedia LLC, Philadelphia

1. How are companies using social media analytics in the area of customer service?

The analysis of social media is still in its infancy. People use social media as a way to talk to each other and express themselves. A lot of companies are beginning to use those conversations to understand more about their customers. On a very basic level, companies can analyze whether a post or a comment is positive or negative and track that over time.

That's on a macro scale. On a micro scale, the more sophisticated companies are actually responding to posts or becoming involved in individual conversations as a customer service.

The ones doing that are really smart. It takes an extraordinary investment of labor and time and energy, but it pays its rewards. A lot of people would say, well that could be automated. It can be automated, but in the world of social media. authenticity matters. Most savvy posters will see right through an automated response.

2. Is there a way to do automated responses well?

There's a trend of using bots. Take GEICO as an example. GEICO could have a bot on social media that allows you to ask GEICO a question about insurance. "I just got into an accident. Am I covered?" Instead of hearing from a live person, which is expensive, you might get a response from a bot that uses artificial intelligence to understand the nature of your question. You could actually have this back and forth conversation with a bot.

3. What types of situations warrant the investment of a live person?

Many companies are setting up social media command posts during major events like the Super Bowl or the Olympics. The idea is that the companies can respond to events as they unfold in real time. When the power went out during the Super Bowl at the Superdome several years ago, Oreo tweeted, "Power out? No problem. You can still dunk in the dark." It was retweeted 10,000 times in one hour.

There's a lot of human labor involved. Organizations that are using social media in real time literally have desks of people sitting at their computers responding. You have a job in social media where you are basically doing customer support.

It's another channel for customer service. Instead of the chat or working in a call center, you're working in a social media command center.

MORE INFORMATION

International Customer Service Association
1110 South Avenue, Suite 50
Staten Island, NY 10314
347.273.1303
info@icsatoday.org
www.icsatoday.org

National Customer Service Association
1714 Pfitzer Road
Normal, IL 61761
Phone: 309-454-3038
309.452.8831
www.nationalcsa.com/

Kylie Hughes/Editor

Database Administrator

Snapshot

Career Cluster(s): Finance, Information Technology, Science, Technology, Engineering & Mathematics

Interests: Computer technology, solving problems, detail-oriented work, numbers

Earnings (2016 median pay): $84,950 per year; $40.84 per hour

Employment & Outlook: Faster Than Average Growth Expected

OVERVIEW

Sphere of Work

Database administrators manage computer databases and networks for businesses, government agencies, hospitals, universities, and other organizations. They set up computer networks according to the needs of the client, integrate data from old systems into new networks, and perform troubleshooting activities as needed. Their responsibilities include organizing, accessing, and increasing storage space for data, adding and deleting users, and purging outdated programs. They

are also charged with the security of the networks on which they work, periodically installing and updating firewalls and virus protection software. Database administrators train employees on new systems and communicate with employees on any changes to or issues with the network.

Work Environment

Database administrators work in offices, computer labs, and similar environments. These facilities are generally clean, well lit, and well ventilated. Many administrators' offices are large rooms that contain a company's central server as well as work stations. In some cases, telecommuting may be an option. Database administrators typically work a standard forty-hour week, although those hours may be increased when major issues occur in the company's network or a new network is brought on line. Some administrators work longer hours also because they are on call, standing by outside of business hours in case any problems with the network arise.

Profile

Interests: Data
Working Conditions: Work Inside
Physical Strength: Light Work
Education Needs: Bachelor's Degree
Licensure/Certification: Required
Physical Abilities Not Required: Not Climb, Not Kneel, Not Hear and/or Talk
Opportunities for Experience: Internship, Military Service, Part Time Work
Holland Interest Score*: IRE

* See Appendix A

Occupation Interest

Somebody interested in database administration should be good at problem solving, pay close attention to detail, and find satisfaction in working independently. Database administrators are in high demand, a trend that is expected to continue. Even during challenging economic times, businesses are less likely to lay off their database administrators in light of the major roles they play in operations. Database administrators are needed in virtually every industry, giving graduates a wide range of professional environments in which to seek employment.

A Day in the Life—Duties and Responsibilities

Database administrators are in charge of storing and managing a business's computer networks and maintaining up-to-date Internet security programs. Administrators meet with key employees to determine their needs. Based on the information provided, they design new systems, write new code, upgrade existing networks and programs, install new programs, and remove outdated files and software to free up space and improve speed. Database administrators run periodic tests on programs and networks in order to monitor efficiency and processing speed, check for problems, or locate both full and unused data files. Administrators frequently train new employees on the systems and, when bringing a new feature or database online, train current employees as well. Administrators may be asked to man a help desk to resolve any individual user issues or be on call after business hours to safeguard against network failures or crashes.

In addition to managing the database, administrators must develop and install firewalls that prevent the spread of viruses, spam, and other Internet-based problems. Database administrators must research the most effective virus protection software, write code that blocks unwanted entry into e-mail systems, and keep abreast of new viruses and hacker tactics.

Duties and Responsibilities

- Working with clients to determine the types of databases needed
- Designing and creating database tables
- Defining data relationships between tables
- Designing application interfaces and data entry systems
- Writing the code that allows comparing and cross-referencing of data
- Testing to make sure steps are correct and will produce the desired results
- Debugging and rewriting programs if unexpected results are received

WORK ENVIRONMENT

Immediate Physical Environment

Database administrators work in computer labs, offices, and similar professional environments. These areas are generally clean, well lit, and well ventilated. Depending on the company, some database administrators may be able to work from home. There is not very much physical activity involved with these positions, although administrators may be asked to move hard drives, monitors, and other hardware over short distances.

Transferable Skills and Abilities

Communication Skills
- Speaking effectively
- Writing concisely

Interpersonal/Social Skills
- Being able to work independently

Organization & Management Skills
- Organizing information or materials
- Paying attention to and handling details
- Performing routine work

Research & Planning Skills
- Identifying problems
- Solving problems
- Using logical reasoning

Human Environment

Database administrators work with all levels and types of employees within their respective organizations, including executives, managers, entry-level employees, administrative personnel, and salespeople. They also interact with external software and hardware vendors as well as off-site network administrators.

Technological Environment

Database administrators must be skilled with both desktop and laptop computer hardware (including printers, disk drives, and external hard drives), servers and data storage systems, and other devices. They should also be capable of using a wide range of computer software, including virus prevention, archival, database management, metadata (which provides information about the data collected by a network), and other programs.

EDUCATION, TRAINING, AND ADVANCEMENT

High School/Secondary

High school students should study computer science and mathematics such as algebra, calculus, geometry, and trigonometry. Additionally, business and accounting courses will help database administrators understand the particular companies for which they will work, as well as how business is conducted in general.

Suggested High School Subjects
- Accounting
- Algebra
- Applied Communication
- Applied Math
- Bookkeeping
- Business & Computer Technology
- Business Data Processing
- Calculus
- College Preparatory
- Computer Programming
- Computer Science
- English
- Geometry
- Keyboarding
- Mathematics
- Statistics
- Trigonometry

Related Career Pathways/Majors
Finance Cluster
- Banking & Related Services Pathway

Information Technology Cluster
- Information Support & Services Pathway

Science, Technology, Engineering & Mathematics Cluster
- Engineering & Technology Pathway

Famous First

Edgar Codd is the creator of the relational databases model. In the 1960s and 1970s, Codd worked out his theories of data arrangement, based on mathematical set theory. He wanted to store data in cross-referenced tables, allowing the information to be presented in multiple permutations. It was a revolutionary approach. Codd's concept of data arrangement was seen within IBM as an "intellectual curiosity" at best and, at worst, as undermining IBM's existing products. Codd's ideas however were picked up by local entrepreneurs and resulted in the formation of firms such as Oracle (today the number two independent software firm after Microsoft), Ingres, Informix and Sybase.

Source: history-computer.com/ModernComputer

"key"		
login	first	last
mark	Samuel	Clemens
lion	Lion	Kimbro
kitty	Amber	Straub

login	phone
mark	555.555.5555

"related table"

Postsecondary

Most database administrators complete a two-year associate's degree or a four-year bachelor's degree in computer science, management information systems (MIS), or similar fields. The bachelor's degree is preferred in a competitive job market. A master's degree in business administration with a focus on information systems, though not necessary, will provide even more of an advantage. Postsecondary students are encouraged to seek internships at professional organizations.

Related College Majors
- Computer Engineering
- Computer Engineering Technology
- Computer Maintenance Technology
- Computer Programming
- Computer Science
- Data Processing Technology
- Information Sciences & Systems
- Management Information Systems & Business Data Processing

Adult Job Seekers

Individuals with limited experience as database administrators are encouraged to start out as computer programmers, software developers, and help desk technicians in order to gain more experience, which can lead to internal promotion to the position of database administrator. Qualified and experienced database administrators should apply directly to companies, government agencies, and other organizations. Additionally, there are a number of job placement agencies that specialize in placing information systems professionals such as database administrators in open positions.

Professional Certification and Licensure

Many software companies and universities provide certification programs for database administrators. Microsoft, for example, offers an intensive certification course on usage of their SQL (structured query language) databases. Some companies require such certification; even when this is not the case, being certified will certainly enhance a candidate's competitiveness regarding open positions.

Additional Requirements

Database administrators must be able to analyze complex systems and address intricate issues. They should have strong research skills, which are critical in monitoring new developments in viruses, hacker attacks, and programs that can block these threats. Because the technology changes so often, database administrators should be prepared to take occasional classes in order to stay up to date. They must also have excellent communications skills, with the ability not only to help others with system problems but also to train them in how to maximize their use of the network.

EARNINGS AND ADVANCEMENT

Earnings depend on the size and location of the employer and the education and experience of the employee. Median annual earnings of database administrators was $84,950 in May 2016. The lowest 10 percent earned less than $47,300, and the highest 10 percent earned more than $129,930.

Database administrators may receive paid vacations, holidays, and sick days; life and health insurance; and retirement benefits. These are usually paid by the employer.

EMPLOYMENT AND OUTLOOK

There were about 119,500 database administrators employed nationally in 2016. Employment of database administrators (DBAs) is projected to grow 11 percent from 2016 to 2026, faster than the average for all occupations. Growth in this occupation will be driven by the increased data needs of companies in all sectors of the economy. Database administrators will be needed to organize and present data in a way that makes it easy for analysts and other stakeholders to understand.

The increasing popularity of database-as-a-service, which allows database administration to be done by a third party over the Internet, could increase the employment of DBAs at cloud computing firms in the data processing, hosting, and related services industry. Employment of DBAs in this industry is projected to grow 17 percent from 2016 to 2026.

Employment of DBAs in the computer systems design and related services industry is projected to grow 20 percent from 2016 to 2026.

The increasing adoption of cloud services by small and medium-sized businesses that do not have their own dedicated information technology (IT) departments could increase the employment of DBAs in establishments in this industry.

Related Occupations
- Computer & Information Systems Manager
- Computer Engineer
- Computer Network Architect
- Computer Operator
- Computer Programmer
- Computer Support Specialist
- Computer Systems Analyst
- Computer-Control Tool Programmer
- Information Security Analyst
- Information Technology Project Manager
- Network & Computer Systems Administrator
- Web Administrator

Related Military Occupations
- Computer Programmer
- Computer Systems Specialist

MORE INFORMATION

Association for Computing Machinery
2 Penn Plaza, Suite 701
New York, NY 10121-0701
800.342.6626
acmhelp@acm.org
www.acm.org

Data Management Association International
19239 N. Dale Mabry Highway, #132
Lutz, FL 33548
813.778.5495
www.dama.org

IEEE Computer Society
2001 L Street, NW, Suite 700
Washington, DC 20036-4928
202.371.0101
help@computer.org
www.computer.org

Institute for the Certification of Computer Professionals
2400 East Devon Avenue, Suite 281
Des Plaines, IL 60018-4610
800.843.8227
office@iccp.org
www.iccp.org

League of Professional System Administrators
P.O. Box 5161
Trenton, NJ 08638
www.lopsa.org

Network Professional Association
1401 Hermes Lane
San Diego, CA 92154
888.672.6720
www.npa.org

Professional Association for SQL Server
203 North LaSalle, Suite 2100
Chicago, IL 60601
425.967.8000
www.sqlpass.org

Michael Auerbach/Editor

Film & Video Editor & Camera Operator

Snapshot

Career Cluster(s): Arts, A/V Technology & Communications, Manufacturing, Science, Technology, Engineering & Mathematics

Interests: Broadcast media and technology, audio/visual techniques, film production

Earnings (Yearly Average): $59,040 per year; $28.39 per hour

Employment & Outlook: Faster Than Average Growth Expected

OVERVIEW

Sphere of Work

Film and video editors and camera operators manipulate images that entertain or inform an audience. Camera operators capture a wide range of material for TV shows, motion pictures, music videos, documentaries, or news and sporting events. Editors take footage shot by camera operators and organize it into a final product. They collaborate with producers and directors to create the final production.

Work Environment

Film and video editors and camera operators typically work in studios or in office settings. Camera operators and videographers often shoot raw footage on location.

Film and video editors work in editing rooms by themselves, or with producers and directors, for many hours at a time. Cinematographers and operators who film movies or TV shows may film on location and be away from home for months at a time. Operators who travel usually must carry heavy equipment to their shooting locations.

Some camera operators work in uncomfortable or even dangerous conditions, such as severe weather, military conflicts, and natural disasters. They may have to stand for long periods waiting for an event to take place. They may carry heavy equipment while on shooting assignment.

Many camera operators have one or more assistants working under their supervision. The assistants set up the camera equipment and may be responsible for its storage and care. They also help the operator determine the best shooting angle and make sure that the camera stays in focus. Likewise, editors often have one or more assistants. The assistants support the editor by keeping track of each shot in a database or loading digital video into an editing bay. Assistants also may do some of the editing tasks.

Most operators prefer using digital cameras because these smaller, more inexpensive instruments give them more flexibility in shooting angles. Digital cameras also have changed the job of some camera assistants: Instead of loading film or choosing lenses, they download digital images or choose a type of software program to use with the camera. In addition, drone cameras give operators an opportunity to film in the air, or in places that are hard to reach.

Nearly all editing work is done on a computer, and editors often are trained in a specific type of editing software.

Profile

Interests: Data, Things
Working Conditions: Work Inside, Work Both Inside and Outside
Physical Strength: Light Work
Education Needs: Junior/Technical/Community College, Bachelor's Degree
Licensure/Certification: Recommended
Physical Abilities Not Required: Not Climb, Not Kneel
Opportunities for Experience: Apprenticeship, Military Service, Volunteer Work, Part Time Work
Holland Interest Score*: RCE

* See Appendix A

Occupation Interest

Film and video editors and camera operators play an integral role in ensuring that broadcasts are transmitted properly, making their work a fulfilling career for individuals who thrive in a complex and fast-paced technological environment. The broad range of equipment used in radio and television, including microphones, sound recorders, lights, cameras, and transmitters, provides technicians with the opportunity to gain hands-on experience in a variety of areas or choose to specialize in one particular field.

A Day in the Life—Duties and Responsibilities

Film and video editors and camera operators coordinate with station managers, producers, and directors to ensure that audiovisual systems operate properly while radio or television programs are running. To this end, they monitor the strength and clarity of outgoing and incoming signals, regulate sound and visual effects using sound boards and video monitors, and report any equipment failures or issues.

Studio camera operators work in a broadcast studio and videotape their subjects from a fixed position. There may be one or several cameras in use at a time. Operators normally follow directions that give the order of the shots. They often have time to practice camera movements before shooting begins. If they are shooting a live event, they must be able to make adjustments at a moment's notice and follow the instructions of the show's director. The use of robotic cameras is common among studio camera operators, and one operator may control several cameras at once.

Cinematographers film motion pictures. They usually have a team of camera operators and assistants working under them. They determine the angles and types of equipment that will best capture a shot. They also adjust the lighting in a shot, because that is an important part of how the image looks.

Cinematographers may use stationary cameras that shoot whatever passes in front of them, or they may use a camera mounted on a track and move around the action. Some cinematographers sit on cranes to film an action scene; others carry the camera on their shoulder while they move around the action.

Some cinematographers specialize in filming cartoons or special effects. For information about a career in animation, see multimedia artists and animators.

Videographers film or videotape private ceremonies or special events, such as weddings. They also may work with companies and make corporate documentaries on a variety of topics. Some videographers post their work on video-sharing websites for prospective clients. Most videographers edit their own material.

Many videographers run their own business or do freelance work. They may submit bids, write contracts, and get permission to shoot on locations that may not be open to the public. They also get copyright protection for their work and keep financial records.

Many editors and camera operators, but particularly videographers, put their creative work online. If it becomes popular, they gain more recognition, which can lead to future employment or freelance opportunities.

Duties and Responsibilities

- Shoot and record television programs, motion pictures, music videos, documentaries, or news and sporting events
- Organize digital footage with video-editing software
- Collaborate with a director to determine the overall vision of the production
- Discuss filming and editing techniques with a director to improve a scene
- Select the appropriate equipment, such as the type of lens or lighting
- Shoot or edit a scene based on the director's vision

OCCUPATION SPECIALTIES

Video Operators

Video Operators control video consoles to regulate the transmission of television screens and control the quality, brightness, and contrast of the video output.

Audio Operators

Audio Operators control audio equipment to regulate volume level and sound quality during television broadcasts.

Field Engineers

Field Engineers install and operate portable field transmission equipment to broadcast programs or events originating outside the studio.

Transmitter Operators

Transmitter Operators are responsible for monitoring and logging outgoing signals and for operating the transmitter.

Plant and Maintenance Technicians

Plant and Maintenance Technicians repair, adjust, set up, and service electronic broadcasting equipment. It is their job to determine the cause of signal breakdown and repair it.

Recording Engineers

Recording Engineers operate and maintain video and sound recording equipment. They operate the disk or recording machine to record music, dialogue, or sound effects during recording sessions, radio and television broadcasts or conferences.

WORK ENVIRONMENT

Immediate Physical Environment

Film and video editors and camera operators primarily work in television and radio stations. However, they often work outdoors, either with on-site shooting crews or on outdoor equipment, such as transmitters, located away from the station. Film and video editors and camera operators face some danger of electrocution or other injury when working with high voltages and equipment that is difficult to access.

Transferable Skills and Abilities

Communication Skills
- Speaking effectively (SCANS Basic Skill)
- Writing concisely (SCANS Basic Skill)

Interpersonal/Social Skills
- Working as a member of a team (SCANS Workplace Competency Interpersonal)

Organization & Management Skills
- Following instructions
- Paying attention to and handling details

Technical Skills
- Applying the technology to a task (SCANS Workplace Competency Technology)
- Performing scientific, mathematical and technical work
- Working with machines, tools or other objects

Human Environment

Depending on their area of work, film and video editors and camera operators may interact with directors, producers, camera and microphone operators, set construction crews, electricians, or on-air personalities. In addition, they may work closely with film and video editors and camera operators specializing in particular tasks.

Technological Environment

The equipment used by film and video editors and camera operators varies based on their responsibilities or specialty and may include sound mixers, cameras, lighting systems and towers, boom microphones, transmitter equipment, master control switchers, oscilloscopes, satellite receivers, and video editors. Technicians may also use video creation, graphic and photo imaging, and office suite computer software.

EDUCATION, TRAINING, AND ADVANCEMENT

High School/Secondary

High school students interested in becoming film and video editors and camera operators should take industrial arts courses related to radio and television repair and electronics. Courses in geometry, trigonometry, and algebra are also highly useful for aspiring technicians. Participation in the school's audiovisual department, as well as theater and other extracurricular activities focused on lighting or sound, is strongly encouraged.

Suggested High School Subjects
- Algebra
- Applied Communication
- Applied Math
- Applied Physics
- College Preparatory
- Electricity & Electronics
- English
- Geometry
- Physics
- Radio & TV Repair
- Theatre & Drama
- Trigonometry

Related Career Pathways/Majors
Arts, A/V Technology & Communications Cluster
- Journalism & Broadcasting Pathway

Manufacturing Cluster
- Maintenance, Installation & Repair Pathway
- Manufacturing Production Process Development Pathway

Science, Technology, Engineering & Mathematics Cluster
- Engineering & Technology Pathway
- Science & Mathematics Pathway

Famous First

The first portable movie cameras came out in 1923, manufactured separately by Kodak and the Victor Animatograph Company of Davenport, IA. Each company claimed to be the first in the field. Such cameras were operated by means of a hand crank that the photographer had to turn twice per second to achieve the desired effect. Within a few years Bell & Howell offered the first "ladies' camera," a thin, lightweight, and handsomely embossed item called the Filmo 75.

Postsecondary

Following high school, aspiring film and video editors and camera operators frequently complete a technical training program at a vocational school or similar institution. A growing number of film and video editors and camera operators hold associate's or bachelor's degrees, which give those candidates an edge in this highly competitive field and opens up possibilities for career advancement. Some senior-level technicians even hold advanced degrees in engineering.

Related College Majors
- Broadcast Journalism
- Radio & Television Broadcasting
- Radio & Television Broadcasting Technology

Adult Job Seekers

Experienced film and video editors and camera operators are encouraged to apply directly to open positions, while candidates who are new to the field can gain hands-on experience in a variety of areas through internships or entry-level jobs at smaller stations. Unions and trade associations, such as the National Association of Broadcast Employees and Technicians (NABET) and the National Association of Broadcasters (NAB), offer training, resources, and valuable networking opportunities.

Professional Certification and Licensure

No certification is required in order to become a broadcast technician. However, technicians may choose to become certified by the Society of Broadcast Engineers (SBE). As with any voluntary certification process, it is beneficial to consult credible professional associations within the field and follow professional debate as to the relevancy and value of any certification program.

Additional Requirements

Film and video editors and camera operators must have strong mechanical skills, with an ability to quickly analyze often-complex electronic systems and equipment. They must demonstrate both dexterity and monitoring skills, which help identify and correct mechanical issues while under strict time constraints. Some film and video editors and camera operators may be required to lift heavy equipment or climb high structures when necessary, so a degree of physical fitness is helpful.

Fun Fact

It seems like YouTube has been around forever. It arrived on the scene in 2005, revolutionizing video sharing.

Source: Smallbiztrends.com

EARNINGS AND ADVANCEMENT

Earnings of film and video editors and camera operators can vary greatly depending on the size and geographic location of the city or town. Television stations usually pay better than radio stations; commercial broadcasting usually pays more than educational broadcasting; and stations in large markets pay more than those in small ones.

Median annual earnings of camera operators, television, video, and motion picture was $55,080 in May 2016. The lowest 10 percent earned less than $26,940, and the highest 10 percent earned more than $109,200.

Film and video editors and camera operators may receive paid vacations, holidays, and sick days; life and health insurance; and retirement benefits. These are usually paid by the employer.

EMPLOYMENT AND OUTLOOK

There were a total of approximately 59,300 television, video, and motion picture camera operators and editors employed nationally in 2016. Employment of film and video editors is projected to grow 17 percent from 2016 to 2026, much faster than the average for all occupations.

Employment of camera operators is projected to grow 7 percent from 2016 to 2026, about as fast as the average for all occupations.

The number of Internet-only platforms, such as streaming services, is likely to increase, along with the number of shows produced for these platforms. This growth may lead to more work for editors and camera operators.

In broadcasting, the consolidation of roles—such as editors who determine the best angles for a shoot, the use of robotic cameras, and the increasing reliance on amateur film footage—may lead to fewer jobs for camera operators. However, more film and video editors are expected to be needed because of an increase in special effects and overall available content.

Related Occupations
- Broadcast and sound engineering technicians
- Editors
- Journalist
- Producer and director

Related Military Occupations
- Audiovisual & Broadcast Technician

Conversation About . . .
VIDEO IN SOCIAL MEDIA
Kiki L'Italien

Host and Podcaster, Association Chat
Alexandria, VA

1. When is video most called for in social media?

Some people would argue it's almost always called for. Video is taking off and the reason is movement and contrast. Our primitive brains respond to movement. We're naturally drawn to what's moving.

If you're trying to evoke emotion and make people feel, using the power of video and the power of story is probably the best thing you can do because moving images can say so much. Create video content when you want to compel people through a story, or when you might lose people if you're trying to convey something complicated, like blockchain, through language. You could read a lot of articles about it or watch the online video, "Blockchain made simple."

2. What's a technical must-know when doing video?

Audio. If you're incorporating audio into your video—say, doing an interview—people will sit through a shaky camera but they're not going to sit through screeching or weird audio problems. Don't use poor quality audio.

3. Do you use much text in your videos?

Yes. It's important to always be thinking about how audiences are taking in social media. People are using mobile devices, primarily their phone. When you're creating video, include some kind of text to explain what's happening, because most people are watching that video with the sound off. They might be standing in line at the grocery store, or sitting on the couch at home across from someone.

4. What shape: vertical or horizontal?

People don't watch TV sideways, but your phone isn't your TV. People look at smartphones in a vertical position, so square or vertical videos are ideal for making the most of that space. Square works both horizontally and vertically. Don't you hate it when you have to turn your phone to horizontal?

5. What's next?

Video is only going to get stronger. Virtual reality and movies are being created with 360-degree video, where the video changes as you turn your head. Then we have augmented reality: you won't have to walk into a store to see if that watch is going to look good on your arm. People who know how to use video well need to refine their skills to stay on top, and the more ability to do editing, the better. That's going to have a lot of value to anyone who wants to hire them, or even working on a project they're doing themselves.

MORE INFORMATION

Alliance for Women in Media
1760 Old Meadow Road, Suite 500
McLean, VA 22102
703.506.3290
www.allwomeninmedia.org

Broadcast Education Association
1771 N Street, NW
Washington, DC 20036-2891
888.380.7222
beainfo@beaweb.org
www.beaweb.org

Federal Communications Commission
445 12th Street, NW
Washington, DC 20554
888.225.5322
fccinfo@fcc.gov
www.fcc.gov

International Brotherhood of Electrical Workers
900 Seventh Street, NW
Washington, DC 20001
202.833.7000
www.ibew.org

National Association of Broadcast Employees and Technicians
501 3rd Street, NW
Washington, DC 20001
202.434.1254
mtiglio@cwa-union.org
www.nabetcwa.org

National Association of Broadcasters
1771 N Street NW
Washington, DC 20036
202.429.5300
www.nab.org

National Cable Television Association
Careers in Cable
1724 Massachusetts Avenue, NW
Washington, DC 20036
202.222.2300
webmaster@ncta.com
www.ncta.com

Society of Broadcast Engineers
9102 North Meridian Street
Suite 150
Indianapolis, IN 46260
317.846.9000
www.sbe.org

Michael Auerbach/Editor

General Manager & Top Executive

Snapshot

Career Cluster(s): Business, Management & Administration, Government & Public Administration

Interests: Having a lot of responsibility, working long hours, running an organization, communicating with others

Earnings (2016 median pay): $103, 950 per year; $49.97 per hour

Employment & Outlook: Average Growth Expected

OVERVIEW

Sphere of Work

General managers and top executives are responsible for making strategic business decisions to ensure that their organizations run smoothly and profitably. They occupy the very top tier of management and, as such, bear the ultimate responsibility to the owners and stakeholders for the organization's performance. Highly compensated, they are expected to provide a corresponding level of leadership and direction to other senior executives and managers, as well as to formulate and

communicate high-level policy. General managers and top executives in private enterprises may be known by more specific job titles, such as president, chief executive officer, or director. In the non-profit and government sectors, they may have job titles such as agency director, chief, or superintendent.

Work Environment

General managers and top executives usually spend most of their work day in office environments. Typically, they have their own office or suite of offices close to other members of the organization's executive management team. General managers and top executives can expect to spend a considerable amount of time traveling away from home, especially if their organization is national or multinational. They are frequently expected to put in as many hours as required to fulfill their duties. As a result, many top executives work sixty or more hours a week, including evenings, weekends, and holidays.

Profile

Interests: Data, People
Working Conditions: Work Inside
Physical Strength: Light Work
Education Needs: Bachelor's Degree, Master's Degree, Doctoral Degree
Licensure/Certification: Usually Not Required
Physical Abilities Not Required: Not Climb, Not Kneel
Opportunities for Experience: Internship, Military Service, Part Time Work
Holland Interest Score*: ESR

* See Appendix A

Occupation Interest

This occupation suits people who combine technical knowledge and abilities relevant to the industry they work in with sophisticated business and leadership skills and the desire and commitment needed to effectively run an organization. They must have the experience, foresight, and ability to develop an organization's strategic direction by taking into account the competitive environment, market opportunities and challenges, micro- and macroeconomics, sociopolitical factors, resource requirements, and operations. Strong analytical abilities and the capacity to set goals for short- and long-term planning are a must in this profession. This job usually requires long hours and a level of responsibility that may cause stress.

A Day in the Life—Duties and Responsibilities

A top executive's day may be dedicated to dealing with one issue or a wide variety of issues. It is likely, however, that a significant proportion of the day will be spent communicating with others, either one-on-one or in group meetings. The general manager is likely to schedule regular meetings with key staff and committees about issues such as budgets, financial results, sales forecasts, and special projects. He or she will meet regularly with the key staff who report to them. This may include, for example, the chief financial officer, human resources director, operations director, sales and marketing directors, and any other key staff. The general manager is likely to delegate duties as needed to his or her support staff, as well as task them with special projects, research, and analysis. Individuals in this position are additionally responsible for developing lower-level employees into future managers.

The organization's top executives may also be involved at a strategic level in special projects and initiatives. Depending on the type of organization, this may include, for example, crisis and reputation management, new product development and launches, mergers and acquisitions, site openings and closures, strategic operational and logistic changes, and policy development.

The general manager is responsible for reporting to the company's board of directors, owners, and investors. In the case of publicly listed companies, this includes shareholders. The general manager is responsible for ensuring that the company fulfills its legal and fiduciary responsibilities. In doing so, the general manager makes a personal guarantee to the company's board and shareholders that the information provided in official legal and financial reports is accurate and reliable.

Duties and Responsibilities

- Setting general goals and policies in collaboration with other top executives and the board of directors
- Meeting with business and government leaders to discuss policy-related matters
- Directing the operations of firms and agencies
- Overseeing department executives
- Achieving organizational goals quickly and economically

OCCUPATION SPECIALTIES

Chief Executive Officers/Presidents

Chief Executive Officers/Presidents decide policies and direct operations of organizations.

Department Store Managers

Department Store Managers direct activities, formulate, and implement policies for sales and other departments.

Bank Presidents

Bank Presidents plan and direct policies and practices of banks or other financial institutions.

Special Agents

Special Agents recruit sales agents and coordinate agencies and home offices of insurance companies.

College Presidents

College Presidents plan and direct the administration of a school, college, or university.

School Superintendents

School Superintendents direct and coordinate the administration of school systems.

Police Chiefs

Police Chiefs direct and coordinate the activities of a municipal police department.

Harbor Masters

Harbor Masters direct and coordinate the activities of a harbor police force.

Library Directors

Library Directors plan and administer library services with the approval of a board of directors.

WORK ENVIRONMENT

Immediate Physical Environment

General managers and top executives usually work from their own office, which tends to be pleasant and well-appointed. The general manager's physical environment will be influenced by the size and type of employer and the industry in which they operate.

Human Environment

This role involves a great amount of interaction with others. General managers and top executives must possess advanced oral and written communication skills, including the ability to collaborate, negotiate, and resolve conflict. They must be able to conduct themselves with diplomacy and tact and interact confidently with powerful people.

Transferable Skills and Abilities

Communication Skills
- Speaking effectively
- Writing concisely

Interpersonal/Social Skills
- Asserting oneself
- Cooperating with others
- Motivating others

Organization & Management Skills
- Making decisions

Research & Planning Skills
- Developing evaluation strategies
- Solving problems

Work Environment Skills
- Traveling

Technological Environment

Daily operations may demand the use of standard office technologies, including computers, telephones, e-mail, photocopiers, and the Internet. General managers and top executives are supported by an executive secretary or administrative team who completes much of the more routine paperwork and requests. The technology used by someone in this position can vary depending on the industry the organization occupies.

EDUCATION, TRAINING, AND ADVANCEMENT

High School/Secondary

High school students can best prepare for a career as a general manager and top executive by taking courses in applied communication subjects such as business writing as well as computer science. Foreign languages may also be beneficial. Courses that develop general business skills may include accounting, entrepreneurship, bookkeeping, business management, and applied mathematics. Administrative skills may be developed by taking subjects such as business computing and typing. Becoming involved in part-time administrative or clerical work after school or during the weekends builds people skills and is a helpful way to begin learning about business operations and management. Leadership experience can be developed through taking part in extracurricular activities.

Suggested High School Subjects
- Applied Communication
- College Preparatory
- Composition
- Computer Science
- English
- Entrepreneurship

Related Career Pathways/Majors

Business, Management & Administration Cluster
- Business Analysis Pathway
- Management Pathway
- Marketing Pathway

Government & Public Administration Cluster
- Foreign Service Pathway
- Governance Pathway
- Planning Pathway
- Public Management & Administration Pathway
- Regulation Pathway
- Revenue & Taxation Pathway

Famous First

Mark Zuckerberg, founder of Facebook, began programming at a young age—when he was 12 he created a messaging program that his father used in his dental office, allowing the receptionist to notify him of new patients without yelling across the office.

Source: www.facebook.com/indianeers

Postsecondary

In keeping with the level of responsibility of the position, most employers expect their general managers and top executives to possess postsecondary qualifications. The minimum requirement is considered to be a bachelor's degree in business or another relevant field. A master's degree in business administration is sometimes, but not always, considered to be a requirement. Because this position is extremely results-oriented, some individuals earn more advanced degrees, while others advance as a result of proving their abilities through on-the-job experience.

Related College Majors
- Aviation Management
- Business
- Business Administration & Management, General
- Education Administration & Supervision, General
- Enterprise Management & Operation
- Entrepreneurship
- Finance, General
- General Retailing & Wholesaling Operations & Skills
- Sport & Fitness Administration/Management
- Travel-Tourism Management

Adult Job Seekers

Adults seeking a career as a general manager and top executive should emphasize any prior management experience or advanced knowledge of the core competencies of business management, such as financial management, human resource management, operations, and sales and marketing. Adult job seekers may need to supplement their current skill set by taking classes in relevant areas. Candidates should keep in mind that many companies promote their existing managers into top executive positions. Networking, job searching, and interviewing are, therefore, critical, and this should include registering with executive recruitment agencies.

Professional Certification and Licensure

There are no formal professional certifications or licensing requirements for general managers and top executives. Professional associations offer general manager certifications and some industry authorities require staff to hold special licenses. The American Management Association (AMA) and National Management Association (NMA) provide certificate programs in a range of specialty areas, as well as general management.

Additional Requirements

The workload and pressures placed on general managers and top executives are often relentless or intense, so these individuals should be highly motivated, confident, and able to thrive under pressure. Work/life balance may be difficult to achieve or maintain in such a demanding and responsible role, which often requires a great commitment of time and energy.

Fun Fact

In the fall of 2006, Facebook launched to the general public—meaning people with an email address over age 13—and by 2014, Facebook drove nearly one-fourth of total visits websites received.

Source: Wikipedia and Shareaholic.com

EARNINGS AND ADVANCEMENT

General managers and top executives are among the highest paid workers in the nation. Earnings depend on the level of managerial responsibility, length of service, and type, size and geographic location of the firm. Salaries in manufacturing and finance are generally higher than in state and local government.

Median annual earnings of chief executives was $181,210 in May 2016. The lowest 10 percent earned less than $69,780, and the highest 10 percent earned more than $208,000.

The median annual wage for general and operations managers was $99,310 in May 2016. The lowest 10 percent earned less than $44,290, and the highest 10 percent earned more than $208,000.

General managers and top executives receive paid vacations, holidays, and sick days; life and health insurance; and retirement benefits. These are paid by the employer. They may also receive the use of company aircraft and cars, expense allowances and stock options.

EMPLOYMENT AND OUTLOOK

General managers and top executives held about 2.6 million jobs nationally in 2016. Overall employment of top executives is projected to grow 8 percent from 2016 to 2026, about as fast as the average for all occupations. Employment growth will vary widely by occupation (see table below) and industry, and is largely dependent on the rate of industry growth.

Top executives are essential for running companies and organizations and their work is central to the success of a company.

Generally, employment growth will be driven by the formation of new organizations and expansion of existing ones, which will require more managers and executives to direct these operations.

However, improving office technology and changing organizational structures have increased the ability of the chief executive officer to manage the day-to-day operations of a business. In addition, the rate of new firm creation has slowed in recent years, with economic activity and employment becoming increasingly concentrated in larger, more mature companies. The demand for chief executives is projected to decline slightly because of the expectation that these trends are likely to continue over the next ten years.

Related Occupations

- City Manager
- Computer & Information Systems Manager
- Education Administrator
- Financial Manager
- Human Resources Specialist/Manager
- Information Technology Project Manager
- Management Analyst & Consultant
- Medical & Health Services Manager
- Online Merchant
- Postmaster & Mail Superintendent
- Public Administrator
- Public Relations Specialist
- Retail Store Sales Manager

Related Military Occupations

- Law Enforcement & Security Officer
- Law Enforcement & Security Specialist
- Military Police

Conversation With . . .
SREE SREENIVASAN

Chief Digital Officer
City of New York, New York, New York
IT, over 25 years

1. What was your individual career path in terms of education/training, entry-level job, or other significant opportunity?

I studied history at St. Stephen's College in Delhi and was a professional journalist in India. Eventually, I moved to the U.S. and taught journalism at Columbia University for 20 years. In 2012, I became the first Chief Digital Officer of Columbia University and, about a year later, became the first CDO of the Metropolitan Museum of Art, which I did for three years before being hired by the City of New York in 2016.

Along the way, I founded the social media educational programs Social Media One-Night Stand and Social Media Weekend. I was part of the founding team at DNAinfo.com, named one of the six hottest startups of 2010 by BusinessInsider. My podcast on CBS Radio's PlayIt is the "@Sree Show: Talking tech, culture, entrepreneurship."

My role as Chief Digital Officer is to help make New York City the most tech-savvy, the most transparent, and the most digitally equitable city in the world. That's what the mayor tweeted when I was hired.

Digital technology has already changed the world and will continue to change the world.

2. What are the most important skills and/or qualities for someone in your profession?

A Chief Digital Officer (CDO) is different from a Chief Technology Officer (CTO). A CDO usually deals with public engagement, whereas a CTO mainly deals with infrastructure and planning and wires and wireless and computers and devices. The CDO works more on the overall strategy of connecting with the public. The CDO role is relatively new. It's still being created and adapted, so it's different in different industries. It requires a deep understanding of technology, a deep understanding of the potential of specific platforms, and a deep understanding of the problems and pitfalls of those platforms. You also need an understanding of how technology has evolved and where consumers and industries are going.

3. What do you wish you had known going into this profession?

I wish I had known how big the Internet was going to be. I understood a little bit, but not the scale and how it would transform the world. I would have understood and been able to do a lot more with the technology. Hey, I would have invested in some of these things. I might have joined one of these companies.

4. Are there many job opportunities in your profession? In what specific areas?

Lots and lots of companies are excited about getting a CDO into their company. But while there are a lot of opportunities, it's not like there are a lot of CDO jobs; every company will have only one CDO. But getting on that path is really important. That means figuring out where things are going, where technology is changing, so that you can understand and prepare for the changes that are coming.

5. How do you see your profession changing in the next five years? What role will technology play in those changes, and what skills will be required?

I believe that all the changes we've seen in the last 10 years, we're going to see even more in the next 10 years—faster, more deep and more meaningful changes. And that's hard to believe because we've had so many changes already.

One of the ways things are going to change is that the expertise of the folks who are in this role is going to get more complicated. I'm lucky that I entered when I did. The next generation is going to have to know a lot more technology, a lot more hands-on technology.

6. What do you enjoy most about your job? What do you enjoy least about your job?

What I enjoy most is the ability to work with people. You help people every day and make their lives better. That's what you do every morning—you think of how you can reduce red tape, make things better, faster, easier for people. Reduce aggravation. That's a wonderful thing. The hardest thing about being a CDO is you have to work very closely with lots of different people, which is exciting, but it also means you don't have full control. It's not like you're the CEO. You have to depend on other people to execute a lot of the things you want to do.

7. Can you suggest a valuable "try this" for students considering a career in your profession?

What they can try is internships at big organizations that have CDOs. Or working with a company that doesn't have a CDO, but working with the Chief Technology Officer or Chief Information Officer and thinking about occasions where if somebody's priority was not technology, where they would have benefited by having a digital strategy. By the time you get into your career, there's a good chance there'll be a CDO for that company. There are hundreds and hundreds and soon thousands of CDOs.

I would also read all the archives of www.cdosummit.com. I think that'll help.

MORE INFORMATION

Business and Professional Women's Foundation
1718 M Street NW, #148
Washington, DC 20036
202.293.1100
foundation@bpwfoundation.org
www.bpwfoundation.org

Career Advancement Scholarship
Program
www.free-4u.com/bpw-career_
advancement_scholarship_program.htm

National Management Association
2210 Arbor Boulevard
Dayton, OH 45439
937.294.0421
nma@nma1.org
www.nma1.org

Various national awards; eligibility is
contingent on membership
www.nma1.org/Awards/NMA_Awards.
html#National_Awards

Kylie Hughes/Editor

Graphic Designer

Snapshot

Career Cluster(s): Arts, A/V Technology & Communications, Business, Management & Administration, Information Technology

Interests: Visual arts, advertising, marketing, being creative, communicating with others

Earnings (2016 median pay): $47,640 per year; $22.90 per hour

Employment & Outlook: Slower than Average Growth Expected

OVERVIEW

Sphere of Work

Graphic designers create visually appealing products and promotional materials that range from simple logos or business cards to entire corporate branding campaigns. Their work is intended to convey a commercial message or otherwise draw attention to an idea, which they accomplish mostly with sophisticated graphic design and animation software. Traditional artistic mediums, such as printmaking or painting, continue to be used, but sporadically. A designer interested in a long-term career must also learn skills in animation, digital video

production, copywriting, web design, or marketing, or collaborate frequently with people who possess these skill sets or perform these job functions.

Work Environment

Graphic designers work mostly in the publishing, advertising, and marketing industries, but some work for graphic design firms or government agencies. Many are self-employed. They spend much of their time working on computers, but may also have access to a full art studio. If self-employed, they interact heavily with clients. If employed in a design firm or design department, they interact with a team of professionals and staff and have less direct contact with clients; however, some customer service is necessary when choosing the final design—a process that can take anywhere from a couple of days to several weeks.

Profile

Interests: People, Things
Working Conditions: Work Inside
Physical Strength: Light Work, Medium Work
Education Needs: Bachelor's Degree
Licensure/Certification: Usually Not Required
Physical Abilities Not Required: Not Climb, Not Kneel, Not Hear and/or Talk
Opportunities for Experience: Part Time Work
Holland Interest Score*: AES

* See Appendix A

Occupation Interest

People who are attracted to graphic design tend to be creative thinkers who are interested in solving problems with images or in making the world more visually interesting. They are artistic and have a good eye for detail, but are also capable of seeing the big picture and being flexible in their presentation of multiple design ideas for a single project. They must have excellent interpersonal and communication skills since they almost always work closely with members of a team. They must be able to handle criticism and work under pressure to meet deadlines.

A Day in the Life—Duties and Responsibilities

Graphic designers are responsible for planning and carrying out projects that fulfill their clients' needs. A major specialty today is branding, in which the designer works with a team of writers, artists, market researchers, and others to create a company's image, including a recognizable logo, stylized advertisements, catchy slogans, and high-tech trade show displays. The designer will suggest colors, images, fonts, and other artistic elements, then create several sample designs for each element of the branding campaign.

Graphic designers create the covers and interior layout for magazines, books, brochures, newspapers, and other print materials. Typically, they work with editors to acquire the articles and advertisements, and then fit them into the allotted space in the most appealing manner. Graphic designers select fonts, graphics, and other design elements (in collaboration with the client or author if the project is a book) and also design internal advertisements that are presented with the final product.

Study of graphic design discipline includes the option to learn website design skills, so some graphic designers specialize in web design and are able to earn a living without working on any print design projects. Some graphic designers collaborate with programmers to create computer games, with authors to create graphic novels, with interior decorators to plan the interiors of businesses, or with architects to design public spaces.

Self-employed graphic designers must also spend some of their time marketing their services, billing customers, preparing contracts, and handling other administrative and business management tasks.

Duties and Responsibilities

- Designing images that convey a message or identify a product or organization
- Creating designs by hand or using computer software
- Meeting with clients to determine their needs
- Deciding on the message that a design should portray
- Giving advice to clients on ways to reach an audience through visual means

OCCUPATION SPECIALTIES

Cartoonists

Cartoonists draw political cartoons, newspaper comics, or comic books.

Fashion Artists

Fashion Artists draw stylish illustrations of new clothing fashions for newspapers or related advertisements.

Illustrators

Illustrators create pictures for books, magazines, billboards, posters and record albums.

Medical and Scientific Illustrators

Medical and Scientific Illustrators draw precise illustrations of machines, plants, animals, or parts of the human body or animal bodies for business and educational purposes.

Set Illustrators

Set Illustrators build and decorate sets for movies, television, and theatrical productions.

Motion Picture Cartoonists

Motion Picture Cartoonists draw series of pictures for animated films shown on TV and in movies.

WORK ENVIRONMENT

Immediate Physical Environment

Graphic designers usually work in studios or offices surrounded by art samples and design reference materials. If a project has a tight deadline, the graphic designer can expect to work some evening hours or work on the design from their home computer until the project is done.

Transferable Skills and Abilities

Communication Skills
- Expressing thoughts and ideas
- Speaking effectively
- Writing concisely

Creative/Artistic Skills
- Being skilled in art, music or dance

Interpersonal/Social Skills
- Being able to work independently
- Perceiving others' feelings

Organization & Management Skills
- Managing time
- Meeting goals and deadlines

Human Environment

In larger design firms and departments, a graphic designer is often one member of a creative team comprised of photographers, illustrators, web developers, and others who collaborate on projects under the supervision of a creative director. Designers may also work with market researchers, architects, interior designers, content editors, clients, authors, and other professionals outside the firm.

Technological Environment

Graphic designers most often use Adobe Creative Suite software (Photoshop, Illustrator, and InDesign) for cover design, manipulating and creating illustrations, page layout design, editing and placing digital photographs, and other purposes. They also use digital photography and video cameras, scanners, printmaking equipment, printing and publishing equipment, and other tools. Each design project is different and may require different resources, so graphic designers should enjoy learning new skills.

EDUCATION, TRAINING, AND ADVANCEMENT

High School/Secondary

Students should pursue a comprehensive college-preparatory program that includes courses in art, graphic design, computer science, and the social sciences. Other relevant courses include film, new media, photography, and industrial arts. Awareness of contemporary graphic design, web design, and animation software programs is extremely important. Most college admissions programs require a portfolio of artistic work, which might include digital designs, as well as hand-drawn sketches or paintings, sculpture, and other sample work.

Suggested High School Subjects
- Applied Communication
- Applied Math
- Arts
- Composition
- Computer Science
- English
- Graphic Communications
- Industrial Arts
- Literature
- Metals Technology
- Pottery
- Woodshop

Related Career Pathways/Majors
Arts, A/V Technology & Communications Cluster
- Audio & Video Technologies Pathway
- Printing Technologies Pathway
- Visual Arts Pathway

Business, Management & Administration Cluster
- Marketing Pathway

Information Technology Cluster
- Interactive Media Pathway

Famous First

The first graphic design to receive a patent was a typeface designed by George Bruce of New York in 1842. The typeface was used in printed school primers. The first company logo to receive a trademark was that of the Bass brewery of England, which still uses its distinctive red triangle on its label.

Postsecondary

Most entry-level positions require a bachelor's degree from an art school or program. Graphic design programs include courses in studio art, design, computer graphics, printing, and other graphic design specialties. Programs should include the option to work an internship. A general awareness of contemporary design is also helpful. The development of a portfolio for use in future job searches is essential, so many graphic design students make an effort to obtain freelance work.

Related College Majors

- Design & Visual Communications
- Graphic Design/Commercial Art & Illustration
- Industrial Design

Adult Job Seekers

Adults with a background in fine art, illustration, photography, typography, or another creative discipline can learn the fundamentals of graphic design and update their skills by taking graphic arts courses, which some schools offer in the evenings and on weekends to accommodate adult professionals. A portfolio can be assembled independently and/or in conjunction with classes.

Advancement for graphic designers comes with experience or taking classes in new software or techniques to supplement current skills. Some designers choose to establish their own firms. Advanced degrees can help experienced designers begin to obtain design work in a different specialty, such as web animation.

Professional Certification and Licensure

There are no licenses or nationally recognized certificates required for graphic designers; however, the idea of professional certification has gained popularity, so it is advisable to follow the issue as it progresses. Adult education programs and computer software companies offer their own certificates upon satisfactory completion of their courses.

Additional Requirements

Graphic artists must have good eyesight, be extremely creative, enjoy art and design, and find satisfaction in continuing professional development. They should be willing to follow trends in advertising, web media, and design, and should enjoy brainstorming for a single project. Although creativity is a plus, graphic designers must be able to distance themselves from their work enough to accept a client's criticism and revisions of design ideas. Excellent people skills are a must in this collaborative field, which can be highly competitive and requires the ability to make and maintain good contacts with clients and colleagues.

Fun Fact

Did you know Twitter's logo—the well-known blue bird—is called Larry? He's named after basketball legend Larry Bird.

Source: Huffingtonpost.com

EARNINGS AND ADVANCEMENT

Earnings for self-employed graphic designers vary widely. Those struggling to gain experience and a reputation may be forced to charge less for their work. Well-established freelancers may earn much more than salaried artists. The median salary for graphic designers was $47,640 in May 2016. The lowest 10 percent earned less than $27,950, and the highest 10 percent earned more than $82,020.

Graphic designers on salary may receive paid vacations, holidays, and sick days; life and health insurance; and retirement benefits. These are paid by the employer. Self-employed graphic designers must arrange for their own ways of meeting these costs.

EMPLOYMENT AND OUTLOOK

Graphic designers held about 266,300 jobs nationally in 2016. About one-third were self-employed. Some graphic designers do freelance work on the side while holding down a salaried position in a design field or another occupation field that is not design-related. The projected change in employment of graphic designers from 2016 to 2026 varies by industry. For example, employment of graphic designers in newspaper, periodical, book, and directory publishers is projected to decline 22 percent from 2016 to 2026. However, employment of graphic designers in computer systems design and related services is projected to grow 20 percent over the same period. Companies are continuing to increase their digital presence, requiring graphic designers to help create visually appealing and effective layouts of websites.

Related Occupations
- Art Director
- Designer
- Electronic Commerce Specialist
- Floral Designer
- Industrial Designer
- Interior Designer
- Medical & Scientific Illustrator
- Multimedia Artist & Animator
- Online Merchant
- Software Developer
- Web Developer

Related Military Occupations
- Graphic Designer & Illustrator

MORE INFORMATION

American Institute of Graphic Arts
164 Fifth Avenue
New York, NY 10010
212.807.1990
www.aiga.org

Graphic Artists Guild
32 Broadway, Suite 1114
New York, NY 10004-1612
212.791.3400
communications@gag.org
www.graphicartistsguild.org

National Art Education Association
1806 Robert Fulton Drive, Suite 300
Reston, VA 20191-1590
703.860.8000
info@arteducators.org
www.naea-reston.org

National Association of Schools of Art & Design
11250 Roger Bacon Drive, Suite 21
Reston, VA 20190-5248
703.437.0700
info@arts-accredit.org
nasad.arts-accredit.org/index.jsp

Society for Environmental Graphic Design
1000 Vermont Avenue NW, Suite 400
Washington, DC 20005
202.638.5555
segd@segd.org
www.segd.org/#/home.html

Sponsors awards for professionals:
www.segd.org/#/design-awards/index.html

Sponsors continuing education courses:
www.segd.org/#/learning/index.html

Society of Publication Designers
27 Union Square W., Suite 207
New York, NY 10003
212.223.3332
mail@spd.org
www.spd.org/

Sponsors student photography and design competitions:
www.spd.org/student-outreach/

Sally Driscoll/Editor

Information Security Analyst

Snapshot

Career Cluster(s): Information Technology, Science, Technology, Engineering & Mathematics

Interests: Electronics, computers, analyzing data

Earnings (2016 median pay): $92,600 per year; $44.52 per hour

Employment & Outlook: Much Faster Than Average Growth Expected

OVERVIEW

Sphere of Work

Information security analysts design and monitor technological systems that shield computer networks from outside threats. They encrypt system data, erect firewalls, and utilize a wide variety of hardware and software tools to ensure that homes, businesses, and government agencies remain protected from criminals, viruses, hackers, and other security threats.

Work Environment

Information security analysts work primarily in administrative and office settings. Analysts work at a variety of locations in and around offices and organizational complexes, most often at their own private workstations. They may also spend time working at the workstations of other employees, servicing their computers or installing equipment. Information security analysts also work in temperature-controlled server housing rooms and may be required to work remotely.

Profile

Interests: Data
Working Conditions: Work Inside
Physical Strength: Light Work
Education Needs: Bachelor's Degree
Licensure/Certification:
  Recommended
Physical Abilities Not Required: Not
  Climb
Opportunities for Experience:
  Internship, Military Service, Volunteer
  Work, Part Time Work
Holland Interest Score*: IRC

* See Appendix A

Occupation Interest

The field of information security attracts critical thinkers with a passion for electronics and computing who enjoy tackling complex problems. Information security analysts often get a tremendous amount of satisfaction from staying ahead of and repeatedly outsmarting security threats. Analysts also possess the patience to scrutinize extremely complicated data.

A Day in the Life—Duties and Responsibilities

Information security analysts handle a wide variety of duties and responsibilities on an everyday basis. Their main responsibility is to commandeer computer systems through constant outside threats. They are also tasked with identifying new potential security threats and encrypting archival data.

Data encryption is one of the central tasks of information security analysts. They are also responsible for constructing firewalls to protect organizational information. Some information security analysts are responsible for building, monitoring, and maintaining custom firewall and encryption systems for specific organizations and businesses, while others operate standard network-based firewall applications for a collection of clients.

Information security analysts are constantly on the lookout for security breaches, evidenced by the presence of outside influences on a computer network or traces of past network violations. In the event of a security breach, analysts will alert senior staff members and recommend enhancements to prevent future violations. This constant need for adaptation requires analysts to stay abreast of new developments in computer security technology through ancillary academic coursework, industry publications, annual meetings, and training seminars.

In addition to constantly monitoring the potential security risks that may target their business or organization, information security analysts must also stay informed of legislation and political developments related to digital security, particularly those that affect the rights of business clients and the civil liberties of individuals.

Duties and Responsibilities

- Monitoring the use of all data files to protect information from unauthorized access and security violations
- Performing regular system tests to ensure that all security measures are functioning properly
- Educating users about security awareness
- Updating virus protection programs as necessary when new computer viruses emerge
- Encrypting data and erecting firewalls to keep information confidential
- Maintaining current records of all security policies and procedures

WORK ENVIRONMENT

Transferable Skills and Abilities

Communication Skills
- Speaking effectively
- Writing concisely
- Listening attentively
- Reading well
- Being able to work independently

Organization & Management Skills
- Paying attention to and handling details
- Managing time
- Managing equipment/materials
- Coordinating tasks
- Making decisions
- Handling challenging situations

Research & Planning Skills
- Identifying problems
- Determining alternatives
- Gathering information
- Solving problems
- Defining needs
- Analyzing information
- Developing evaluation strategies

Technical Skills
- Performing scientific, mathematical and technical work
- Using technology to process information
- Understanding which technology is appropriate for a task
- Applying the technology to a task

Immediate Physical Environment

Information security analysts predominantly work in office settings with occasional off-site work. They work in almost every industry, from business and finance to education, government, transportation, communications, and the military.

Human Environment

Many of the tasks of information security analysts are conducted individually. However, the explanation of different security systems to coworkers and clients requires group and one-on-one interactions.

Technological Environment

Information security analysts are highly trained in technology. They utilize a variety of computer science technologies, including software, hardware, and network technology. They must also be well adept at computer programming languages and web communication.

EDUCATION, TRAINING, AND ADVANCEMENT

High School/Secondary

High school students can best prepare for a career as an information security analyst by completing courses in algebra, calculus, geometry, trigonometry, and computer courses such as introductory programming. Exposure to computer systems via internships or volunteer work can also build an important foundation for students interested in being employed in computer science.

Suggested High School Subjects
- Algebra
- Applied Communication
- Applied Math
- Business & Computer Technology
- Business Data Processing
- Calculus
- College Preparatory
- Computer Programming
- Computer Science
- English
- Geometry
- Keyboarding
- Mathematics
- Statistics
- Trigonometry

Related Career Pathways/Majors

Information Technology Cluster
- Network Systems Pathway

Science, Technology, Engineering & Mathematics Cluster
- Engineering & Technology Pathway

Famous First

When Rich Skrenta created Elk Cloner as a prank in February 1982, he was a 15-year-old high school student with a precocious ability in programming and an overwhelming interest in computers. The boot sector virus was written for Apple II systems, the dominant home computers of the time, and infected floppy discs. If an Apple II booted from an infected floppy disk, Elk Cloner became resident in the computer's memory. Uninfected discs inserted into the same computer were given a dose of the malware just as soon as a user keyed in the command catalog for a list of files. Computer viruses had been created before, but Skrenta's prank app was the first to spread in the wild, outside the computer system or network on which it was created.

Source: www.theregister.co.uk

Postsecondary

A bachelor's degree is a standard requirement for nearly all employment vacancies in the information security profession. Most candidates arrive to the field after academic training in general computer science, programming or software development while others prepare for the role by completing degree programs dedicated specifically to computer and network security. Postsecondary students who study information security complete coursework in such topics as network design, intrusion detection, wireless security, system administration, and cryptography. Additional related coursework also includes system administration and architecture and firewall construction.

Related College Majors
- Computer Installation & Repair
- Computer Maintenance Technology
- Computer Programming
- Computer Science
- Data Processing Technology
- Information Sciences & Systems
- Management Information Systems & Business Data Processing

Adult Job Seekers

The field of information security requires extensive academic and professional training. Individuals with no background in a related field should enroll in a college or a technical or vocational school that offers a program in computer security. Technical schools are also a great place for job seekers to network. Communication technologies and standards are always changing, so information security analysts should be willing to continue learning throughout their career.

Professional Certification and Licensure

There are numerous professional certifications available for information security professionals, each of which expands their frame of reference while making them attractive candidates for professional vacancies. They include Certified Information Systems Security Professional (CISSP), Certified Ethical Hacker (CEH), Certified Information Security Manager (CISM), and Global Information Assurance Certification (GIAC).

Additional Requirements

Information security is a constantly evolving field. Those interested in a career as an information security analyst must possess the patience and professionalism to stay up to date on rapidly emerging developments in a variety of technical disciplines, notably mobile communications, network diagnostics, software development, and hardware design.

EARNINGS AND ADVANCEMENT

Median annual earnings of information security analysts was $92,600 in May 2016. The lowest 10 percent earned less than $53,760, and the highest 10 percent earned more than $147,290.

Information security analysts may receive paid vacations, holidays and sick days; life and health insurance; and retirement benefits. These are usually paid by the employer.

EMPLOYMENT AND OUTLOOK

Information security analysts, web developers, and computer network architects as a group held about 302,000 jobs nationally in 2016. Employment of information security analysts is projected to grow 28 percent from 2016 to 2026, much faster than the average for all occupations.

Demand for information security analysts is expected to be very high. Cyberattacks have grown in frequency, and analysts will be needed to come up with innovative solutions to prevent hackers from stealing critical information or creating problems for computer networks.

Banks and financial institutions, as well as other types of corporations, will need to increase their information security capabilities in the face of growing cybersecurity threats. In addition, as the healthcare industry expands its use of electronic medical records, ensuring patients' privacy, and protecting personal data are becoming more important. More information security analysts are likely to be needed to create the safeguards that will satisfy patients' concerns.

Employment of information security analysts is projected to grow 56 percent in computer systems design and related services from 2016 to 2026. The increasing adoption of cloud services by small and medium-sized businesses and a rise in cybersecurity threats will create demand for managed security services providers in this industry

Related Occupations

- Computer & Information Systems Manager
- Computer Engineer
- Computer Network Architect
- Computer Programmer
- Computer Support Specialist
- Computer Systems Analyst
- Computer-Control Tool Programmer
- Database Administrator
- Information Technology Project Manager
- Software Developer
- Web Administrator
- Web Developer

Related Military Occupations

- Computer Programmer
- Computer Systems Officer
- Computer Systems Specialist

Conversation With . . .
HAYLEY KAPLAN

Owner, What is Privacy?
Los Angeles, CA
Privacy Expert, 7 years

1. What was your individual career path in terms of education/training, entry-level job, or other significant opportunity?

I majored in psychology with a business emphasis. My first job was International marketing for a large software company. Over the years, I've done bookkeeping, real estate, and owned a retail gift business. I attended UCLA for a marketing certificate in 2010 and had to create a blog for a social media class. Around that time, I posted an adorable photo of my naked 6-month-old nephew lying on his tummy on Facebook. My brother saw it and was irate because of potential online predators. I deleted the photo and realized this was one of many social media mistakes I had made or had heard of, so I created a blog about solutions to technology problems and social media mistakes.

Initially I made a little money with ads on my site, but my focus was on helping people protect themselves. I wrote tutorials for removing personal online information, but readers asked if I'd do it for them for a fee. That's what led to my current successful business of removing all sorts of online information.

My most common service is removal from 50 to 75 data broker, phone, and property directories. It's labor intensive, takes at least 60 hours and my fee begins at about $3,500 per person. My work gives people peace of mind. It also gives them second chances when I can remove information pertaining to a misstep or indiscretion they've already paid dearly for. It's unfortunate that the internet makes some people pay for mistakes indefinitely.

2. What are the most important skills and/or qualities for someone in your profession?

Key skills include tenacity, the ability to learn new things, and the ability to adapt to a changing environment. "No" does not always mean "no" and you have to be able to communicate in a professional and skilled way in order to accomplish what seems impossible. You must be discreet and respectful and self-motivated.

3. What do you wish you had known going into this profession?

I was ahead of the curve and should have capitalized on the business end from the start. But at the time family-related matters were calling for my attention and I couldn't focus on my business as much as I would have liked. But I'm making up for it now.

4. Are there many job opportunities in your profession? In what specific areas?

Yes! There is a huge need for cyber privacy, cybersecurity, and cyber safety professionals to help protect businesses from cyber threats and losses. Businesses need to comply with regulations and privacy expectations for their employees and customers or patients, because the alternative comes with high costs and risks.

There also are jobs setting up firewalls and secure networks. There are opportunities helping parents, children, educators, and everyone else stay safe. Reputation management is exploding and people in all sorts of professions are in need of this service.

People (and businesses) need help recovering from identity theft. Ransomware and cyber breaches have reached ridiculous proportions. Social media is constantly manipulated, with dangerous results—as illustrated by the manipulation of the presidential election and the gun debate. New technologies have benefits, but also give rise to new problems. People who can figure out solutions will thrive.

5. How do you see your profession changing in the next five years? How do you envision platforms evolving? What skills will be required?

It could go in two completely different directions. We could find there's no way to maintain privacy because of an explosion of directory and data broker sites and because of insistence on complete governmental transparency, which has a downside. On the other hand, it's possible things will change for the better. I'm hopeful that regulations such as the EU's General Data Protection Regulation (GDPR) will find their way here and Americans will get a shot at privacy again. Pending lawsuits against broker sites could eventually improve our privacy. Lastly, I'm hopeful that the government will stop making personal information so easily accessible online.

6. What do you enjoy most about your job? What do you enjoy least about your job?

I love the relief I'm able to provide with my free online tools, and of course to those who hire me to do the removal. I enjoy the variety of people I deal with and the fact that I learn new things regularly. Each client has different needs and requires a customized plan to solve their problem(s). That keeps me engaged.

What I enjoy least is witnessing the helplessness of people who, undeservedly, are in predicaments due to the cruel and unforgiving nature of the internet. Not all damaging information is removable.

I also fear that privacy is diminishing so quickly that a time may come where it is impossible to maintain or achieve.

7. Can you suggest a valuable "try this" for students considering a career in your profession?

Start by understanding your own privacy situation. See: https://what-is-privacy. com/2015/10/how-to-find-your-personal-information-on-the-internet/. Check your privacy settings. When you view your Facebook profile the way a stranger can see it, is everything okay for any stranger to see? If not, delete posts or alter the settings for posts intended for a limited audience.

Test your ability to delete some of your own information by using one of my online tutorials. See: https://what-is-privacy.com/category/opt-out-2/.

MORE INFORMATION

Applied Computer Security Associates
c/o Dr. Marshall Abrams, Chairman
2906 Covington Road
Silver Spring, MD 20910
abrams@acsac.org
www.acsac.org

Computer Security Institute
350 Hudson Street, Suite 300
New York, NY 10014
610.604.4604
csi@ubm.com
www.gocsi.com

Computer Security Resource Center
National Institute of Standards and Technology
100 Bureau Drive
Mail Stop 8930
Gaithersburg, MD 20899-8930
301.975.6478
csrc.nist.gov

IT Governance Institute
3701 Algonquin Road, Suite 1010
Rolling Meadows, IL 60008
847.660.5700
info@itgi.org
www.itgi.org

League of Professional System Administrators
P.O. Box 5161
Trenton, NJ 08638-0161
202.567.7201
board@lopsa.org
www.lopsa.org

National Security Institute
165 Main Street, Suite 215
Medway, MA 02053
508.533.9099
infoctr@nsi.org
www.nsi.org

National Workforce Center for Emerging Technologies
Bellevue College
3000 Landerholm Circle SE, N258
Bellevue, WA 98007-6484
425.564.4229
mmajury@bellevuecollege.edu
www.nwcet.org

John Pritchard/Editor

Information Technology Project Manager

Snapshot

Career Cluster(s): Business, Management & Administration, Information Technology, Science, Technology, Engineering & Mathematics

Interests: Science, technology, mathematics, computer science, multi-tasking, communicating with others

Earnings (2016 median pay): $135,800 per year; $65.29 per hour

Employment & Outlook: Faster than Average Growth Expected

OVERVIEW

Sphere of Work

Information technology project managers, often abbreviated as IT project managers, oversee the design and implementation of information technology systems and related infrastructure. Today's IT professional manages cloud-based strategies, wireless and mobile systems, blockchain technology, virtual team technologies, and cybersecurity. IT project managers work closely with social media strategists and

other managers in their organization to understand the company's IT needs. They then direct and supervise the technical staff in implementing the necessary hardware or software to address those needs, be they deployment or development of tools to handle social media networks and platforms; data collection, storage, and analysis; content management and delivery; information security; safeguarding and backing up sensitive customer or client information; or inventory management. IT project managers are also responsible for ensuring that all IT projects are completed within budget and on schedule.

Profile

Interests: Data, People
Working Conditions: Work Inside
Physical Strength: Light Work
Education Needs: Bachelor's Degree, Master's Degree
Licensure/Certification: Recommended
Physical Abilities Not Required: Not Climb, Not Kneel
Opportunities for Experience: Internship, Military Service, Volunteer Work, Part Time Work
Holland Interest Score*: ECI

* See Appendix A

Work Environment

IT project management professionals work primarily in administrative and office settings, though their exact locations may vary depending on their area of expertise and the type of company that employs them. The work of IT project managers requires extensive interaction with coworkers, outside vendors, and technical staff members. IT project managers must be able to draw out and interpret the specific IT needs of a department or organization and utilize that feedback to develop customized systems. Project managers are also supervisors charged with ensuring that their staff of IT professionals is continually contributing to project advancement in a timely and organized manner.

Occupation Interest

IT project managers are results-oriented multi-taskers who thrive in environments where numerous tasks and objectives are active simultaneously. IT project management covers a diverse array of scientific, technical, and managerial knowledge and skills. The majority of IT project management professionals are graduates and professionals who have a strong foundation in mathematics, computer engineering, programming, or computer science. Many IT professionals also possess an academic or professional background in software development, database management, or IT project administration.

Many universities now offer specific undergraduate and postgraduate programs in information technology and project management, but many professionals enter the field with professional and academic backgrounds that span a wide variety of computer-science disciplines. IT project managers must have strong communication and interpersonal skills as well as excellent management skills.

A Day in the Life—Duties and Responsibilities

A day in the life of an IT project manager involves planning future projects, monitoring the progress of projects that are currently active, and overseeing system maintenance, upkeep, and security tasks. These numerous responsibilities require IT managers to work in close concert with their staff, which can vary in size and scope depending on their organization of employment and particular realm of industry.

In addition to monitoring the progress of active projects, IT project managers also spend a considerable amount of time developing project plans for new initiatives in collaboration with other departmental and organizational staff members. Before work begins on new IT projects, the entire scope of each initiative must be outlined, with specific focus on the systems, schedules, funding, and required staff for each project.

IT project managers hold frequent meetings with subordinates to gauge the progress of active projects. In addition to providing technological and strategic input to resolve project delays or other concerns, IT project managers must also be able to prevent future problems through forethought and a reliance on previous project experience.

IT project managers are often responsible for reporting to executive management in order to outline the successes of previously implemented projects and to address any IT-related concerns relevant to a company or organization as a whole.

Duties and Responsibilities

- Implementing and coordinating project schedules
- Consulting with department heads to create and understand organization needs
- Training and supervising technical staff
- Monitoring the progress of projects to achieve time, budgetary and quality assurance goals
- Meeting with outside consultants, vendors and clients

WORK ENVIRONMENT

Transferable Skills and Abilities

Communication Skills
- Speaking effectively
- Writing concisely
- Listening attentively
- Reading well

Interpersonal/Social Skills
- Motivating others
- Cooperating with others
- Asserting oneself
- Being able to work independently

Organization & Management Skills
- Paying attention to and handling details
- Performing duties which change frequently
- Managing people/groups
- Managing time
- Managing equipment/materials
- Demonstrating leadership

Immediate Physical Environment

IT project managers work in a variety of settings across all types of business and industry, including corporate offices, schools, government offices, transportation centers, and industrial or medical settings.

Human Environment

IT project managers must be savvy communicators who can successfully supervise, manage, and coordinate a variety of professionals on a daily basis.

- Making decisions
- Meeting goals and deadlines
- Working quickly when necessary

Research & Planning Skills

- Analyzing information
- Developing evaluation strategies
- Using logical reasoning
- Setting goals and deadlines
- Defining needs
- Identifying problems
- Solving problems

Technical Skills

- Performing scientific, mathematical and technical work
- Using technology to process information
- Understanding which technology is appropriate for a task
- Applying the technology to a task

Technological Environment

IT project managers utilize a broad range of technologies, including collaborative operational software, application servers, networking servers, web-development software, and programming languages.

EDUCATION, TRAINING, AND ADVANCEMENT

High School/Secondary

High school students can prepare for a career in IT project management by completing course work in algebra, calculus, geometry, trigonometry, computer programming, and computer science. Advanced placement (AP) classes in computer-related subjects are especially recommended.

Participation in volunteer work, charities, or team sports can help foster the leadership and managerial skills necessary for large-scale project management. Many IT professionals gain additional experience through summer jobs or internships with computer-related organizations. Supplemental information technology courses offered by universities and community colleges are also helpful.

Suggested High School Subjects

- Accounting
- Algebra
- Applied Communication
- Applied Math
- Business & Computer Technology
- Business Data Processing
- Calculus
- College Preparatory
- Computer Programming
- Computer Science
- English
- Geometry
- Keyboarding
- Mathematics
- Statistics
- Trigonometry

Related Career Pathways/Majors

Business, Management & Administration Cluster
- Management Pathway

Information Technology Cluster
- Programming & Software Development Pathway

Science, Technology, Engineering & Mathematics Cluster
- Engineering & Technology Pathway

Famous First

John W. Tukey writes in "The Future of Data Analysis" in 1962: "For a long time I thought I was a statistician… But as I have watched mathematical statistics evolve… I have come to feel that my central interest is in data analysis… Data analysis, and the parts of statistics which adhere to it, must…take on the characteristics of science rather than those of mathematics… data analysis is intrinsically an empirical science… How vital and how important… is the rise of the stored-program electronic computer? In many instances the answer may surprise many by being 'important but not vital,' although in others there is no doubt but what the computer has been 'vital.'"

Postsecondary

Undergraduate programs related to IT include core course work in UNIX system administration software and programming languages such as Java and C+. In addition to a survey of wireless-network technology and database-management techniques, undergraduate IT students also study business models, network security systems, and infrastructure, as well as information-security management.

Postgraduate and doctoral-level programs in information technology are traditionally dedicated to the exploration and discovery of new strategies and technologies, grounded in a strong foundational knowledge of the history of the field. Graduate students are required to complete a thesis or capstone project related to an emerging trend in information technology; this is often highly specialized work that can be an important precursor for their professional growth and eventual career path.

Related College Majors
- Computer Programming
- Computer Science
- Information Sciences & Systems
- Management Information Systems & Business Data Processing

Adult Job Seekers

Like many supervisory and management professionals, IT project managers work extensive hours. The role often requires evening and weekend work. Due to the vast amount of academic and professional experience required, IT project management is not a traditional choice for those seeking to begin a new career path. The long hours required of the position, particularly in large organizations and corporations, may also pose difficulty for adult professionals eager to achieve a harmonious work-life balance.

Professional Certification and Licensure

Specific certification and licensure is not required for a career as an IT project manager, though numerous national and international professional organizations exist. Voluntarily completing a certification program will give professionals in the field a competitive advantage.

Additional Requirements

IT project managers are talented multi-taskers who can simultaneously execute a wide variety of managerial responsibilities. In addition to being able to monitor all active projects, IT project management professionals must also possess the professional and academic experience necessary to predict and eliminate potential pitfalls before they occur in order to ensure that the systems and infrastructure continue to operate effectively and efficiently.

EARNINGS AND ADVANCEMENT

The median annual wage for computer and information systems managers was $135,800 in May 2016. The lowest 10 percent earned less than $82,360, and the highest 10 percent earned more than $208,000.

Information technology managers may receive paid vacations, holidays and sick days; life and health insurance; and retirement benefits. These are usually paid by the employer.

EMPLOYMENT AND OUTLOOK

Computer and information systems managers, of which information technology project managers are a part, held about 367.600 jobs nationally in 2016. Employment of computer and information systems managers is projected to grow 12 percent from 2016 to 2026, faster than the average for all occupations.

Demand for computer and information systems managers will grow as firms increasingly expand their operations to digital platforms. Computer and information systems managers will be responsible for implementing these goals.

Employment growth will result from the need to bolster cybersecurity in computer and information systems used by businesses. Industries such as retail trade will need to implement more robust security policies as cyber threats increase.

An increase in the popularity of cloud computing may result in firms outsourcing services from in-house IT departments to cloud-computing companies. This will shift IT services from IT departments in noncomputer industries, such as financial firms or schools, to firms engaged in computer systems design and related services and those in data processing, hosting, and related services.

Related Occupations
- Computer & Information Systems Manager
- Computer Engineer
- Computer Network Architect
- Computer Support Specialist
- Computer Systems Analyst
- Database Administrator
- General Manager & Top Executive
- Information Security Analyst
- Medical Records Administrator
- Network & Computer Systems Administrator
- Operations Research Analyst
- Software Developer
- Web Administrator
- Web Developer

Related Military Occupations
- Computer Programmer
- Computer Systems Officer

Conversation With . . .
MICHAEL TANENBAUM

Co-Founder and Director of Strategy
Duplex Social, Los Angeles, California
Social Media Strategist, 10 years

1. What was your individual career path in terms of education/training, entry-level job, or other significant opportunity?

The field was in its infancy when I began. My formal marketing training as an MBA student at Pepperdine University included statistics and Excel, but nearly all of my strategy and analytics education occurred on the job. My most significant career transition was going from being an independent contractor deploying Facebook, Twitter, and blog strategies for local businesses to working with globally recognized brands at a social media agency. I learned a tremendous amount from scouring leading social media blogs and attending conferences such as Social Media Week.

2. What are the most important skills and/or qualities for someone in your profession?

The social media strategist role builds upon that of the social media analyst. The skills required are broader and at a higher level, with a strong emphasis on quantitative analytical and statistical methods, as well as qualitative analysis.

A good strategist will use social media listening tools such as Sysomos or Crimson Hexagon; competitive analytics tools such as Simply Measured, Fan Page Karma, Stylophane, or Social Bakers; survey tools such as Qualtrics, Google Forms, or Survey Monkey; and Microsoft Excel or Google Sheets.

The role requires solid communication skills, excellent presentation design skills, and strong attention to detail. It is highly client-facing, as opposed to a social media analyst, who typically remains in the background. The strategist interfaces with the art director, copywriters and content creators, the account team, and often the new business lead. The strategist is often present in new business pitch meetings.

3. What do you wish you had known going into this profession?

I wish I had known how taxing this career would be on my personal life, in terms of hours worked, creative energy expended, and staying abreast of constant changes in technology. Regardless, I still would have pursued the profession.

4. Are there many job opportunities in your profession? In what specific areas?

Strategists are among the most in-demand professionals in the social media field. As such, there are many job opportunities, both at agencies and in-house. However, the role is quite competitive and job functions vary wildly across the marketplace. The best place to begin is at a large agency, where a budding strategist can get his or her feet wet while working with numerous clients. There tend to be a lot of agency positions available for entertainment and Consumer Packaged Goods (CPG) brands.

5. How do you see your profession changing in the next five years? How do you envision platforms evolving? What skills will be required?

The role will continue evolving to a higher level, with less emphasis on writing copy and posting to social networks and more focus on how social media ties into overall business strategy and objectives.

Social will continue its integration with the shopping experience. Virtual Reality and Artificial Intelligence (AI) will become mainstream and bots will become the norm for customer service. These changes will require the strategist to create campaigns, content, and paid advertising for these technologies in Messenger, WhatsApp, Reddit, and other emerging channels. And the aftermath of the Facebook ads scandal in 2017 will require that more attention be given to government regulations on paid media.

6. What do you enjoy most about your job? What do you enjoy least about your job?

Social media strategists tell the account or marketing team which campaigns to run, where to invest the brand's ad dollars, which social channels to actively use, what the art department should design, what insights to look for and why. I find this level of involvement quite exhilarating.

As someone who has worked on the agency side, I most enjoy the freedom to create, the opportunity to work cross-functionally with other team members, and the ability to interface directly with the client.

The downside is that social media strategy, like analytics, is by its nature a sedentary profession. Since nearly all the work is done on a computer, it is deceptively easy to sit in a chair all day and work without moving. Also, the technology advances very rapidly. It's a challenge to keep up with new social network features, updates to existing features, and shifting regulations around acceptable content.

7. **Can you suggest a valuable "try this" for students considering a career in your profession?**

Practice doing both a brand audit and a competitive analysis of a favorite brand that you follow. Look at how that brand's posts are performing on Facebook, Instagram, Pinterest, Twitter, Tumblr, and YouTube. Track the fan growth for two to three months. Measure the monthly post engagement rate (by adding total likes, comments and shares, dividing by the number of posts and then dividing by the followers), break down the content into different buckets (such as quotes, marketing/product posts, influencer content, etc.). Pay attention to the content they are posting. Is it "on-brand"? Does it tell a compelling and unique story? Are they posting consistently? Do they appear to be boosting the posts on Facebook? How is the customer service, based on the comments and time it takes to respond? Compare this with one or two key competitors to determine ways that your brand could be doing better or to discover an opportunity or campaign idea that's not being exploited by the competitors.

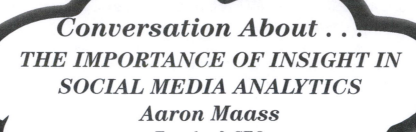

Conversation About . . .
THE IMPORTANCE OF INSIGHT IN SOCIAL MEDIA ANALYTICS
Aaron Maass
Founder & CEO
MaassMedia LLC, Philadelphia

1. How are companies using social media analytics to plan?

They're mining the historical data for insights. Let's say you're J. Crew and you're looking to predict the next season's fashion trends. Potentially you could mine Facebook and Instagram and Twitter for conversations that might lead to, "Oh, this is trending. This is hot." Most companies, to predict trends, will bring in focus groups or they'll survey a panel. But the intelligence that you can get from that is limited to the size of your panel or focus group, whereas in the world of social media, you have access to billions of data points.

2. What's unique about social media data?

When you typically think of data, you think of numbers. But in the world of social media, the data is text, which adds further complexity to it. How many times was the word "bad" mentioned versus "good'? That's taking text and turning it into a numerical data point that can then be analyzed. There's a special skill involved there; that's what we're training our people on and looking for when we're hiring people.

3. Given the nuances of language, can that analysis be automated?

We, as a company, have experimented with machine learning algorithms to help automate the process, but that, too, starts as a very human-centered activity. You take an algorithm that's programmed to look for patterns and mentions of certain words, let's say "bad" and "good." But then there are combinations of words. "Sucks" could be considered bad, but it could be good if it were used in a different context. So somebody needs to review that. You have to look, for instance, at the references that were scored as bad; are they actually negative? A human can retrain these algorithms. Eventually they get better.

4. So are both math and verbal skills required in social media analytics?

Yes. This is good news for people who are in the Humanities, because there's a real place for them. The kind of work that we do is very multi-disciplinary, interdisciplinary. We need people who have quantitative and qualitative skill sets— left brain and right brain. Some of the people we've hired have double-majored in mathematics and creative writing or statistics and psychology. And even those who majored in just psychology or sociology or anthropology are attractive if they have used research and scientific methods in their studies. These are people who are attracted to the world of understanding human behavior and who've been trained in the science of that.

Our work is about understanding why people do what they do—specifically why did somebody buy and why did they buy that, or why didn't they buy? How do we apply what we learn from understanding that experience to the greater population and find more people who exhibit similar attributes? Those people are going to be predisposed to buy. So what incentives can you put in their path to conversion to get them to actually buy? Someone who is a pure mathematician may see the numbers and see the trend line, but because of the way they think or because of the way they've been trained, they don't necessarily understand how to read between the lines and connect the dots. If the data is trending up, it's very important to ask why. What caused that?

I was a philosophy major in college, and I've found I'm not the only philosophy major in this field. The reason, I suspect, is because people who study philosophy are curious by nature and that's a very important skill to have in the world of analytics: the ability to ask critical, insightful, meaningful questions about the data. "Why did this happen?" And to further answer the question "Why does it matter?" And then the all-important third question, "Now what? What are we going to do with it?"

5. What would you recommend as a major for someone interested in social media analytics?

Study a curriculum that's as broad as possible, but do it in an intentional way. Take a psychology course because it helps you understand why people make decisions. Take a statistics course because it helps you understand how to correlate behaviors with actions.

But there's never any substitute for hands-on experience. If you're a member of the glee club or the Ultimate Frisbee club, volunteer to maintain the website and experiment with tools that help you track how people use it. Even selling your textbooks online can give you really good experience. If you're good at selling your textbooks, you've probably thought about what the pictures look like, what the title of your ad should be, the description of the items you're selling, and how to price those items.

When people interview with us, I ask them, "Have you ever sold anything online? Have you bought things online? Do you pay your bills online?" We live in an increasingly digital world and I want to make sure the people we hire understand that digital world. You'd think that every kid coming out of college these days is digitally savvy—they're on their phones, they play games all day long—but not necessarily. If all you do is play games, unless you're thinking about the business of the games or building your own game, your experience is very limited.

MORE INFORMATION

Association of Information Technology Professionals
330 N. Wabash Avenue, Suite 2000
Chicago, IL 60611
800.224.9371
aitp_hq@aitp.org
www.aitp.org

Network Professional Association
1401 Hermes Lane
San Diego, CA 92154
888.672.6720
www.npa.org

John Pritchard/Editor

Journalist

OVERVIEW

Sphere of Work

The field of journalism involves reporting news, events, and ideas to a wide audience through various media, including the Internet (podcasts, streaming media, news websites and blogs); print (newspapers and magazines), or broadcasting (television and radio). Journalists usually start out as reporters, covering anything from sports and weather to business, crime, politics, and consumer affairs.

Later, they may become editors, helping to direct the process of gathering and presenting stories.

Journalists can operate on many different levels local, regional, national, or international. It is common for a journalist to start out working on the local or regional level and then move up the ladder as his or her career progresses. Journalists spend the bulk of their time investigating and composing stories, observing events, interviewing people, taking notes, taking photographs, shooting videos, and preparing their material for publication or broadcast. This work can happen in a matter of minutes, or it can take days or weeks to gather information and build a story.

Profile

Interests: People, Things
Working Conditions: Work Both Inside and Outside
Physical Strength: Light Work
Education Needs: Bachelor's Degree Master's Degree
Licensure/Certification: Usually Not Required
Physical Abilities Not Required: Not Climb, Not Kneel
Opportunities for Experience: Internship, Apprenticeship, Military Service, Volunteer Work, Part Time Work
Holland Interest Score*: EAS

* See Appendix A

Work Environment

A journalist's work environment is fast-paced and competitive, subject to tight and changing deadlines, irregular work hours, and pressure to get breaking news on the air or on-line before other news organizations. Journalists covering "hard news"—current events that directly affect people's lives, such as crime, politics, or natural disasters—typically work with stories that are moving and changing constantly; their challenge is to present as much relevant and verifiable information as possible under the circumstances. Journalists covering less pressing subjects, like economic and social trends, popular culture, or "human interest" stories, are subject to less immediate time pressures, but are under no less of an obligation to get their facts straight.

Journalists must therefore be able to adapt to unfamiliar places and a variety of people. They must be accustomed to interruptions and have the ability to pick up and process new information at all times.

Occupation Interest

Successful journalists are curious by nature. Some are generalists, able to work comfortably with a wide variety of subjects. Others may specialize, even to the point of being known as "micro-niche specialists." They enjoy writing and presenting stories, and they have a great respect for principles that define a free society. These principles include the public's right to know and to question government, business, and social institutions. They also respect an individual's desire to feel connected to what is going on in society. Journalists have to be adept at dealing with people, and successful journalists often have a competitive nature that drives them to try to get the "scoop" before other journalists.

Journalism can be multifaceted work—it can be a low-key, local position for a community newspaper, or it can be international in scope. Reporting can be a fast-paced in- or out-of-office experience driven by publication editors or producers.

Finally, journalists have to exhibit tenacity and a tough skin, able to pursue a story to its natural end with a commitment to fair and accurate reporting, even when dealing controversial topics or evasive interview subjects.

A Day in the Life—Duties and Responsibilities

On any given day, journalists are researching and developing story ideas, checking facts, writing articles for publication, maintaining an active social media presence, all on a tight deadline. Journalists uncover news, information, statistics, and trends that they incorporate into news stories, broadcasts, feature stories, and editorials. They meet regularly with editors and get assignments based on the day's or week's happenings. Depending where a journalist works, a typical day can vary.

Some news outlets and newswire services have an almost instant presence, with live streaming media available to viewers twenty-four hours a day, requiring journalists to work at all hours to follow and update breaking and ongoing news stories. Longform journalism calls for more in-depth reporting. This form of journalism, as well as reporters who write for weekly or monthly publications, may have longer deadlines, but all journalists face constant pressure to meet deadlines while creating stories that are well-crafted and accurate.

Some journalists work in the field as correspondents, perhaps traveling with a camera crew and conducting "man-on-the-street" interviews, or gathering information about rapidly developing events, which they then submit electronically to newspaper editors or radio or television producers. Since the rise of the Internet, the distinction between print and broadcast journalism has become less sharp: newspaper websites today often include video feeds, and television news stations may stream their content live or have websites where their stories appear in a variety of forms.

The most important part of a journalist's job is making sure that the stories he or she presents are based on solid, verifiable facts, rather than rumors or misinformation. Inaccuracies can creep into news stories in many ways honest mistakes, the reporter's own conscious or unconscious biases, and sources attempting to deceive the public are just a few. For this reason, journalists must invest a good deal of time in making sure their stories are correct before they reach the public.

Duties and Responsibilities

- **Researching public records**
- **Interviewing people**
- **Writing stories and fact-checking**
- **Specializing in one or more fields of news**
- **Covering news in a particular location**
- **Taking photographs**
- **Writing headlines**
- **Laying out pages**
- **Editing wire service copy**
- **Writing editorials**
- **Investigating leads and news tips**

OCCUPATION SPECIALTIES

News Writers

News Writers write news stories from notes recorded by reporters after evaluating and verifying the information, supplementing it with other material and organizing stories to fit the platform on which it will appear.

Reporters and Correspondents

Reporters and Correspondents gather and assess information, organize it and write news stories in prescribed style and format. They may also take photographs for stories and give broadcast reports, or report live from the site of events.

Columnists

Columnists analyze news and write columns or commentaries based on personal knowledge and experience with the subject matter. They gather information through research, interviews, experience, and attendance at functions such as political conventions, news meetings, sporting events, and social activities.

Critics

Critics write critical reviews of literary, musical, or artistic works and performances.

Editorial Writers

Editorial Writers write comments on topics of reader interest to stimulate or mold public opinion in accordance with the viewpoints and policies of publications.

WORK ENVIRONMENT

Immediate Physical Environment

A journalist's work environment can be anywhere, from a crime scene to a press conference to a desk in an office. News outlets usually house journalists in large, well-lit rooms filled with work stations, computer equipment, and the sounds of keyboards and printers. "Boots-on-the-ground" reporting can take a journalist anywhere, though: embedded war correspondents may travel with a military unit right into battle; a journalist reporting on the fishing industry may spend several days on a fishing boat at sea; the next week, that same journalist may tour a farm or a factory or a school to get the next story.

Transferable Skills and Abilities

Communication Skills
- Speaking effectively
- Writing concisely

Interpersonal/Social Skills
- Asserting oneself
- Being flexible
- Being persistent
- Cooperating with others
- Working as a member of a team

Organization & Management Skills
- Managing time
- Meeting goals and deadlines
- Paying attention to and handling details

Research & Planning Skills
- Analyzing information
- Gathering information
- Solving problems

Unclassified Skills
- Discovering unusual aspects of stories

Human Environment

Journalists deal with people. They are constantly interviewing people and collecting and analyzing information; therefore, they can usually be found speaking with anyone who has something to do with the story at hand, be it politicians, company officials, protesters, or an average person.

Technological Environment

Today, journalists submit their stories electronically and can therefore be anywhere in the world, collecting information. They often carry their technology on their back, with just a smartphone, tablet, or laptop computer; or they may travel with a crew of broadcast professionals, including camera operators and sound engineers, who can put the journalist on the air live at any time.

EDUCATION, TRAINING, AND ADVANCEMENT

High School/Secondary

High school students can prepare to be a journalist by working for the school newspaper or yearbook, producing their own podcasts or blogs, volunteering with local broadcasting stations, and participating in internships with news organizations. Coursework should include a strong focus on writing and communication, through classes such as English, social studies, political science, history, and psychology.

Knowledge of foreign languages can also be highly useful in many journalism jobs.

Practical experience is highly valued and can be found through part-time or summer jobs, summer journalism camps, work at college broadcasting stations, and professional organizations. Work in these areas can help in obtaining scholarships, fellowships, and assistantships for college journalism majors.

Local television stations and newspapers often offer internship opportunities for up-and-coming journalists to improve their craft by reporting on town hall meetings or writing obituaries and human-interest stories.

Suggested High School Subjects
- Business
- College Preparatory
- Composition
- Computer Science
- Economics
- English
- Government
- Journalism
- Keyboarding
- Literature
- Photography
- Political Science
- Social Studies
- Speech

Related Career Pathways/Majors
Arts, A/V Technology & Communications Cluster
- Journalism & Broadcasting Pathway

Famous First

The first war correspondent was George Wilkins Kendall of the New Orleans Picayune (which he cofounded). Kendall participated with the American army during the Mexican War of 1846–50, and began filing reports carried by Pony Express. Wounded, he later embarked on a different career and became known as the father of Texas sheep ranching.

Postsecondary

Most, but not all, journalists have a bachelor's degree in journalism, English, or another liberal arts-related field. There are many journalism schools within colleges and universities across the country. Many schools also offer master's and doctoral degrees, which are especially useful for those interested in journalistic research and teaching.

Bachelor degree program coursework should include broad liberal arts subjects, a general overview of journalism, and then specialty courses that correspond with the highly important requirements for good writing and communication. These can include classes in social media, broadcast writing, news editorial writing, magazine writing, copy editing, interviewing, media ethics, blogging, feature writing, news reporting, and news photography.

All college and university students should make the effort to use career centers, academic counselors, and professors when seeking opportunities for advancement through volunteering or interning.

Related College Majors
- Broadcast Journalism
- Journalism

Adult Job Seekers

Almost anyone can become a journalist if they can find a local newspaper or public access cable channel willing to let them try writing a story. Adults can seek continuing journalism education and ongoing opportunities to volunteer in various capacities, perhaps by writing guest newspaper columns, or helping produce a local newsletter, or writing for a blog. These options mean it is entirely viable to seek journalism jobs after having been out of the workplace for a while. Prospective journalists will need to have updated resumes, preferably with portfolios showing relevant work.

More experience leads to more specialized and challenging assignments. Large publications and news stations prefer journalists with several years of experience. With more experience, journalists can advance to become columnists, correspondents, announcers, reporters, or publishing industry managers.

Becoming adept at freelancing—where reporters work independently by selling stories to any interested media outlet—is another way to stay involved in the journalism field.

Professional Certification and Licensure

In the United States, professional certification is not necessary to be a journalist; however, involvement in the Society of Professional Journalists or other professional organizations can help journalists network and raise their profile.

Additional Requirements

It is extremely useful for journalists to have experience with computer graphics and desktop skills, as well as proficiency in all forms of multimedia. Familiarity with databases and knowledge of news photography is an added plus.

EARNINGS AND ADVANCEMENT

The median annual wage for broadcast news analysts was $56,680 in May 2016. The lowest 10 percent earned less than $25,690, and the highest 10 percent earned more than $163,490. The median annual wage for reporters and correspondents was $37,820 in May 2016. The lowest 10 percent earned less than $22,120, and the highest 10 percent earned more than $86,610.

Journalists may receive paid vacations, holidays, and sick days; life and health insurance; and retirement benefits. These are usually paid by the employer.

EMPLOYMENT AND OUTLOOK

Journalists held about 50,400 jobs nationally in 2016. Overall employment of reporters, correspondents, and broadcast news analysts is projected to decline 9 percent from 2016 to 2026. Employment of reporters and correspondents is projected to decline 10 percent, while employment of broadcast news analysts is projected to show little or no change from 2016 to 2026. Declining advertising revenue in radio, newspapers, and television will negatively affect the employment growth for these occupations.

Readership and circulation of newspapers are expected to continue to decline over the next decade. In addition, television and radio stations are increasingly publishing content online and on mobile devices. As a result, news organizations may have more difficulty selling traditional forms of advertising, which is often their primary source of revenue. Some organizations will likely continue to use new forms of advertising or offer paid subscriptions, but these innovations may not make up for lost print ad revenues.

Declining revenue will force news organizations to downsize and employ fewer journalists. Increasing demand for online news may offset some of the downsizing. However, because online and mobile ad revenue is typically less than print revenue, the growth in digital advertising may not offset the decline in print advertising, circulation, and readership.

News organizations also continue to consolidate and increasingly are sharing resources, staff, and content with other media outlets. For example, reporters are able to gather and report on news for a media outlet that can be published in multiple newspapers owned by the same parent company.

As consolidations, mergers, and news sharing continue, the demand for journalists may decrease. However, in some instances, consolidations may help limit the loss of jobs. Mergers may allow financially troubled newspapers, radio stations, and television stations to keep staff because of increased funding and resources from the larger organization.

Reporters, correspondents, and broadcast news analysts are expected to face strong competition for jobs. Those with experience in the field— experience often gained through internships or by working for school newspapers, television stations, or radio stations—should have the best job prospects.

Multimedia journalism experience, including recording and editing video or audio pieces, should also improve job prospects. Because stations and media outlets are increasingly publishing content on multiple media platforms, particularly the web, employers may prefer applicants who have experience in website design and coding.

Related Occupations
- Copywriter
- Radio/TV Announcer and Newscaster
- Technical Writer
- Writer & Editor

Conversation With . . .
JASON KOLNOS

Digital Editor/Social Media Manager
Cape Cod Times
Hyannis, MA
Digital journalist, 11 years

1. What was your individual career path in terms of education/training, entry-level job, or other significant opportunity?

My high school journalism teacher inspired me to become a storyteller. Under his tutelage, I became the editor of our student newspaper. When I was a junior and senior, I started an internship at the *Cape Cod Times*, working mostly for the business section. I've loved working there so much, I haven't left yet. Summer internships continued while I attended Boston University, where I graduated with a bachelor's degree in journalism. I wrote for the school's *Daily Free Press*, was its business editor, and, while studying in London, worked at *The Independent* newspaper. After college, I took a full-time job with the *Cape Cod Times* and worked as a reporter for four years. In 2007, I was promoted to multimedia reporter after teaching myself all sorts of technical skills. Since then, I've been a digital leader at the newspaper, filming and producing thousands of videos—including our award-winning webcast called *CapeCast*, which features fun community stories and has 26 million total views on our YouTube channel. One of my main roles is managing our social media.

2. What are the most important skills and/or qualities for someone in your profession?

A quality journalist must have a passion for telling good stories, and in order to achieve that, you have to do plenty of listening and connecting with people in the community. It's also important to understand the type of stories that your audience wants to read. In the digital world, the ability to engage your readers is essential. Jack-of-all-trades journalists will be the ones who will succeed as the profession evolves. You'll be in good shape if you can report on and write a story, use your phone to take photos and videos, package it all together, and quickly and accurately send it out to online audiences and through social media platforms like Facebook, Twitter, and Instagram.

3. **What do you wish you had known going into this profession?**

I wish I had known how much and how quickly the profession was going to change. Digital-driven newsrooms are the ones that will survive. Many people only use their phones or tablets to digest news, so you have to adjust storytelling strategies. Perhaps you write and present a story in a different way than a long narrative, like an easy-to-understand story that resonates with your mobile audience. Or you infuse graphics or videos into your stories.

4. **Are there many job opportunities in your profession? In what specific areas?**

While the industry has had rough patches during all these transitions, it's clear that the public still wants to read newspapers. They need journalists to uncover truths, expose falsehoods, and write stories that speak to the heart of their community. If you have good social media skills, it should be easier for you to get a job in journalism. Many news sites are on the web only, so there will be opportunities to work remotely if you have quality digital reporting skills. If you can shoot and edit videos, there are ample opportunities for visual storytellers, from newsrooms to public relations or marketing.

5. **How do you see your profession changing in the next five years, how do you see platforms evolving, and what skills will be required?**

People will be consuming news in ways that we probably haven't even thought of yet. But if you have a solid understanding of how to use social sites and the tools to tell good stories, you'll be able to master emerging technologies because always, at the heart, will be the good story or subject that you are writing about. Telling stories using virtual reality, augmented reality, and digital assistants like Alexa will be an interesting and exciting new challenge.

6. **What do you enjoy most about your job? What do you enjoy least about your job?**

Without a doubt, it's the excitement that every day will bring a new challenge or adventure. One day I could be taking a video of researchers tagging great white sharks and the next day I could be recording a Facebook Live of an active fire. I love the variety of responsibilities. The downsides? Newsrooms are like a busy bee's nest of activity, so the long and inconsistent hours, stress related to deadlines, and sheer volume of information and responsibilities that flow through a normal day can sometimes be a drag.

7. **Can you suggest a valuable "try this" for students considering a career in your profession?**

Those looking to get into social media managing should follow some of the better Twitter and Facebook accounts for news organizations, like the *New York Times*, *Vox*, *The Washington Post*, and Associated Press (and the *Cape Cod Times*, of course!) to understand how they effectively share their stories with their audiences. Listen to plenty of good podcasts to get examples of how really good stories develop. Start with the pros from National Public Radio (NPR). Learn how to strengthen your video and editing skills by filming a simple project about your favorite pet. (My first video involved my cat Max). Hone your interviewing skills by writing a profile of the person closest to you who is not a direct family member. And if you want to become a journalist, embrace every opportunity you can to spend time in an active newsroom by doing internships or shadowing a seasoned reporter.

MORE INFORMATION

Accred. Council on Education in Journalism & Mass Comm.
University of Kansas
Stauffer-Flint Hall
1435 Jayhawk Boulevard
Lawrence, KS 66045-7575
785.864.3973
www2.ku.edu/~acejmc

Association for Women in Communications
3337 Duke Street
Alexandria, VA 22314
703.370.7436
info@womcom.org
www.womcom.org

Dow Jones Newspaper Fund, Inc.
P.O. Box 300
Princeton, NJ 08543-0300
609.452.2820
djnf@dowjones.com
www.newsfund.org

Association of Broadcasters
1771 N Street NW
Washington, DC 20036
202.429.5300
nab@nab.org
www.nab.org

Investigative Reporters and Editors
141 Neff Annex
Missouri School of Journalism
Columbia, MO 65211573 882 2042
Twitter: @IRE_NICAR
info@ire.org
www.ire.org

Knight Foundation
Suite 3300
200 S. Biscayne Blvd.
Miami, FL 33131-2349
(305) 908-2600
Twitter: @knightfdn
www.knightfoundation.org

National Federation of Press Women
P.O. Box 34798
Alexandria, VA 22334-0798
800.780.2715
presswomen@aol.com
www.nfpw.org

National Newspaper Association
P.O. Box 7540
Columbia, MO 65205-7540
800.829.4662
briansteffens@nna.org
www.nnaweb.org

National Press Club
529 14th Street NW, 13th Floor
Washington, DC 20045
202.662.7500
www.press.org

Newspaper Association of America
4401 Wilson Boulevard, Suite 900
Arlington, VA 22203-1867
571.366.1000
membsvc@naa.org
www.naa.org

Newspaper Guild-CWA
Research and Information
Department
501 Third Street NW, 6th Floor
Washington, DC 20001-2797
202.434.7177
guild@cwa-union.org
www.newsguild.org

Online News Association
1111 North Capitol Street NE
Second Floor
Washington, DC 20002
(202) 503-9222
Twitter: @ONA
https://journalists.org

Poynter Institute
801 3rd Street S.
St. Petersburg, FL 33701
727.821.9494
www.poynter.org

Society of Professional Journalists
Eugene S. Pulliam National
Journalism Center
3909 N. Meridian Street
Indianapolis, IN 46208
317.927.8000
cvachon@spj.org
www.spj.org

Tow Center for Digital Journalism
Columbia University
Graduate School of Journalism
Pulitzer Hall, 6th Floor
116 and Broadway
New York NY 10027
Twitter: @TowCenter
towcenter@columbia.edu
www.towcenter.org

Market Research Analyst

Snapshot

Career Cluster(s): Business, Management & Administration, Human Services, Marketing, Sales & Service

Interests: Marketing, advertising, analyzing data, computer science, communicating with others, sales

Earnings (2016 median pay): $62,560 per year; $30.08 per hour

Employment & Outlook: Faster Than Average Growth Expected

OVERVIEW

Sphere of Work

Market research analysts collect and interpret information about consumers, sales, employee satisfaction, and other facets of the business market. Their findings and analyses are used by clients to target specialized markets, develop brand allegiance, determine profitability and pricing, and prepare marketing and advertising campaigns.

Market research analysts are skilled communicators who interact with consumers in a variety of ways. Analysts obtain consumer or employee data through one-on-one interviews, focus group meetings, questionnaires, and polls. Market researchers are also skilled in

numerical data analysis and mathematical problem solving. One of their primary tasks is to present large quantities of complex data in a clear and cohesive manner.

Work Environment

Market research analysts work primarily in professional environments, either as independent consultants or as employees of consulting firms, corporations, or government organizations. Data collection may take place in any number of locations depending on the company or product being analyzed, and fieldwork is often required to establish direct contact with consumers.

Profile

Interests: Data, People
Working Conditions: Work Inside
Physical Strength: Light Work
Education Needs: Bachelor's Degree
Licensure/Certification: Usually Not Required
Physical Abilities Not Required: Not Climb, Not Kneel
Opportunities for Experience: Internship
Holland Interest Score*: ISC

* See Appendix A

Occupation Interest

Market research analysis is a diverse field encompassing a variety of disciplines. As such, the field attracts scholars and professionals with academic and work experience in marketing, advertising, analytics, computer science, communication, public relations, business, and sales.

Some research analysts come to the field after lengthy careers in sales and marketing. Conversely, many young professionals spend an early portion of their careers as market analysts to build a foundation for future work in advertising, sales, or public relations.

A Day in the Life—Duties and Responsibilities

The day-to-day duties of market research analysts are traditionally divided into three major areas of concentration: data collection, data interpretation, and presentation of results.

The data collection tasks of market research analysts vary from product to product and company to company. Some market researchers collect consumer or employee data from data-mining, mobile applications, fieldwork, one-on-one interviews, or focus groups. Other tactics include disseminating survey questionnaires, cold-calling, or conducting public opinion polls.

When the desired data has been collected, market research analysts must next interpret the study's findings. Analysts break down data and use reports and visual aids in order to identify particular consumer opinions, product demand, and potential avenues for improvement in product development, internal operations, design, and marketing strategy.

The information acquired by analysts is then presented to clients and businesses in the form of a written report, an oral presentation with accompanying graphics, or a combination of the two. Many market research firms also use their data to forecast future customer opinion, sales trends, and market fluctuation. These predictions are often crucial to the development of new marketing programs and sales strategies.

Duties and Responsibilities

- Designing questionnaires to collect customer opinion
- Gathering data through personal, telephone, or online surveys
- Analyzing information gathered from customers and the company
- Consulting sources such as records, journals, reports, financial publications, and industry statistics
- Interpreting information and presenting an oral or written report of findings
- Making recommendations or proposing alternatives based on findings

WORK ENVIRONMENT

Immediate Physical Environment

Market research analysts primarily work in office settings. Data collection work may entail field surveys and direct interaction with consumers. Market research analysts may also work in retail locations, at public venues and events, and on university campuses. Analysts traditionally work regular business hours, though survey and research projects may require extended hours and weekend work.

Transferable Skills and Abilities

Communication Skills
- Speaking effectively
- Writing concisely

Interpersonal/Social Skills
- Being objective
- Cooperating with others
- Working as a member of a team

Organization & Management Skills
- Making decisions
- Paying attention to and handling details

Research & Planning Skills
- Analyzing information
- Creating ideas
- Solving problems

Human Environment

Focused interaction with other people is one of the most important aspects of market research analysis. The job entails asking extensive questions regarding personal habits, spending, and consumer beliefs. Excellent communication skills are paramount.

Technological Environment

Market research analysts use online survey and questionnaire tools, cloud computing, content management systems, telephones, scanners, e-mail, web conferencing applications, databases, presentation software, and analytic software to organize and present data and relevant findings.

EDUCATION, TRAINING, AND ADVANCEMENT

High School/Secondary

High school students can prepare to enter the field of market research analysis with courses in algebra, calculus, public speaking, and computer science. English and writing courses are also important, as they hone written presentation skills.

Internships and summer volunteer work can provide students with experience and knowledge about the field. Marketing interns are often charged with disseminating surveys, collecting and keying data, or distributing information to focus groups and target markets at public events.

Suggested High School Subjects
- Algebra
- Applied Math
- Business Law
- Calculus
- College Preparatory
- Computer Science
- Economics
- English
- Mathematics
- Psychology
- Social Studies
- Sociology
- Statistics

Related Career Pathways/Majors
Business, Management & Administration Cluster
- Business Analysis Pathway
- Marketing Pathway

Human Services Cluster
- Consumer Services Pathway

Marketing, Sales & Service Cluster
- Marketing Information Management & Research Pathway

Famous First

Social media at a minimum has seven layers of data. Out of the seven layers, some are visible or easily identifiable (e.g., text and actions), and other are invisible (e.g., social media and hyperlink networks): 1)Textual data (such as Tweets and comments) 2)Network data (such as Facebook Friendship Network, and Twitter follow-following network) 3) Actions (such as likes, shares, views) 4) Hyperlinks (e.g., hyperlinks embedded within text) 5) Mobile data (e.g., mobile application data 6) Location data 7) Search engines data. Social media analytics can also be referred as social media listening, social media monitoring or social media intelligence.

Source: https://ipfs.io

Postsecondary

Postsecondary education is traditionally a prerequisite for job openings in market research analysis. Employees enter the field from a variety of postsecondary fields of study, including communications, advertising, marketing, public relations, social science, statistics, finance, and business management.

Undergraduate courses in research methodology, rhetorical communication, statistics, psychology, and sociology are all effective building blocks for a career in market analysis. Students should also complete coursework focused on traditional marketing strategies, including global market segmentation, response modeling, and marketing ethics. Advanced mathematical coursework helps students record and interpret patterns in data, while coursework in marketing instructs students in putting such findings to use in a commercial environment. Landmark marketing research and key historical developments in the field are also traditionally surveyed.

Some colleges and universities in the United States offer graduate-level programs specializing in market research. Admission into such programs is difficult. Graduate students study advanced analysis methods ranging from perceptual mapping, customer loyalty development, data mining, and website traffic metrics. Graduate work in market research allows students to gain hands-on experience in marketing analysis research, interpretation, and presentation and to develop contacts and relationships that can provide an important foundation for a career in the field.

Related College Majors

- Applied & Resource Economics
- Business Marketing/Marketing Management
- Econometrics & Quantitative Economics
- Economics, General
- Marketing Research

Adult Job Seekers

Transitioning to a career in market research analysis can be difficult for adults seeking new opportunities or new career paths, given the amount of academic and professional experience that is often required. Transitioning is easier for experienced professionals transferring to the field from similar or relevant professional realms such as advertising, marketing, or media. Advanced degrees in market research, marketing, business management, statistics, or other related fields can give market research analysts a competitive edge when seeking higher level positions.

Professional Certification and Licensure

No professional certification or licensure is required for market research analysts, but many nationwide professional organizations, such as the American Marketing Association and the Marketing Research Association, offer voluntary certifications to their members. These certifications typically require a specified amount of experience in the field, completion of a written exam, and ongoing coursework for certification renewal.

Additional Requirements

In addition to the analytical and mathematical prowess inherent to the role, excellent conversation skills, amicability, and patience are qualities that help professionals excel at market research. Market research analysts must be able to form trusting relationships with consumers in order to acquire honest information about their thoughts, opinions, and buying habits, much of which can be considered personal information.

Fun Fact

Researchers are keeping an eye on how social media impacts a person's social life. One study found that having more friends on social media does not necessarily improve your social life. Other studies have looked into whether social media harms people by prompting them to compare their lives with others.

Source: Forbes.com

EARNINGS AND ADVANCEMENT

Graduate training increasingly is required for many market research analyst jobs and for advancement to more responsible positions. In government, industry, research organizations, and consulting firms, market research analysts who have a graduate degree can usually qualify for more responsible research and administrative positions.

Median annual earnings of market research analysts was $62,560 in May 2016. The lowest 10 percent earned less than $33,950, and the highest 10 percent earned more than $121,720.

Market research analysts entering careers in higher education may receive benefits such as summer research money, computer access, money for student research assistants, and secretarial support. Those who work in the private sector may receive paid vacations, holidays, and sick days; life and health insurance; and retirement benefits. These are usually paid by the employer.

EMPLOYMENT AND OUTLOOK

Market research analysts held about 595,400 jobs nationally in 2016. Employment of market research analysts is projected to grow 23 percent from 2016 to 2026, much faster than the average for all occupations.

Employment growth will be driven by an increasing use of data and market research across all industries. They will be needed to help understand the needs and wants of customers, measure the effectiveness of marketing and business strategies, and identify the factors affecting product demand.

Market research provides companies and organizations with an opportunity to increase sales and cut costs. Companies increasingly use research on consumer behavior to develop improved marketing strategies. By doing so, companies are better able to market directly to their target population.

Market research also lets companies monitor customer satisfaction and gather feedback about how to improve products or services, allowing companies to build an advantage over their competitors. They may use research to decide the location of stores, placement of products, and services offered.

The increase in the collection and analyses of "big data"—extremely large sets of information, such as social media comments or online product reviews— can provide insight on consumer behaviors and preferences. Businesses will need market research analysts to conduct analyses of the data and information.

Related Occupations
- Economist
- Electronic Commerce Specialist
- Online Merchant
- Sociologist
- Urban & Regional Planner

Conversation With . . .
LYNETTE CHEN

Senior Consultant
MaassMedia, LLC
Philadelphia, Pennsylvania
Social Media Analyst, 4 years

1. What was your individual career path in terms of education/training, entry-level job, or other significant opportunity?

I went to Northwestern University in Illinois and studied economics. Throughout college, the internships that I had helped me understand my passions. A content marketing internship at Groupon made me realize that while I was interested in marketing, I was hungry for a role that involved data because I felt it was crucial in order to make smart decisions. Additionally, I was most excited about social media because it was such a new and constantly evolving space.

2. What are the most important skills and/or qualities for someone in your profession?

As a social media analyst, I believe it is most important to have a curious mindset. Too often, marketers make decisions based on hunches. However, to really excel in the field, you need to understand what is working and why. If you see a spike in social content engagement, what caused it? Was it a new campaign? If so, what was special about this campaign?

Communication skills are also crucial because your insights are only as good as your presentation. Often, individuals who are creating content are not numbers-savvy, so it's important to understand how to deliver your findings to them in a way that they both understand and find interesting.

3. What do you wish you had known going into this profession?

Sometimes you are the bearer of bad news. Not all campaigns will perform well and the data will reveal the truth. Having the conversation where you share the bad news is difficult. It's important to focus on how the brand can improve from there.

4. Are there many job opportunities in your profession? In what specific areas?

Yes, every brand wants to be on social media today. Consumer facing brands have been on social media for years, but B2B brands are still catching up and learning how to best leverage and reach a more niche audience.

5. How do you see your profession changing in the next five years? How do you envision platforms evolving? What skills will be required?

Social media platforms come and go and it's important to be able to adapt. For example, Google+ was quickly replaced by Instagram as the third platform that brands had to be on (following Facebook and Twitter). A new platform comes with new features, and even existing platforms continue to roll out additional functionalities. As an analyst, you need to be flexible in how you think about success as the landscape continuously changes. If you continue to measure content engagement with the same formula you did a few years ago, you could potentially make wrong recommendations. To elaborate, in the past, users could only "like," comment, and share Facebook posts. Now, users can not only "like" content, but express additional emotions like anger and sadness. If a brand were to assume the additional emotion engagements were the same thing as "likes," it could result in a recommendation of creating more content that actually makes people angry, despite receiving more total overall engagements.

As the world demands more transparency and greater access to data from the platform giants, we will also be able to better inform decisions. For example, two years ago, Twitter did not share data on how many times people saw your posts (impressions), but now that is available and is a key data point to consider when evaluating content.

6. What do you enjoy most about your job? What do you enjoy least about your job?

I enjoy discovering actionable insights that help shape strategy. After mining through thousands of rows of data, it is extremely rewarding to be able to come up with a recommendation that gets used. Even more exciting is when you are then able to see from the data the impact that your recommendation was able to make.

Analysts joke that sometimes we're "data janitors." In order to analyze data, you first have to ensure that it's in the right format and has all the pieces you need. This prep work that you have to do is my least favorite part because it's time consuming— but necessary.

7. Can you suggest a valuable "try this" for students considering a career in your profession?

Twitter has an easily accessible analytics interface that allows you to analyze the data from your Tweets. Take a look and see if you can identify any trends in the Tweets you've posted that received the most engagement from your followers. This will give you a glimpse of the type of work social analysts perform as well as help you identify opportunities to optimize your own social media presence.

MORE INFORMATION

American Marketing Association
311 S. Wacker Drive, Suite 5800
Chicago, IL 60606
800.262.1150
info@ama.org
www.marketingpower.com

Offers the professional certified marketer
certification program
www.marketingpower.com/Careers/
Pages/ProfessionalCertifiedMarketer.
aspx

**Council of American Survey
Research Organizations**
170 North Country Road, Suite 4
Port Jefferson, NY 11777
631.928.6954
casro@casro.org
www.casro.org

Marketing Research Association
1156 15th Street NW, Suite 302
Washington, DC 20005
202.800.2545
membership@marketingresearch.org
marketingresearch.org

Offers the professional researcher
certification program
www.marketingresearch.org/certification-
about

John Pritchard/Editor

Motion Picture/Radio/TV Art Director

Snapshot

Career Cluster(s): Arts, A/V Technology & Communication, Business, Management & Administration
Interests: Set design and building, marketing and advertising, management, art, illustration, architectural research
Earnings (2016 median pay): $89,820 per year; $43.18 per hour
Employment & Outlook: Average Growth Expected

OVERVIEW

Sphere of Work

Art directors for motion pictures, radio, and television work in collaboration with producers, writers, and directors to bring concepts from the page to the screen or airwaves. They oversee a studio's art department and typically play a major role in hiring the creative staff, which can include artists, graphic designers, model makers, and set builders. Sometimes known as production designers, they often directly assist in the construction of sets and props. Motion picture, radio, and television art directors are also responsible for the management and allocation of the art department's budget, ensuring that the work performed on a given project stays within the production's overall financial

framework. In addition, they are frequently called upon to assist in the marketing and advertisement of their projects.

Work Environment

Motion picture, radio, and television art directors commonly work in studios and sound stages that allow for little contact with individuals not involved in the production. Studios are busy locations in which many different working groups operate in concert with one another, so art directors should be comfortable interacting with others on a regular basis. Some art directors also spend a great deal of time in an office environment, working on advertising and marketing plans and designing sets. Frequently, art directors travel to off-site locations to scout filming or recording spots and must be prepared to encounter potentially unpleasant weather and climate conditions. Art directors often work irregular hours, particularly when working on a production set, but may work fewer and more consistent hours during pre-production periods prior to the start of shooting or recording. Due to the expectations of producers and directors to stay on schedule and within budget, art directors in the entertainment industry may experience work-related stress.

Profile

Interests: Data, Things
Working Conditions: Work Inside
Physical Strength: Light Work
Education Needs: Bachelor's Degree
Licensure/Certification: Usually Not Required
Physical Abilities Not Required: Not Climb, Not Kneel
Opportunities for Experience: Internship, Part Time Work
Holland Interest Score*: AES

* See Appendix A

Occupation Interest

Art direction is a critical facet of the entertainment industry, and the seniority afforded by the position allows the art director creative input into the ways in which films, television programs, and radio shows are made and marketed. As such, this career attracts those who have a strong interest in the behind-the-scenes workings of media. The nature of the work requires that a large number of diverse responsibilities be managed simultaneously, so art directors are frequently masters of organization, leadership and delegation, and multi-tasking.

A Day in the Life—Duties and Responsibilities

Art directors are responsible for bringing the collective creative vision of producers, directors, and writers to life. They begin by meeting and consulting with these individuals during the pre-production stage, months in advance of shooting or recording. Using computer technologies as well as their own artistic abilities, they design set blueprints, present sketches and illustrations, and when applicable, conduct research on architectural styles to ensure historical accuracy. In addition to designing and building project-specific sets, they scout potential shooting or recording locations in both outdoor and indoor environments. Art directors also work with advertising managers to create a marketing strategy for the film, program, or show.

During the shoot or recording session, art directors assist in set building and design, directing artists, model makers, and other members of the crew in accordance with the director and producer's desires. They often contribute to the design of costumes, makeup, lighting effects, and other aspects of the production. Art directors must also manage the internal operations of the art department, including establishing departmental budgets; hiring, training, and terminating team members; and monitoring individual assignments to ensure that the department is operating efficiently, on time, and within budget parameters.

Duties and Responsibilities

- Designing set blueprints and creating illustrations
- Consulting with writers, producers and directors
- Assisting in the marketing and advertising of products
- Managing budgets and ensuring that projects meet budget requirements

WORK ENVIRONMENT

Immediate Physical Environment

Motion picture, radio, and television art directors typically work in studios and office environments, which are generally well organized and highly controlled to ensure no interference from uninvolved individuals. They also work on location, which can either be an existing structure, such as a hotel, museum, or office building, or an outdoor setting, which can be remote and susceptible to various weather conditions.

Human Environment

Art directors work with and oversee a wide range of crew and cast members, including actors and extras, directors, producers, writers, creative directors, electricians, painters, construction crews, lighting and sound crews, unit publicists, camera operators, costume designers, and makeup artists. Therefore, they must have excellent interpersonal skills and the ability to work past any personality conflicts.

Technological Environment

Art directors must use a wide range of technologies. Off the set, they rely on many computer-based systems, including software devoted to computer-aided design (CAD), animation, graphic design, and special effects. On the set, they may use hand tools, photography and filming equipment, lighting systems, and sound recording equipment.

Transferable Skills and Abilities

Communication Skills
- Speaking effectively
- Writing concisely

Creative/Artistic Skills
- Being skilled in art, music or dance

Interpersonal/Social Skills
- Being persistent
- Cooperating with others
- Working as a member of a team

Organization & Management Skills
- Coordinating tasks
- Managing people/groups
- Managing time
- Meeting goals and deadlines

Research & Planning Skills
- Creating ideas

EDUCATION, TRAINING, AND ADVANCEMENT

High School/Secondary

High school students should study theater as well as explore the technical and creative arts through mechanical drawing, graphics, drafting, photography, and audio-visual courses. English, art history, the industrial arts, and mathematics are also highly useful for aspiring art directors. High school students can also gain experience in art direction through participation in school- or community-based theater and media productions.

Suggested High School Subjects
- Arts
- Audio-Visual
- Drafting
- English
- Graphic Communications
- Mathematics
- Mechanical Drawing
- Photography
- Theatre & Dram

Related Career Pathways/Majors
Arts, A/V Technology & Communications Cluster
- Visual Arts Pathway

Business, Management & Administration Cluster
- Marketing Pathway

Famous First

On 19 June, 1878, Eadweard Muybridge took a series of photographs of a horse, using 12 cameras. As the horse galloped, it tripped a series of wires, triggering each camera. The images were then copied onto plates and animated by projecting them using his invention, the zoopraxiscope. Simply called 'Sallie Gardner', it is considered the oldest surviving motion picture made with multiple cameras.

Source: www.biography.com

Postsecondary

Art directors for motion pictures, radio, and television generally have a bachelor's degree in fine arts, theater, or a similar field. During postsecondary schooling, many aspiring art directors assemble a portfolio of their work, which can be used to fulfill the admission requirements for specialized undergraduate and graduate art programs that provide training in photography, graphic design, design, and other relevant fields. A strong portfolio also demonstrates the future art director's knowledge and skill to prospective employers. Students can gain practical experience and build a portfolio by participating in school-based or independent film, radio, and television productions.

Related College Majors

- Advertising
- Design & Visual Communications
- Graphic Design, Commercial Art & Illustration

Adult Job Seekers

The film, radio, and television job market is very competitive. While some individuals find work through placement offices at art schools or colleges, most art directors attain their positions after having acquired and worked in lower-level jobs within an art department. Internships, frequently unpaid, serve as a common entry point into the industry. Aspiring art directors can build their portfolios by working on commercials, independent film projects, and music videos, as well as through employment with entertainment-oriented advertising and marketing firms. As with many other entertainment careers, networking is essential.

Professional Certification or Licensure

No certification is required to work as a motion picture, radio, and television art director. Some art directors may pursue voluntary certification in specialized areas, such as design, digital technology, and art direction. As with any voluntary certification process, it is beneficial to consult credible professional associations within the field and follow professional debate as to the relevancy and value of any certification program.

Additional Requirements

Motion picture, television, and radio art directors should be excellent communicators and managers. They must be creative and detail oriented, and they should possess strong computer and budgeting skills. In order to succeed in this fast-paced environment, art directors must be decisive and able to handle stressful situations.

EARNINGS AND ADVANCEMENT

People who have become art directors do so after acquiring much experience in the advertising field. Salaries and job opportunities depend on the size and geographic location of the employer and the individual's experience and ability.

The median annual wage for producers and directors was $70,950 in May 2016. The lowest 10 percent earned less than $32,940, and the highest 10 percent earned more than $189,870.

Art directors may receive paid vacations, holidays, and sick days; life and health insurance; and retirement benefits. These are usually paid by the employer.

EMPLOYMENT AND OUTLOOK

Art directors held about 74,000 jobs nationally in 2016. Employment is expected to grow slower than the average for all occupations through the year 2026, which means employment is projected to increase 3 percent to 9 percent. Producers of information, goods, and services will continue to place increased emphasis on visual appeal in product design, advertising, marketing, and television. Competition for good jobs will be strong.

Related Occupations
- Advertising Director
- Art Director
- Cinematographer
- Photographer

Conversation About . . . Bloggers And Webcomic Artists: Careers In Online Creativity

The expansion of the Internet has created many new opportunities for people to share their talents. Many people share just for fun—but some do it for fun and money. Online, these artists can reach a global audience. The rapid growth of online media excites many people working in the field. "There are a billion new opportunities that weren't there 5 years ago," says Greg Wyshynski, editor of hockey blog *Puck Daddy*. This article describes careers for digital media workers. The first section focuses on two online occupations: bloggers and webcomic artists. The second section discusses why bloggers and webcomic artists enjoy their work and some of the challenges that they face. A final section suggests sources for more information.

Jobs in digital media

The growth of the Internet and the availability of simple Web publishing tools have made it easy to share content online. Many people create websites as a hobby or as a way to share news with family and friends. Artists— including photographers, writers, filmmakers, and musicians—put their work online in the hopes of attracting attention and building a following. These artists enjoy sharing their creations with people around the world. Some artists, however, are able to make a living creating content for their websites. Workers in the occupations covered in this article, bloggers and webcomic artists, produce online content as their primary source of revenue. The U.S. Bureau of Labor Statistics has no employment or wage data for bloggers or webcomic artists. Their wages vary significantly depending on their employer and the size of their audience.

Bloggers

Bloggers are writers who regularly post content on a Web log, or blog. These blog posts can be of any length and on any topic. Some bloggers post many times a day; others post less frequently. In their posts, bloggers occasionally use other media and content that aren't possible in print. Cooking blogs might include instructional videos of cooking techniques, for example, or news blogs provide interactive maps. Bloggers can be self-employed, employed by print media or other companies, or work as contractors.

Depending on their interests, self-employed bloggers write on a number of topics, such as offering financial advice or reviewing restaurants. They have complete creative control over their own content and set their own schedules. Most self-employed bloggers make money through advertising on their websites. The amount of money they make from ads depends on the number of times people visit their website, called traffic. As traffic increases, advertisers pay bloggers more. Well-known bloggers may also make money through sponsorships, book or product sales, and speaking fees.

When employed by traditional print media companies, such as newspapers and magazines, bloggers may write for both print and online editions. For example, Brier Dudley, technology blogger for *The Seattle Times*, writes a weekly column in addition to his regular blog entries. According to Dudley, the tone of his blog differs from that of his column. "Blog items tend to be more conversational and casual," he says.

Bloggers who work for newspapers or magazines are more like traditional journalists than are self-employed bloggers. News bloggers receive guidance from editors who review their posts. And like traditional journalists, news bloggers need to be ready to write whenever news occurs. Many readers turn to the Internet for breaking news, so bloggers often race to be the first to post news. "You're like a doctor on call at all times," says Wyshynski. "You have to be on the story first." Some bloggers work on a contract basis, not as employees of news media companies. These contractors usually write for online news websites that publish posts from many bloggers. Like news bloggers, these contractors submit their posts to editors for review. They are usually paid per post, similar to freelance reporters. Many contract bloggers write for several different sites to increase their income. They may also earn bonuses for writing posts that attract particularly high traffic.

Skills and training. As professional writers, bloggers must be excellent communicators and need to understand what content most appeals to their audiences. Bloggers also have to be disciplined to produce high-quality research and writing, while trying to meet deadlines or to post breaking news. Bloggers employed by newspapers usually have a journalism degree or previous newspaper experience. Some contract bloggers have journalism degrees, but it is not a requirement. Like freelance journalists, contract blogger's posts are judged on their own merit. There are no formal education requirements for self-employed bloggers. However, self-employed bloggers are usually experts in the field they blog about. They previously may have worked in a job related to their blog's topic. For example, a professional blogger who runs a home decorating blog may have experience with many different decorating or remodeling techniques.

Bloggers who are self-employed or who work with a small staff usually need experience with multimedia tools. Newspapers may have photographers and video editors on staff, but many bloggers lack these resources and produce the photos and videos themselves. "A lot of online media isn't just about being talented as a writer or a journalist," says Wyshynski. "You might have to shoot and edit your own video and audio."

Webcomic artists

Although most comic artists work for newspaper syndicates or comic book companies, webcomic artists post their strips for readers online. Some webcomic artists post new strips daily; others post less frequently. Creating a widely read webcomic requires more than excellent artwork. Webcomic artists must also write scripts for their strips before they begin drawing. In some webcomics, called one-shots, each strip is a self-contained story. Other webcomics are serials, which have long-running plots and regularly occurring characters.

For webcomic artists, developing a good script can be a quick or lengthy process. Sometimes, inspiration strikes early in the creative process, and they get an idea for a script immediately. Other times, webcomic artists may spend hours—or more— struggling to craft a script that their audiences will enjoy.

Webcomic artists may turn to outside influences for inspiration when they're having difficulty writing a script. For example, Tim Buckley, artist of *Ctrl + Alt + Del*, frequently uses video game humor in his comic. To find ideas, Buckley researches what new games are scheduled to be released and what issues are of interest to the gaming community. He also draws inspiration from his personal life. "I've gotten many ideas from interactions with my friends and family," he says.

After they've written the script for a strip, webcomic artists begin drawing. All artists have their own style. Some draw highly detailed characters and landscapes; others use a minimalist style. Many webcomics are in full color, but some artists prefer to work in black and white. Depending on the complexity of the artwork, drawing a strip may take anywhere from a few minutes to many hours. Most webcomics are available online at no cost, so comic artists have to find alternative sources of revenue. Like bloggers, many webcomics make money through advertisements.

Webcomic artists also earn money from selling products, such as t-shirts and compilation books of their comics, to fans. When they're not planning or drawing comic strips, webcomic artists are frequently creating new products to sell to fans. According to Jeph Jacques, artist of *Questionable Content*, coming up with good products can be a challenge. "Coming up with a t-shirt design is like making a comic," he says. "It can be quick, but it usually takes a long time." Webcomic artists are able to communicate directly with readers, which allows them to understand which products and scripts appeal most to their audience. Many webcomic artists spend part of their day replying to email from fans. Some webcomics also have message boards that allow artists to communicate with their fans. To share information with readers, webcomic artists sometimes write personal blogs on their websites.

Many webcomic artists also connect with readers by meeting them at conventions. Artists may travel to conventions to speak on panels and interact with fans and peers. Many artists also bring their products to conventions, where they can sell their merchandise directly.

Skills and training. Not all webcomic artists are formally trained. In fact, many are self-taught and have refined their artwork through years of practice. The artwork of different webcomics varies widely, and practice is essential for each artist to develop a unique style.

Excellent artwork alone does not ensure success as a webcomic artist; artists also must write scripts that appeal to their audience. To improve their scripts, many artists practice writing dialogue and developing characters. Because each webcomic operates as his or her own small business, operating it successfully also requires skill in business and math. These skills help artists evaluate companies to find the right manufacturer for their products, to price merchandise, and to complete tax forms for their small businesses.

Rewards and Challenges

Sharing content online is often rewarding. Bloggers and webcomic artists can gain a global audience for their work, and they frequently develop close relationships with their fans. Unlike traditional media, digital media workers who post online can communicate directly with readers from all over the world. "You can get feedback instantly," says Dudley. "And you're having a conversation with people everywhere."

Self-employed bloggers and webcomic artists enjoy having control over their work and making their own decisions. They set their own schedules and write or draw without supervision. "I have the freedom to work and to write stories and jokes that entertain me," says Buckley.

But establishing a popular blog or webcomic is difficult. New blogs and webcomics face competition from an immense crowd of previously existing sites. With so many competitors, new sites struggle to stand out. Even the best blog or webcomic may never be read by an audience large enough to make it profitable.

Blogs and webcomics that are able to attract a following usually have to wait years before they're financially stable. Bloggers and webcomic artists frequently develop and maintain their websites as side projects while working full time in another job. But building a large audience usually takes a while. "You have to be willing to be poor," warns Jacques. "There aren't any instant millions."

Bloggers and webcomic artists constantly search for ways to monetize the work they put online. Even online advertising, the most common way to make money, isn't a guaranteed source of revenue anymore. To view blog and webcomics, many people now use Rich Site Summary (RSS) feeds to see updates from their favorite websites all in one place. RSS feeds frequently remove advertisements from posts and don't count towards a webpage's traffic totals. This decreased traffic reduces the amount of money bloggers and webcomic artists make from advertisers. In response to the increasing use of RSS feeds, bloggers and webcomic artists are searching for new ways to make money while continuing to put their content online for free.

Despite these challenges, many bloggers and webcomic artists are passionate about sharing their work directly with readers. "Even if I couldn't make the living I do," says Buckley, "I'd still want to do this because I enjoy it so much."

Tips for developing your own blog or webcomic

Creating a popular blog or webcomic takes both hard work and luck. Here are some tips to help you be successful.

Find your niche. There are already many blogs and webcomics online. To distinguish yours, develop your own style or become an expert in a specific subject matter. If your content is unique and entertaining, casual browsers are more likely to become regular readers. To cultivate a group of fans, it may be beneficial to limit your scope. For example, if you want to write a blog of restaurant reviews, you might focus on restaurants in your local area or on a specific type of cuisine.

Update regularly. The more frequently you add content, the more often regular readers will come back to your website. If you post several times a day, regular readers might check the site multiple times, increasing your web traffic. This doesn't mean that you must update the website constantly. But if you have a published update schedule, such as one new comic strip a week, stick to it. If readers see that you're not following your own schedule, they might stop visiting your site.

Engage your audience. Communicate with your readers through e-mail, message boards, or social media. If your audience feels personally invested in your blog or webcomic, they're more likely to read it regularly and support you financially. And the more you understand your audience, the better you'll be able to create content and products that appeal to them.

Search for revenue. Find creative ways to make money. If your blog or webcomic attracts a large audience, you can make money through advertising. However, even a smaller group of dedicated readers can be profitable. Dedicated readers are more likely to financially support your blog or webcomic, either through donations or product purchases.

MORE INFORMATION

Advertising Research Foundation
432 Park Avenue, 6th Floor
New York, NY 10016-8013
212.751.5656
Thearf.org

Advertising Women of New York
25 West 45th Street, Suite 403
New York, NY 10036
212.221.7969
awny@awny.org
www.awny.org

American Advertising Federation
1101 Vermont Avenue, NW
Suite 500
Washington, DC 20005-6306
800.999.2231
aaf@aaf.org
www.aaf.org

American Association of Advertising Agencies
405 Lexington Avenue, 18th Floor
New York, NY 10174-1801
212.682.2500
OBD@aaaa.org
www.aaaa.org

Art Directors Club
106 West 29th Street
New York, NY 10001
212.643.1440
www.adcglobal.org

Art Directors Guild
11969 Ventura Boulevard, 2nd Floor
Studio City, CA 91604
818.762.9995
www.adg.org

Association for Women in Communications
3337 Duke Street
Alexandria, VA 22314
703.370.7436
btijerina@womcom.org
www.womcom.org

Association of National Advertisers
708 Third Avenue, 33rd Floor
New York, NY 10017-4270
212.697.5950
info@ana.net
www.ana.net

Set Decorators Society of America
7100 Tujunga Avenue, Suite A
North Hollywood, CA 91605
818.255.2425
www.setdecorators.org

Michael Auerbach/Editor

Multimedia Artist & Animator

Snapshot

Career Cluster(s): Arts, A/V Technology & Communications

Interests: Art, illustration, web design, current trends, being competitive, communicating with others

Earnings (2016 median pay): $65,300 per year; $31.40 per hour

Employment & Outlook: Average Growth Expected

OVERVIEW

Sphere of Work

Commercial artists may design artwork for product packaging, billboards, media advertisements, and other marketing tools, or create illustrations for magazines, books, GIFs, memes, and other forms of media. Some are self-employed, working from home offices, while others work for advertising and design agencies of varying sizes.

Work Environment

Commercial artists often work in settings such as design firms, advertising companies, and corporate offices for manufacturers, in environments that are generally clean and comfortable. Their hours vary based on the size and scope of the project on which they are working, as well as the time constraints established in a contract. Smaller companies and independent, self-employed artists tend to work longer hours to manage not only their projects, but also the issues associated with a small business.

Profile

Interests: Data, People, Things
Working Conditions: Work Inside
Physical Strength: Light Work
Education Needs: On-The-Job Training, Junior/Technical/Community College, Apprenticeship, Bachelor's Degree
Licensure/Certification: Usually Not Required
Physical Abilities Not Required: Not Climb, Not Kneel, Not Hear and/or Talk
Opportunities for Experience: Internship, Apprenticeship, Military Service, Volunteer Work, Part Time Work
Holland Interest Score*: AEI

* See Appendix A

Occupation Interest

Commercial artists must combine a talent for art and creative thinking with good research and communication skills, close attention to detail, and the ability to meet deadlines and work in a competitive atmosphere, all while remaining true to the needs of the client. They should be aware of general public attitudes and keep up with current trends. Many independent commercial artists set their own hours and act as small business entrepreneurs as well as creative artists.

A Day in the Life—Duties and Responsibilities

The duties and responsibilities of commercial artists vary based on the area and the size of the business in which they work. Commercial artists may specialize as graphic designers, illustrators, cartoonists, photographers, web designers, medical or scientific illustrators, police and forensic artists, or art directors. Many commercial artists work for larger marketing and advertising companies, focusing on one particular discipline or type of client. Others are self-employed, and must run a successful small business in addition to their other responsibilities.

In general, commercial artists first confer with clients to establish the preferred design approach, budget, and anything else that needs to be taken into account. They then develop the requested design, often showing samples to the client at different points in the process. The artist may work independently, or as part of a team overseen by an art director. In a team setting, the art director's job is to assign tasks, give the artists advice and feedback, and approve and present the final product.

Duties and Responsibilities

- Conferring with clients, other animators and designers, and directors to determine budgets and timelines
- Creating graphics and animation using computer programs
- Developing storyboards that lay out the main scenes in the animation

OCCUPATION SPECIALTIES

Cartoonists

Cartoonists draw comic or editorial cartoon and comic strips to amuse readers and illustrate or comment upon political events, advertising, stories or articles.

Illustrators

Illustrators draw or paint illustrations for use by various media to explain or adorn the printed or spoken word.

WORK ENVIRONMENT

Immediate Physical Environment

Commercial artists work primarily in design firms, studios, or office spaces in marketing and advertising companies. These environments are well lit and well ventilated, with computers and Internet access. Many commercial artists are independent consultants who work from studios and office spaces in their own private residences.

Transferable Skills and Abilities

Communication Skills
- Expressing thoughts and ideas
- Persuading others
- Speaking effectively
- Writing concisely

Interpersonal/Social Skills
- Being able to remain calm
- Respecting others' opinions

Organization & Management Skills
- Making decisions
- Paying attention to and handling details

Research & Planning Skills
- Analyzing information
- Creating ideas
- Gathering information

Technical Skills
- Performing scientific, mathematical and technical work
- Working with machines, tools or other objects

Unclassified Skills
- Performing work that produces tangible result

Human Environment

Depending on their areas of expertise, commercial artists meet and interact with a wide range of individuals. These parties include marketing and advertising professionals, business executives, editors, decorators, medical professionals, and other specialized commercial artists.

Technological Environment

Commercial artists might use computer programs such as graphics and animation software, as well as publishing and editing software. A scanner may be necessary in order to send prospective designs to clients. Other materials used can include traditional art media such as pencils, pens, inks, and paints; designers' tools such as T-squares and parallel rules; and books of type styles and other reference sources.

EDUCATION, TRAINING, AND ADVANCEMENT

High School/Secondary

High school students should study art, including drawing, photography, and design; math, including geometry; and computer science, including graphic design and drafting. They should also take advantage of any subject areas of interest to them as artists; for example, future medical illustrators are advised to take anatomy and physiology classes.

Suggested High School Subjects
- Applied Math
- Arts
- College Preparatory
- Composition
- Computer Science
- Crafts
- Drafting
- English
- Graphic Communications
- Literature
- Photography
- Pottery
- Woodshop

Related Career Pathways/Majors
Arts, A/V Technology & Communications Cluster
- Visual Arts Pathway

Famous First

The first entirely computer-animated film was Toy Story, released in 1995. It was produced by Pixar Studios under the control of Walt Disney Pictures. The film was an "instant classic," garnering $300 million in its first year and spawning legions of toys, video games, theme-park attractions, and other spin-offs—including two sequels.
Source: www.pixar.com

Postsecondary

Aspiring commercial artists may pursue a bachelor's degree in fine art, design, or a similar field. Alternatively, they may enroll in art or design institutes for programs with more studio time and a greater focus on graphic design, photography, or publishing art. Further education may be warranted depending on how a commercial artist chooses to specialize. For example, a prospective art director may also study management or art administration, while somebody interested in medical or scientific illustration would be well served by a master's degree in a relevant science.

Related College Majors

- Art, General
- Crafts, Folk Art & Artisanry
- Educational/Instructional Media Design
- Educational/Instructional Media Technology
- Fine/Studio Arts
- Graphic Design/Commercial Art & Illustration
- Painting
- Printmaking
- Visual & Performing Arts

Adult Job Seekers

An internship or apprenticeship is a good way to gain necessary experience. Individuals looking for work can apply directly to the art or advertising director of a particular company, and may also find opportunities through professional organizations such as the

American Institute of Graphic Arts (now known as AIGA). Any potential commercial artist must have a portfolio showing his or her best work.

Professional Certification and Licensure

Some organizations provide certification programs to help commercial artists become specialists in their particular fields. For example, the International Association for Identification offers a forensic artist certification program. Such certification can provide a competitive edge for job candidates.

Additional Requirements

Commercial artists should be both creative and extremely knowledgeable of the wide range of media options available to them to meet a client's needs. They should be willing to listen to and communicate with clients who may or may not agree with their ideas. Commercial artists must have self-discipline and a strong work ethic, especially in light of the fact that many are self-employed.

EARNINGS AND ADVANCEMENT

Earnings of multimedia artists and animators depend on skill, education, and the type, size, and geographic location of the employer. Earnings of freelance multimedia artists and animators may vary with the artists' individual fees and reputation, as well as the nature and amount of work sold.

The median annual wage for multimedia artists and animators was $65,300 in May 2016. The lowest 10 percent earned less than $38,520, and the highest 10 percent earned more than $115,960.

Earnings for self-employed multimedia artists and animators vary widely. Those struggling to gain experience and build a reputation may be forced to charge only small fees for their work. Well-established free-lancers may earn much more than salaried artists.

Multimedia artists and animators may receive paid vacations, holidays, and sick days; life and health insurance; and retirement benefits. These are usually paid for by the employer.

EMPLOYMENT AND OUTLOOK

Nationally, there were approximately 673,700 multimedia artists and animators employed in 2016. Employment of multimedia artists and animators is projected to grow 8 percent from 2016 to 2026, about as fast as the average for all occupations. Projected growth will be due to increased demand for animation and visual effects in video games, movies, and television. Job growth may be slowed, however, by companies hiring animators and artists who work overseas. Studios may save money on animation by using lower paid workers outside of the United States.

Consumers will continue to demand more realistic video games, movie and television special effects, and three-dimensional movies. This will create demand for newer computer hardware, which will enhance the complexity of animation and visual effects. Additional multimedia artists and animators will be required to meet this increased demand.

Further, an increased demand for computer graphics for mobile devices, such as smart phones, will lead to more job opportunities. Multimedia artists will be needed to create animation for games and applications for mobile devices.

Related Occupations
- Art Director
- Designer
- Graphic Designer
- Industrial Designer
- Interior Designer
- Medical & Scientific Illustrator

- Merchandise Displayer
- Photographer
- Sign Painter & Letterer
- Software Developer
- Web Developer

Related Occupations

- Graphic Designer & Illustrator

Conversation With . . .
TYLER NAUGLE

MTV Production Assistant
Freelance Animator, 2 years

1. What was your individual career path in terms of education, entry-level job, or other significant opportunity?

At Maryland Institute College of Art (MICA), I majored in 2D Animation with a concentration in Video. After my junior year I was fortunate to get an internship with MTV's On-Air Design department. Shortly before my 2011 graduation, I received a call from my previous supervisor at MTV who offered me a Production Assistant position. I accepted the position and started working at MTV full-time a few weeks after graduation. I work on different projects: it could be animating, it could be editing. Something called a "lower third" is a big thing we work on; it pops out from the corner of the screen and gives information about a show coming out and directs the viewer toward something. I've also done some freelance jobs in my free time.

2. Are there many job opportunities in your profession? In what specific areas?

Animation is a big industry with a lot of opportunities. Corporations, independent film makers, small companies trying to show people what they're about ... people are willing to pay for motion graphics. There is no shortage of people looking for motion graphics or animation in general.

I focus in 2D Animation and there are an assortment of positions available (Key Artist, In-betweener, Background Artist, Effects Artist, Motion Designer). At MTV, I'm specifically in motion graphics. Work assignments are mainly elements for TV, and more subdued than what I do in my spare time, which is very character-based, usually revolving around humor, and much more manic.

3. What do you wish you had known going into this profession?

I wish that I had known more about negotiating pay. That is a topic that's only very briefly touched on in school and is a huge part of working as an artist.

4. How do you see your profession changing in the next five years?

I may be wrong, but it think animation is going toward a more graphic-based presentation even though there is always going to be a market for more experimental animation. Also, independents use Kickstarter. Outside the commercial side of things, that's where all the independent animation is going to be flourishing. That's where people should focus if they just want to do their own projects.

5. What role will technology play in those changes, and what skills will be required?

Technology is huge in the animation industry. Programs are constantly changing so you have to pay attention to what's new and what's being phased out. Depending on what you want to do, your toolkit could be completely different from your fellow animators. For example, I use mostly Flash and After Effects and edit in Premiere. There are people I know who use Toon Boom and edit in Final Cut. We end up with a similar product but how we each get there is completely different.

6. Do you have any general advice or additional professional insights to share with someone interested in your profession?

To work professionally as an animator is to essentially sell your abilities as a product and you need to be able to sell the product successfully. Being confident in your work and knowing what your abilities are worth is very important. Too many animators sell their abilities for way less than they are worth. This is a problem that I have found affects recent graduates more than any other group. It's something that a lot of people are uncomfortable talking about, and though pay varies depending on the type of job you're doing and the client that it's for, it's a good idea to talk about it with your peers to make sure that you're not getting taken advantage of.

7. Can you suggest a valuable "try this" for students considering a career in your profession?

Anyone wanting to go into animation should work with others as often as possible. Commercial animation requires you to work closely with peers. That's quite different from other fields within art and it's an aspect of the industry that some people might find difficult or unusual. Practicing that level of cooperation in school could be particularly useful; it has the potential to provide contacts that could be mutually beneficial in later years.

This interview was originally conducted in 2014, so some details regarding software and computer applications may have changed.

MORE INFORMATION

American Institute of Graphic Arts
164 Fifth Avenue
New York, NY 10010
212.807.1990
www.aiga.org

Color Marketing Group
1908 Mount Vernon Avenue
Alexandria, VA 22301
703.329.8500
www.colormarketing.org

Design Management Institute
101 Tremont Street, Suite 300
Boston, MA 02108
617.338.6380
www.dmi.org

Graphic Artists Guild
32 Broadway, Suite 1114
New York, NY 10004-1612
212.791.3400
communications@gag.org
www.graphicartistsguild.org

National Art Education Association
1806 Robert Fulton Drive, Suite 300
Reston, VA 20191-1590
703.860.8000
info@arteducators.org
www.naea-reston.org

National Association of Schools of Art & Design
11250 Roger Bacon Drive, Suite 21
Reston, VA 20190-5248
703.437.0700
info@arts-accredit.org
nasad.arts-accredit.org/index.jsp

Society of Publication Designers
27 Union Square West, Suite 207
New York, NY 10003
212.223.3332
www.spd.org

Michael Auerbach/Editor

Photographer

Snapshot

Career Cluster(s): Arts, A/V Technology & Communications
Interests: Photography, art, visual imagery, photojournalism, fine arts, media technology
Earnings (2016 median pay): $34,070 per year; $16.38 per hour
Employment & Outlook: Slower than Average Growth Expected

OVERVIEW

Sphere of Work

Photographers capture images of various objects, people, and events using a film or digital camera. They must exhibit a solid understanding of technical camera operation and the fundamental processes behind photography, lighting, and the composition of an image. Most photographers focus on one area of photographic specialty. Photographic specialties include news, portrait, commercial and industrial, scientific, and fine arts photography. Because their profession is based on choosing image composition and creating unique images, creativity is a trait common among all types of photographers regardless of their area of specialization.

Work Environment

A photographer's work environment depends primarily on his or her area of photographic specialty. Some photographers, such as those who take studio portraits of children and families, work primarily out of comfortable, well-lit, indoor studios. Other photographers work outside in a multitude of environments and are subject to various weather conditions. Photographers who work for the government, advertising agencies, or private companies frequently maintain a forty-hour week. Freelance and newspaper photographers, or photojournalists, generally work irregular hours, travel often, and are expected to be on-call for last-minute projects or emergency events.

Profile

Interests: Data, People, Things

Working Conditions: Work Inside, Work Both Inside and Outside

Physical Strength: Light Work, Medium Work

Education Needs: On-the-Job Training, High School Diploma or GED, High School Diploma with Technical Education, Apprenticeship

Licensure/Certification: Usually Not Required

Physical Abilities Not Required: Not Climb, Not Kneel, Not Hear and/or Talk

Opportunities for Experience: Internship, Apprenticeship, Military Service, Volunteer Work, Part Time Work

Holland Interest Score*: AES, ESA, RIC, RSE, SRC

* See Appendix A

Occupation Interest

Potential photographers should demonstrate a passion for artistic creation. They should be compelled to tell stories through photographs and possess a deep desire to analyze, present, and offer a unique perspective on their photographic subjects. They should express a definitive opinion through their photographs, and that opinion should be easily discernible to an audience examining their photography. They should be able to lead and work with different types of people and personalities.

A Day in the Life—Duties and Responsibilities

Most photographers purchase and maintain their own camera equipment, lenses, and accessories, which can be costly at the outset. Photographers usually work independently or with an assistant. They are responsible for the physical positioning of subjects as well as the arrangement of lighting and camera angles. If the photographs are taken with film, the photographer develops the film and prints in either a darkroom or printing facility. Digital photographs may be edited and retouched prior to printing.

Photographers' specialties determine what they photograph and how those images are used. Portrait photographers specialize in photographing people or groups of people. They are generally self-employed and often travel to various locations for special events like weddings, school functions, and other special ceremonies. Commercial and industrial photographers travel to various locations to photograph landscapes, buildings, and merchandise. Their photographs are usually published in books, advertisements, catalogs, or other media. Scientific photographers make a photographic record of data related to science and medicine. These photographers usually have technical training in the sciences as well as the arts. News photographers, or photojournalists, take pictures of relevant people or events for publication in regular newspapers or periodicals. Fine arts photographers are usually highly technically proficient, and may display their photographs in museums, art galleries, or private art shows.

Self-employed and freelance photographers must perform business and administrative tasks in addition to their creative work. Such tasks might include managing employees, handling billing and payments, setting appointments, and obtaining licenses, copyrights, contracts, and other legal documents as needed. They must also arrange their own advertising, marketing campaigns, and self-promotion.

Duties and Responsibilities

- Enlarging, reducing and retouching prints
- Carefully arranging lighting and composition of the picture
- Using makeup, lights, reflectors, screens and props
- Mixing and developing chemicals
- Developing and printing film

OCCUPATION SPECIALTIES

Aerial Photographers

Aerial Photographers photograph segments of earth and other subject material from aircraft.

Scientific Photographers

Scientific Photographers photograph a variety of subject matter to illustrate and record scientific data or phenomena.

Still Photographers

Still Photographers photograph subjects, using still cameras, color or black-and-white film, and a variety of accessories. They normally specialize in a particular area of photography, such as illustrative, fashion, architectural or portrait.

Photojournalists

Photojournalists photograph newsworthy events, locations, people, or other illustrative and educational material for use in publications or telecasts, using a still camera.

Animation Camera Operators

Animation Camera Operators operate special cameras to make animated cartoon motion picture films, by placing the background drawings on a horizontal easel over which the camera is suspended.

WORK ENVIRONMENT

Immediate Physical Environment

A photographer's working conditions vary greatly depending on his or her specialty. Some photographers can work in clean, comfortable, well-ventilated studios. Others work in unpleasant or dangerous outdoor environments. Photographers regularly travel to and from photographic sites. Those who process film and prints, especially in a darkroom, are exposed to potentially harmful chemicals.

Transferable Skills and Abilities

Communication Skills
- Speaking effectively
- Writing concisely

Creative/Artistic Skills
- Being skilled in art, music or dance

Interpersonal/Social Skills
- Being able to remain calm
- Cooperating with others
- Working as a member of a team

Organization & Management Skills
- Handling challenging situations
- Paying attention to and handling details

Research & Planning Skills
- Creating ideas

Human Environment

Photographers work with numerous clients, customers, and subjects. They must interact easily with others, and they should be comfortable directing, evaluating, and occasionally comforting their photographic subjects. Photographers sometimes collaborate with graphic designers, journalists, reporters, and editors. Some may report to a supervisor or direct an assistant.

Technological Environment

Photographers must learn how to operate camera equipment in order to be successful. To create a photograph, photographers use film and digital cameras, film, digital memory and storage devices, tripods, lenses and filters, floodlights, reflectors, light meters, and electronic flash units. Image processing may require computers, imaging and editing software, printers and scanners, photographic paper, darkroom equipment, and chemicals for developing film and prints from film.

EDUCATION, TRAINING, AND ADVANCEMENT

High School/Secondary

High school students interested in becoming photographers should devote time to the study of communications, mathematics, chemistry, art, photography, and technology. Aspiring photographers should also engage in extracurricular activities (like the school newspaper or yearbook) that allow them to practice taking pictures, editing their work, and developing or printing their best photographs. Interested students should pursue part-time work with a photographer or store and consider applying to postsecondary photography programs.

Suggested High School Subjects
- Arts
- Chemistry
- English
- Mathematics
- Photography

Related Career Pathways/Majors
Arts, A/V Technology & Communications Cluster
- Visual Arts Pathway

Famous First

The first modern photographic print in a publication appeared in the New York Daily Graphic in 1873, an image of Steinway Hall in Manhattan published on December 2, 1873. The Graphic then published "the first reproduction of a photograph with a full tonal range in a newspaper" on March 4, 1880 (entitled "A Scene in Shantytown") with a crude halftone screen.. It showed a shantytown in the city. The print was produced by means of the halftone process, which uses tiny dots of different sizes and gradations to create the optical illusion that the viewer is seeing shades of gray along with black and white.

Source: www.historygraphicdesign.com

Postsecondary

Most photographers find it helpful to have an undergraduate degree or certificate in photography from a university, community college, private art school, or vocational institute. Many vocational education programs offer courses in visual imaging technology as well as in the fundamentals of photography. Other postsecondary programs teach students the practical and technical aspects of photography. Coursework may include the history of photography and cinema, camera maintenance, photojournalism, composition, color printing and print finishing, lighting, retouching, and other related subjects. Prospective freelance photographers may benefit from studying courses in business, including marketing, public relations, and business management.

Related College Majors
- Commercial Photography
- Educational/Instructional Media Design
- Educational/Instructional Media Technology
- Fine/Studio Arts
- Photography

Adult Job Seekers

Many prospective photographers find positions as assistants to local, professional photographers after receiving their formal education. Assistants gain valuable technical experience, on-the-job training, and the practical skills needed to start their own businesses. Other job seekers apply for full- or part-time positions at camera shops, local newspapers, or photography studios. Candidates can also participate in apprenticeships, mentorships, or internships through their schools or photography training programs.

Many photographers subscribe to photography newsletters and magazines in order to make contacts in the industry. Networking, mentoring, and professional development opportunities are also frequently available through professional photographer associations.

Professional Certification and Licensure

Photographers are usually not required to obtain professional certification or licensure in their field; to an extent, this is because the work is highly visual, so photographers can easily provide samples of their work to others. Some professional photography organizations offer voluntary certifications, which may enhance a photographer's marketing and job-seeking efforts. To become a Certified Professional Photographer (CPP) through the Professional Photographers of America, candidates must pass a written exam and provide images for critique. Continuing education is typically required for certification renewal.

Additional Requirements

Photography is a well- respected form of artistic expression. Therefore, aspiring and professional photographers should be naturally artistic and able to understand the fundamentals of photographic composition. Because the field is intrinsically subjective, photographers should maintain the integrity and conviction necessary to present effective artwork and subject analysis, without reacting negatively to criticism. Photographers should be patient, have great eyesight, possess boundless imagination, and demonstrate impeccable communication skills when dealing with clients and subjects.

EARNINGS AND ADVANCEMENT

Earnings of photographers depend on geographic location, type of photographic specialty, number of hours worked, photographic skills and marketing ability. Most salaried photographers work full-time and earn more than the majority of self-employed photographers who usually work part-time, but some self-employed photographers have very high earnings. Unlike photojournalists and commercial photographers, very few fine arts photographers are successful enough to support themselves solely through this profession.

Median annual earnings of photographers were $34.070 in 2016. The lowest ten percent earned less than $19,388, and the highest ten percent earned more than $78,202.

Photographers may receive paid vacations, holidays, and sick days; life and health insurance; and retirement benefits. These are usually paid by the employer. Freelance and self-employed photographers must provide their own benefits.

EMPLOYMENT AND OUTLOOK

There were approximately 147,300 photographers employed nationally in 2016. Employment of photographers is projected to decline 6 percent from 2016 to 2026. The decreasing cost of digital cameras and the increasing number of amateur photographers and hobbyists will reduce the need for professional photographers. In addition, stock photographic services available online give individuals and businesses access to stock photographs for a fee or subscription, possibly dampening demand for photographers.

However, the application of newer technologies, such as drone photography, may contribute to increased demand for these workers in a variety of ways. For example, drone photography in the commercial sector enables the capturing of images and information for agricultural land, real estate, and new construction projects. In addition, drone photography enables the photographer to create visuals of tall structures, such as cell towers and bridges that are in need of repair. Drone photography at weddings or special events can also capture scenic aerial portraits.

Employment of self-employed photographers is projected to grow 12 percent from 2016 to 2026. Demand for portrait photographers will remain as people continue to want new portraits. In addition, corporations will continue to require the services of commercial photographers to develop compelling advertisements to sell products.

Declines in the newspaper industry will reduce demand for news photographers to provide still images for print. Employment of photographers in newspaper publishing is projected to decline 34 percent from 2016 to 2026.

Related Occupations

- Art Director
- Camera Operator
- Cinematographer
- Commercial Artist
- Motion Picture Projectionist
- Motion Picture/Radio/TV Art Director
- Photographic Process Worker
- Prepress Technician

Related Military Occupations

- Audiovisual & Broadcast Technician
- Broadcast Journalist & Newswriter
- Diver
- Photographic Specialist

MORE INFORMATION

American Society of Media Photographers
150 North 2nd Street
Philadelphia, PA 19106
215.451.2767
www.asmp.org

American Society of Photographers
3120 N. Argonne Drive
Milwaukee, WI 53222
jonallyn@aol.com
www.asofp.com

National Press Photographers Association, Inc.
3200 Croasdaile Drive, Suite 306
Durham, NC 27705
919.383.7246
info@nppa.org
www.nppa.org

NPPA's Honors and Recognitions:
www.nppa.org/about_us/honors_and_
recognitions/

Sponsors photojournalism competitions:
www.nppa.org/competitions/

Newspaper Guild-CWA
Research and Information
Department
501 Third Street NW, 6th Floor
Washington, DC 20001-2797
202.434.7177
guild@cwa-union.org
www.newsguild.org

Professional Photographers of America, Inc.
229 Peachtree Street, NE, Suite 2200
Atlanta, GA 30303
800.786.6277
csc@ppa.com
www.ppa.com

PPA Awards:
www.ppa.com/competitions/other-awards.
php

Briana Nadeau/Editor

Public Relations Specialist

Snapshot

Career Cluster(s): Business, Management & Administration, Marketing, Sales & Service

Interests: Mass communications, media relations, public opinion, crisis management, marketing, writing

Earnings (2016 median pay): $58,020 per year; $27.89 per hour

Employment & Outlook: Faster Than Average Growth Expected

OVERVIEW

Sphere of Work

Public relations (PR) specialists are communication professionals who handle a wide range of functions to support clients in their efforts to build and maintain a positive public image, seek positive media exposure, and forge strong relationships with the public.

Almost any organization or individual can be a client, such as businesses, industries, non-profit organizations, universities, hospitals, government, or celebrities. PR specialists are responsible for a company's overall social media strategy and for creating and implementing

social media campaigns, along with all other media and community relations, consumer and industry relations, investor and employee relations, and interest-group representation, as well as political campaigns, fundraising, and conflict mediation.

As part of these functions, public relations specialists focus on maintaining contact with online, print, and traditional broadcast media, arranging media interviews, setting up speaker engagements, hosting events, writing speeches and press releases, and planning and conducting press conferences. Public relations specialists communicate key messages that have been strategically crafted. These messages must be approved by the client, be clear and understandable to the audience or market, and should align with short- and long-term client goals.

Profile

Interests: Data, People
Working Conditions: Work Inside
Physical Strength: Light Work
Education Needs: Bachelor's Degree
Licensure/Certification: Required
Physical Abilities Not Required: Not Climb, Not Kneel
Opportunities for Experience: Internship, Apprenticeship, Military Service, Volunteer Work, Part Time Work
Holland Interest Score*: EAS

* See Appendix A

Occupation Interest

The public relations field attracts those who enjoy working with people from all industries and environments—who can easily communicate on many levels. Writing is an essential skill for public relations specialists, as is an ability to gauge public opinion, empathize with particular market segments, and assess the public perception of a given message.

Many colleges and universities offer a degree in public relations. Typical coursework includes core classes in English and writing, with specialty coursework in public relations, journalism, news and speech writing, media relations, communications, planning and analysis, crisis management, and public relations ethics.

A Day in the Life—Duties and Responsibilities

Like all communications experts, public relations specialists are consistently on alert for new and creative ways to achieve client goals and to protect, preserve, or enhance the client's image. In a typical day, public relations specialists will write and distribute news releases, prepare copy for annual reports, take and manage calls from journalists, plan press conferences or events, line up media interviews, provide executives with media training and debriefing after interviews, and attend strategy meetings with clients and public relations managers. Within a corporation, "clients" may be divisions or areas inside the company, with the public relations specialist preparing and disseminating various types of information for different departments, all under the banner of one key message.

Public relations specialists often face pressure from eager clients, and work frequently with outside reporters, producers, bloggers, and other social media specialists. In order to avoid the label of a "spin doctor"—a pejorative term often assigned to PR professionals in corporate or government communications—successful PR specialists do well to earn the trust of those in the media by maintaining a professional demeanor and a strict code of ethics. Successful PR specialists communicate a client's message by delivering it to the public in a truthful manner that provides positive exposure for the client and useful information to the customer.

Public relations specialists are employed in nearly every industry in some form or fashion, which makes this a flexible career option. Additionally, because of advances in technology, and through the use of email, videoconferencing, and online social media, public relations specialists can work from almost any location. Self-employment is common among PR specialists; however, most entry-level candidates do not yet have the experience required to branch out on their own.

Duties and Responsibilities

- **Determining the needs of the organization or individual**
- **Preparing and distributing fact sheets, photographs, articles, news releases and/or promotional booklets**
- **Making speeches and conducting research**
- **Directing advertising campaigns in all types of media**
- **Coordinating special exhibits, contests or luncheons into the total public relations plan**

OCCUPATION SPECIALTIES

Lobbyists

Lobbyists contact and confer with members of the legislature and other holders of public office to persuade them to support legislation favorable to their clients' interests.

Fundraising Directors

Fundraising Directors direct and coordinate the solicitation and disbursement of funds for community social-welfare organizations. They establish fund-raising goals according to the financial need of the agency and formulate policies for collecting and safeguarding the contributions.

Funds Development Directors

Funds Development Directors plan, organize, and coordinate ongoing and special project funding programs for museums, zoos, public broadcasting stations and similar institutions. They prepare a statement of planned activities and enlist support from members of the institution staff and volunteer organizations.

Sales-Service Promoters

Sales-Service Promoters generate sales and create good will for a firm's products by preparing displays and touring the country. They call on merchants to advise them of ways to increase sales and demonstrate products.

WORK ENVIRONMENT

Transferable Skills and Abilities

Communication Skills
- Listening attentively
- Speaking effectively
- Writing concisely

Interpersonal/Social Skills
- Asserting oneself
- Cooperating with others
- Working as a member of a team

Organization & Management Skills
- Coordinating tasks
- Making decisions
- Managing people/groups
- Selling ideas or products

Research & Planning Skills
- Creating ideas
- Developing evaluation strategies
- Solving problems

Immediate Physical Environment

Busy office settings predominate. In an agency environment, public relations specialists cater to the demands of more than one client and can expect a busy atmosphere with many phone calls and tight deadlines. In-office work includes writing and assistance in strategy sessions with clients and the agency itself. Public relations specialists can also work within a company's larger communication department, often as part of a marketing role. The ability to work as a team, providing a comprehensive communication strategy, is essential.

While most public relations specialists usually work in an office setting, it is not necessarily where they spend all their time. They are often on the road, with clients, meeting with journalists, hosting press conferences, or events, and helping executives receive media training. Public relations specialists can be seen at trade shows and conventions, auditoriums, and broadcast or print offices, working with executives from all levels and all industries.

Human Environment

Public relations specialists must have strong interpersonal skills because they are dealing with a wide variety of environments. They work with fast-paced news reporters and bloggers, broadcast producers, freelance writers, engineers, corporate executives, other business specialists, legal counsel, and the general public. At times, this can produce high stress levels and will require the ability to multi-task and delegate. Public relations specialists often work in crisis management, and therefore need to maintain calm while thinking and acting quickly.

Technological Environment

Today, public relations specialists use a wide range of technology to achieve client goals. This technology includes everything from phone and email, to texting, tweeting, blogging, and monitoring online news organization.

EDUCATION, TRAINING, AND ADVANCEMENT

High School/Secondary

It is best for public relations specialists to have a college degree with some experience, such as an internship. High school students can best prepare to be a public relations specialist through Advanced Placement (AP) English courses that include and encourage non-fiction or news editorial writing, creative writing, reading comprehension, public speaking, critical thinking, and decision making. Extracurricular activities, such as working with the school newspaper, can also help high school students gain admission to the universities they want to attend.

Suggested High School Subjects
- Business
- College Preparatory
- Composition
- English
- Graphic Communications
- Humanities
- Journalism
- Keyboarding
- Literature
- Political Science

- Psychology
- Social Studies
- Sociology
- Speech

Related Career Pathways/Majors

Business, Management & Administration Cluster
- Management Pathway
- Marketing Pathway

Marketing, Sales & Service Cluster
- Marketing Communication & Promotion Pathway

Famous First

Public relations (PR) is not a recent invention. The importance of communication with the public and maintenance of positive public image was known as early as in the antiquity but the beginnings of modern PR are traditionally dated in the 18th century London. One of the first PRs was Georgiana Cavendish, Duchess of Devonshire who heavily campaigned for Charles James Fox and his Whig party. PR in the real meaning of the word, however, dates only to the early 20th century. The first real PR specialist was according to some Ivy Lee (1877-1934), while the others see Edward Bernays (1891-1995) as "the father of public relations."

Source: www.ipr.org.uk/

Postsecondary

A bachelor's degree is highly recommended for success as a public relations specialist. Many universities offer communications programs, often specializing in journalism, which can include subspecialties within actual public relations majors.

Universities often provide internship opportunities, with the aim of the internship turning into an official entry-level job offer. College students are encouraged to make use of existing career centers, to question professors with well-thought out ideas, secure mentors, and seek input about studies and the jobs they can lead to.

Advanced degrees, such as a master's or PhD, are not necessary for public relations specialists; after earning a bachelor's degree, most of these professionals move through the job ranks through on-the-job experience and a successful portfolio.

Related College Majors

- Business & Personal Services Marketing Operations
- Business Administration & Management, General
- Mass Communications
- Public Relations & Organizational Communications

Adult Job Seekers

It is useful to maintain an up-to-date resume with other credentials, such as scholarships, internships, awards, and grants. Being prepared with a portfolio of accomplishments from previous jobs is a good way to demonstrate relevant skills.

Those who do well as public relations specialists are able to articulate the written and spoken word, have confidence, and relate easily to others. They are quick learners and thinkers, calm in the face of pressure, and are persuasive communicators.

Professional associations are often useful sources for those transitioning from another career to public relations, in that they track job openings and provide unique networking opportunities. The Public Relations Society of America (PRSA) and the International Association of Business Communicators (IABC) are two such professional associations.

Professional Certification and Licensure

Accreditations for public relations can be helpful but are not necessary. Employers have varying outlooks on certification. The PRSA has an accreditation program for members who have at least five years of professional experience. The IABC offers opportunities for professionals to be internationally recognized for their achievements through a variety of awards. Work portfolios that include accomplishments such as press clippings, published speeches, or bylined articles are helpful in receiving certification. Professional accreditation can indicate competence in the field which then can help people find jobs in the highly competitive environment of public relations. Consult credible professional associations within your field and follow professional debate as to the relevancy and value of any certification program.

Additional Requirements

Understanding clients' audiences and target markets is essential for aspiring public relations specialists. Public relations specialists must research client background and objectives, understand the business, and "sell" key messages to those people who will benefit from the specific product or service.

Fun Fact

Alas, social media may be addictive. The Bergen Facebook Addiction Scale, created by Dr. Cecilie Adraessen of the University of Bergen in Norway, arrived in 2015 and looks at such criteria as whether somebody becomes restless or troubled if they cannot use Facebook.

Source: Medicalnewstoday.com

EARNINGS AND ADVANCEMENT

Earnings of public relations specialists depend on the type of industry in which the individual is employed and the size and geographic location of the employer. Private consulting firms generally pay more than companies that have their own public relations departments. The median annual wage for public relations specialists was $58,020 in May 2016. The lowest 10 percent earned less than $32,090, and the highest 10 percent earned more than $110,560.

Public relations specialists may receive paid vacations, holidays, and sick days; life and health insurance; and retirement benefits. These are usually paid by the employer. Some employers may also provide an expense account.

EMPLOYMENT AND OUTLOOK

Nationally, there were approximately 258259,600 public relations specialists employed in 2016. Employment of public relations specialists is projected to grow 9 percent from 2016 to 2026, about as fast as the average for all occupations.

Organizations will continue to emphasize community outreach and customer relations as a way to maintain and enhance their reputation and visibility. Public opinion can change quickly, particularly because both good and bad news spread rapidly through the Internet. Consequently, public relations specialists will be needed to respond to news developments and maintain their organization's reputation.

The growing use of social media also is expected to increase employment for public relations specialists. This will create more work for public relations specialists as they try to appeal to consumers and the general public in new ways. Public relations specialists will be needed to help their clients use these new types of social media effectively.

Related Occupations
- Advertising Account Executive
- Advertising Agent
- Copywriter
- Electronic Commerce Specialist
- General Manager and Top Executive
- Online Merchant

Related Military Occupations
- Public Information Officer

Conversation With . . .
TAYLOR TITUS

Social Media Specialist
American Urological Association
Linthicum, Maryland
Social Media Specialist, 4 years

1. What was your individual career path in terms of education/training, entry-level job, or other significant opportunity?

I went to Kent State University in Kent, Ohio where I majored in public relations and minored in marketing. During my college career, I took advantage of every resume-building and networking opportunity I could get. I joined the Public Relations Student Society of America, where I held two officer positions. I worked for the university's marketing and communications department and did other extracurricular activities that I could put on my resume, such as being marketing director for the university's television station. I completed an internship that turned into my first job, which was a small PR agency. Since it was a small agency, I was able to get great hands-on experience. After that, I started my current role as Social Media Specialist at the American Urological Association (AUA), where I am responsible for maintaining the AUA's Twitter, Facebook, Instagram, and YouTube accounts every day. I create and post the content that goes out through these channels. I am also responsible for the social media strategy of the AUA and the AUA Annual Meeting, where I tweet every 10 minutes and provide live coverage of the meeting via social media. Last year we had over 20,000 tweets with our meeting hashtag throughout the span of the meeting. I also do some public relations and help with our foundation's social media channels. Experience is key!

2. What are the most important skills and/or qualities for someone in your profession?

Some of the most important skills and qualities for someone working in social media are staying up-to-date on the latest trends in technology—such as the latest feature Twitter launched where you can now edit your tweets—creativity, and being a hard worker, flexible, adaptable, and quick on your feet. You want to come up with creative posts to make your content more engaging and be quick to adapt to changes in the format of a platform. Because it can be time consuming to monitor different accounts and different channels, time management is a must!

3. What do you wish you had known going into this profession?

Since social media is nonstop, it's important to know you're never really off the job. In my position, I can't ignore a negative post that occurs on the weekend because I'm not in the office. I'm always keeping my eye on what chatter is happening on social media. Also, it's not as easy as writing a tweet and pressing send. I develop a yearly social media strategy to support how I run the association's social media accounts.

4. Are there many job opportunities in your profession? In what specific areas?

Yes, the social media industry is constantly growing. In today's world you don't exist if you aren't on social media, and it's not going away anytime soon. Most companies, in any type of industry, have some sort of social media presence. That's what is so cool about the opportunities in the social media world – there's a variety, from non-profit to fashion to finance.

5. How do you see your profession changing in the next five years, how do you see platforms evolving, and what skills will be required?

The social media world changes every day. In the next five years, social media platforms will probably look different than they do today. There will be new platforms that companies will have to jump on and platforms that we use today may not be as popular. I think the skill set required for a social media position won't change. Since the technology is always changing, it's important for social media professionals to be adaptable.

6. What do you enjoy most about your job? What do you enjoy least about your job?

There are so many things I love about my job! I get to do most things in 280 characters. I love interacting with our social media followers. We also have a social media workgroup made up of our association's members that I enjoy working with. I get to spend time on Instagram every day for work—it's awesome. Always being on the job is what is tough about being a social media professional. Your phone goes off at 2 a.m. because someone tagged you in a tweet!

7. Can you suggest a valuable "try this" for students considering a career in your profession?

Follow brands in the industry you would like to work for on social media platforms and watch how they engage on social.

MORE INFORMATION

**American Association of
Advertising Agencies**
405 Lexington Avenue, 18th Floor
New York, NY 10174-1801
212.682.2500

OBD@aaaa.org
www.aaaa.org

**Public Relations Society of
America**
33 Maiden Lane, 11th Floor
New York, NY 10038-5150
212.460.1400
membership@prsa.org
www.prsa.org

PRSA's Silver Anvil awards recognize
the highest level of achievement in public
relations. www.prsa.org/
awards/silveranvil?utm_
campaign=PRSASearch&utm_
source=PRSAWebsite&utm_
medium=SSearch&utm_term=silver%20
anvil

Susan Williams/Editor

Software Developer

Snapshot

Career Cluster(s): Arts, A/V Technology & Communications, Information Technology
Interests: Computer Software Technology, Math, Science, Information Technology
Earnings (2016 median pay): $102,280 per year; $49.17 per hour
Employment & Outlook: Much Faster Than Average Growth Expected

OVERVIEW

Sphere of Work

Software designers develop system, utility, and application software, as well as computer games. They also modify existing programs to improve functionality or to meet client needs. On large-scale projects, software designers typically work with a team of professionals that includes software engineers, software architects, and computer programmers. In these cases, they might be primarily responsible for developing the functional or "front-end" user interface of the program to ensure that it is compatible with a particular platform and related components and that it works reliably and

securely. On smaller jobs, software designers might also handle the programming, engineering, and architecture of the program.

Work Environment

Many software designers are self-employed and work at home or in small businesses. Others work for the military, government agencies, or industries such as telecommunications, health care, aerospace, e-commerce, video games, and education. Software designers working for corporations typically work forty-hour weeks, while those who are self-employed may set their own hours. In either case, strict deadlines or unexpected problems may require software designers to work additional hours as needed.

Profile

Interests: Data, Things
Working Conditions: Work Inside
Physical Strength: Light Work
Education Needs: Bachelor's Degree
Licensure/Certification:
  Recommended
Physical Abilities Not Required: Not
  Climb, Not Kneel, Not Hear and/or Talk
Opportunities for Experience:
  Internship, Apprenticeship, Military
  Service, Part Time Work
Holland Interest Score*: AES, IRE

* See Appendix A

Occupation Interest

People who are attracted to software design careers are analytical and mathematically inclined, with strong problem-solving skills and an aptitude for learning programming languages. They are detail oriented, yet also able to envision the overall design and application of products. Software designers need good communication skills to interact with team members and convey their ideas. Leadership and organizational skills are also important, as is the desire to be knowledgeable about new developments in the industry.

A Day in the Life—Duties and Responsibilities

Most computer programs are born out of a need. Software designers first evaluate that need, usually in consultation with a client, and then conceive of a program to solve the problem. They design computer games, applications for mobile phones, and other highly visible types of software. They also design behind-the-scenes programs known as utilities, which may help users download content from the Internet seamlessly, convert files to different formats, protect computers from malware or keylogging, or free up computer disk space when needed. Some software designers develop programs used in business, education, graphic arts, multimedia, web development, and many other fields, as well as programs intended just for other programmers.

Software designers are often responsible for planning a project within budget and time constraints. They must consider compatibility issues, determining the type of platform or multi-platform on which the software will operate and the oldest version on which it will work reliably. They also consider issues such as the maintainability of the software (how often it will need to be updated).

Software designers then devise a schematic of the program that shows its structure, often displayed as a hierarchy consisting of modules. They develop algorithms, which are sets of instructions or steps needed to solve the problems identified by each module. Designers program the code line by line, or supervise other programmers. They test the modules, locate and correct any errors, and then test the program repeatedly until it is secure, user-friendly, and reliable. They might also add graphics and multimedia components or hand that job over to a graphic designer.

Duties and Responsibilities

- Documenting each step necessary to create software
- Testing to make sure steps are correct and will produce the desired results
- Rewriting programs if desired results are not produced
- Creating graphics, animation and sound effects for software

WORK ENVIRONMENT

Immediate Physical Environment

Software designers usually work in comfortable offices or from their homes, although some may also travel to meet with clients. They are at some risk for carpel tunnel syndrome, back problems, and eyestrain due to prolonged use of computers.

Transferable Skills and Abilities

Organization & Management Skills
- Paying attention to and handling details

Communication Skills
- Speaking effectively
- Writing concisely

Interpersonal/Social Skills
- Being able to work independently
- Working as a member of a team

Organization & Management Skills
- Organizing information or materials
- Performing routine work

Research & Planning Skills
- Creating ideas
- Identifying problems
- Solving problems
- Using logical reasoning

Human Environment

Software designers typically report to a project manager and are usually members of a development team, along with programmers, systems architects, quality assurance specialists, and others. The designer might also manage the team or oversee the work done by programmers. A high level of communication and cooperation is usually necessary for success. Many designers, however, work alone and are responsible only to their clients.

Technological Environment

Software designers use a variety of desktop computers, portable computer devices, video game consoles, and related hardware. They use and interface with various operating systems and database management programs. While software designers do not necessarily do programming, they should be familiar with various computer and markup languages, including C++, Java, ColdFusion, and HTML, as well as related compilers and interpreters.

EDUCATION, TRAINING, AND ADVANCEMENT

High School/Secondary

Students should take a strong college-preparatory program that includes English, chemistry, physics, and four years of mathematics, including trigonometry, calculus, and statistics. Computer science or technology, engineering, and electronics courses are also important. Students interested primarily in designing video games or visual-heavy programs should take computer graphics and drawing courses. Other potentially beneficial subjects include psychology, sociology, and business. Participation in technology clubs, science fairs, mathematics competitions, and other related extracurricular activities is encouraged, as is independent study and creation of programs.

Suggested High School Subjects
- Accounting
- Algebra
- Applied Communication
- Applied Math
- Bookkeeping
- Business & Computer Technology
- Business Data Processing
- Calculus
- College Preparatory
- Computer Programming
- Computer Science
- English
- Geometry
- Graphic Communications
- Keyboarding
- Mathematics
- Statistics
- Trigonometry

Related Career Pathways/Majors
Arts, A/V Technology & Communications Cluster
- Visual Arts Pathway

Information Technology Cluster
- Interactive Media Pathway
- Programming & Software Development Pathway

Famous First

Six Degrees is widely considered to be the very first social networking site. Founded by Andrew Weinreich in May 1996, the site launched the following year and combined popular features such as profiles, friends lists and school affiliations in one service. While the site had millions of registered users, due to the lack of people connected to the Internet, networks were limited. It would be a few years before the Internet's infrastructure could catch up with the concept of social networks. The site was sold in December 2000 to YouthStream Media Networks.

Source: www.cbsnews.com

Postsecondary

Although some employers consider job applicants with an associate's degree, most prefer to hire workers with a bachelor's degree or higher in computer science, computer engineering, or a related technical field. Prospective software designers must be familiar with different types of computers and operating systems, systems organization and architecture, data structures and algorithms, computation theory, and other related topics. Internships and independent projects are recommended.

Related College Majors
- Computer Engineering
- Computer Engineering Technology
- Computer Maintenance Technology
- Computer Programming
- Computer Science
- Design & Visual Communications
- Educational/Instructional Media Design
- Graphic Design, Commercial Art & Illustration
- Information Sciences & Systems
- Management Information Systems & Business Data Processing

Adult Job Seekers

Adults with a computer science or programming background who are returning to the field can update their skills and knowledge by taking continuing education courses offered by software vendors or colleges. Some courses are available online. Those with family obligations might want to consider self-employment, although regular full-time employment may offer more financial stability. Professional associations may provide networking opportunities, as well as job openings and connections to potential clients.

Advancement is partially dependent on the size of the company and the scale of projects. In large companies, software designers with leadership skills typically move into project management and higher-ranked positions as experience and education warrant. Experienced designers may also establish their own businesses, while designers with advanced degrees may move into college teaching.

Professional Certification and Licensure

There are no mandatory licenses or certifications needed for these positions, although voluntary certification from the Institute of Electrical and Electronics Engineers (IEEE), the Institute for Certification of Computing Professionals (ICCP), and other professional organizations can be especially advantageous for job hunting and networking. Software designers can be certified as Software Development Associates (CSDA) or Software Development Professionals (CSDP) through IEEE or as Computing Professionals (CCP) and Associate Computing Professionals (ACP) through ICCP. Software designers are encouraged to consult prospective employers and credible professional associations within the field as to the relevancy and value of any voluntary certification program.

Additional Requirements

Software designers must have excellent keyboarding skills. Some designers might need a driver's license to travel between job sites.

EARNINGS AND ADVANCEMENT

Earnings for software developers vary depending on the size and location of the employer and the education, experience and certification of the employee. The median annual wage for software developers, applications was $100,080 in May 2016. The lowest 10 percent earned less than $58,300, and the highest 10 percent earned more than $157,590. The median annual wage for software developers, systems software was $106,860 in May 2016. The lowest 10 percent earned less than $64,650, and the highest 10 percent earned more than $163,220.

Software developers may receive paid vacations, holidays, and sick days; life and health insurance; and retirement benefits. These are usually paid by the employer.

EMPLOYMENT AND OUTLOOK

Software developers held about 1,256,200 jobs nationally in 2016. Employment of software developers is projected to grow 24 percent from 2016 to 2026, much faster than the average for all occupations. Employment of applications developers is projected to grow 31 percent, and employment of systems developers is projected to grow 11 percent. The increasing use of the Internet and mobile technology such as wireless Internet has created a demand for a wide variety of new products. In addition, information security concerns have created new software needs. Concerns over cyber security should result in businesses and government continuing to rely on security software that protects their networks from attack. The growth of this technology in the next ten years will lead to an increased need for these workers to design this type of software.

Related Occupations

- Commercial Artist
- Computer & Information Systems Manager
- Computer Engineer
- Computer Operator
- Computer Programmer
- Computer Security Specialist
- Computer Support Specialist
- Computer Systems Analyst
- Computer-Control Tool Programmer
- Designer
- Graphic Designer
- Information Technology Project Manager
- Network & Computer Systems Administrator
- Network Systems & Data Communications Analyst
- Web Administrator
- Website Designer

Related Military Occupations

- Computer Programmer
- Computer Systems Specialist
- Graphic Designer & Illustrator

Conversation With . . .
JAY CORREIA

Founder and CEO
DreamCo Design
West Dundee, Illinois
Company owner, 11 years

1. What was your individual career path in terms of education/training, entry-level job, or other significant opportunity?

Simply put, I learned from experience. Every single day provides ample opportunity to learn. I didn't go to college. When I was 18 I wasn't 100 percent certain what, exactly, I wanted to do. I was leaning toward film school but a cosigner on a loan fell through and it never went any further. I contemplated other options but decided it made more sense financially to save money and learn via experience than go into debt without a specific career focus.

My first career-oriented position was with a digital printing company. I worked part-time during high school and though I began doing nothing more than making color copies, I ended up learning skills I still use to this day like Adobe Photoshop for graphic work.

I started DreamCo Design in 2006. After spending multiple years in the print/graphic design field, including working for a start-up, I came to the pragmatic realization that things were going digital. I was a self-taught/intern-taught graphic designer, a computer person, and full of ambition. I'd designed/developed a couple of successful websites and also excelled in sales related roles so I decided to fill a void by providing custom websites.

Within a couple of years, we reached the 7-figure mark for revenue. Our nationally recognized web/app/marketing agency has completed more than 1,500 projects for clients including Grammy Award winning musicians, TV personalities, the National Park Service, and a wide variety of small businesses.

In addition to marketing and web development, our company is, for example, currently developing social media platforms and apps. We've also done smaller networks that operate in a way similar to Facebook.

2. What are the most important skills and/or qualities for someone in your profession?

When being involved with social media, I think it's incredibly important to think like a business owner or decision maker. Social media is used as a reflection of an individual's or business' likeness. Having strong communication skills to extrapolate goals and deliver them digitally is a necessity.

3. What do you wish you had known going into this profession?

That no two clients are alike. While that may seem obvious, the amount of variance between the control some owners want to have as compared to the passiveness of others is striking.

4. Are there many job opportunities in your profession? In what specific areas?

There is a plethora of jobs in the social media industry.

Just as having a professional website is critical for most businesses, so is having a social media presence, especially for business-to-consumer (B2C) companies.

5. How do you see your profession changing in the next five years? How do you see platforms evolving? What skill sets will be required?

I think the concept of social media management will continue to grow, reaching maturity over the next decade.

Entrepreneurs are always dreaming up ideas that often involve social media. Privacy, issues involving who owns content, and users being paid for participating (whether real money, cryptocurrency, or other methods) will all likely play major roles in how the platforms evolve.

As basic as it sounds, having a general business understanding already helps. Social media management is a hybrid of putting technology to use for sales, branding, marketing, and public relations. In some cases, it is also customer service. Having a strong technological backbone will always be key.

6. What do you enjoy most about your job? What do you enjoy least about your job?

On the social media side, I enjoy seeing a campaign directly impact the success of a business or individual in a positive way. I least enjoy having to deal with unrealistic expectations. Not everything will go viral, no matter how much someone may want it to.

7. **Can you suggest a valuable "try this" for a student considering a career in your profession?**

Pick a company that you care about and develop a social media plan based around a hypothetical goal. For example, the goal might be "L.L.Bean wants to sell more boots while proving their boots outlast all of their competitors." With the goal in mind, choose the social media platforms you'd use to connect with consumers and plan the content accordingly. Think about every phase of carrying out the social media campaign. How are you going to get the content (photos, videos, etc.)? Are you going to schedule posts in advance? When are you going to post material? What demographics are you going to try to reach? How are you going to ensure that your strategy will help the company reach its goals?

Thinking through all these questions and putting a plan to paper is a great exercise that can also be hands on.

In addition to that, getting an internship with any marketing agency would also assist.

MORE INFORMATION

American Institute of Graphic Arts
164 Fifth Avenue
New York, NY 10010
212.807.1990
www.aiga.org

Association for Computing Machinery
2 Penn Plaza, Suite 701
New York, NY 10121-0701
800.342.6626
acmhelp@acm.org
www.acm.org

ACM-W scholarships for female students to attend research conferences:
http://women.acm.org/participate/scholarship/index.cfm

Graphic Artists Guild
32 Broadway, Suite 1114
New York, NY 10004-1612
212.791.3400
pr@gag.org
www.gag.org

Institute for the Certification of Computer Professionals
2400 East Devon Avenue, Suite 281
Des Plaines, IL 60018-4610
800.843.8227
office@iccp.org
www.iccp.org

Institute of Electrical and Electronics Engineers (IEEE) Computer Society
2001 L Street, NW, Suite 700
Washington, DC 20036-4928
202.371.0101
help@computer.org
www.computer.org

A variety of IEEE scholarships, grants, and fellowships:
www.computer.org/portal/web/studentactivities/home

Sally Driscoll/Editor

Writers & Authors

Snapshot

Career Cluster(s): Arts, A/V Technology & Communications, Business, Management & Administration, Information Technology, Science, Technology, Engineering & Mathematics

Interests: Language and grammar, proofreading, publishing, communication, journalism

Earnings (2016 median pay): $61,240 per year; $29.44 per hour

Employment & Outlook: As fast as average

OVERVIEW

Sphere of Work

Writers and authors are employed in all realms of business and industry. In addition to journalism, publishing, and media, employment for writers can be found in government, marketing, law, entertainment, and sales. Writers employed by local, state, or federal governments may craft legislation or produce speeches and press releases for elected representatives. Every industrial sector, be it the automobile industry, healthcare, education, retail, agriculture, or mining, utilizes writers to communicate with colleagues and clients and

develop messaging regarding their productivity and business plan. Freelance writing and editing, or writing and editing under temporary contract, is common. Many freelancers work for online publishers, producing content for clients that adheres to specific guidelines.

Work Environment

Most writers and authors work in an office environment. Writers and authors in the media often work in the field, gathering data and interviewing people for news reports. Many freelance writers and authors work from a home office. Some freelance writers work at rented office spaces.

Profile

Interests: Data, People, Things
Working Conditions: Work Inside
Physical Strength: Light Work
Education Needs: Bachelor's Degree
Licensure/Certification: Usually Not Required
Physical Abilities Not Required: Not Climb, Not Handle, Not Kneel
Opportunities for Experience: Internship, Apprenticeship, Military Service, Volunteer Work, Part Time Work
Holland Interest Score*: AES

* See Appendix A

Occupation Interest

Writers and authors enjoy working with language and ideas. They enjoy the challenge of communicating complex ideas in a way that is readily digestible to a specific audience. Writers and authors have a penchant for grammar and the intricacies of publishing formats and editorial guidelines. Those who are employed by a specific industry or business sector should have a passion for that area of communication and commerce. For examples, sports writers need to be knowledgeable about a particular sport's rules and regulations, teams, and players. Individuals interested in writing public policy or producing content for the news media should be interested in government, politics, and current events.

A Day in the Life—Duties and Responsibilities

The daily life of a writer is highly dependent upon the field in which they are employed. Writers must establish their credibility with editors and readers through clean prose, strong research, and the use of appropriate sources and citations. Writers and authors select the material they want to use and then convey the information to readers.

With help from editors, they may revise or rewrite sections, searching for the clearest language and the most appropriate phrasing. Some writers and authors are self-employed or freelance writers and authors. They sell their written content to book and magazine publishers; news organizations; advertising agencies; and movie, theater, and television producers. They may be hired to complete specific short-term or recurring assignments, such as writing a newspaper column, contributing to a series of articles in a magazine, or producing an organization's newsletter.

An increasing number of writers are producing material that is published only on the Internet, such as for digital news organizations or blogs.

Duties and Responsibilities

- Choose subject matter that interests readers
- Write fiction or nonfiction through scripts, novels, biographies, and more
- Conduct research to obtain factual information and authentic detail
- Write advertising copy for internet, social media, newspapers, magazines, and broadcasts
- Present drafts to editors and clients for feedback
- Work with editors and clients to shape the material so it can be published

OCCUPATION SPECIALTIES

The following are examples of types of writers and authors:

Critics

Critics write critical reviews of literary, musical, or artistic works or performances for broadcast or publication.

Fiction and Nonfiction Prose Writers

Fiction and Nonfiction Prose Writers write original prose material for publication.

Screen Writers

Screen Writers write scripts for videos, motion pictures or television.

News Writers

News Writers write news items for newspapers, magazines or news organizations including television and radio broadcasts and online media.

Technical Publications Writers

Technical Publications Writers write about scientific and technical information in clear language.

Copywriters prepare advertisements to promote the sale of a good or service. They often work with a client to produce written content, such as advertising themes, jingles, and slogans.

Content writers write about any topic of interest, unlike writers who usually specialize in a given field. Their work typically appears on social media platforms.

Biographers write a thorough account of a person's life. They gather information from interviews and research about the person to accurately portray important events in that person's life.

Bloggers write posts to a blog that may pertain to any topic or a specific field, such as fashion, news, or sports.

Novelists write books of fiction, creating characters and plots that may be imaginary or based on real events.

Playwrights write scripts for theatrical productions. They come up with a concept, write lines for actors to say, produce stage direction for actors to follow, and suggest ideas for theatrical set design.

Screenwriters create scripts for movies and television. They may produce original stories, characters, and dialogue, or turn a book into a movie or television script.

Speechwriters write speeches for business leaders, politicians, and others who must speak in front of an audience. A speech is heard, not read, which means speechwriters must think about audience reaction and rhetorical effect.

WORK ENVIRONMENT

Immediate Physical Environment

Freelance or contract writers and authors work primarily from home offices or in designated sections of their homes. Freelance work has no set hours or specified work schedule, and freelancers often work atypical hours and on weekends. Some long-term contracts require that writers or authors work at the company who is hiring them, which would require the writer or author to work in an office setting during regular business hours for the length of the project they have been hired to complete.

Writers or authors who are hired as full-time employees for a company or organization work in office settings and during standard business hours and days.

Transferable Skills and Abilities

Communication Skills
- Expressing thoughts and ideas
- Speaking effectively
- Writing concisely

Interpersonal/Social Skills
- Being able to work independently
- Cooperating with others
- Working as a member of a team

Organization & Management Skills
- Managing time
- Meeting goals and deadlines
- Paying attention to and handling details

Research & Planning Skills
- Analyzing information

Technical Skills
- Using technology to process information
- Working with data or numbers
- Working with machines, tools or other object

Human Environment

Writers and authors interact frequently with clients and colleagues and good communication skills are essential to their work. While many writers and authors work alone, nearly all communicate regularly with colleagues and clients about project-specific guidelines and goals.

Technological Environment

Writers and authors utilize a wide range of computer software to produce content. This includes writing and editing platforms such as Microsoft Word. Many publishing companies and media organizations utilize proprietary computer software that is specific to their workflow. The work of a writer and author requires excellent research skills; both web-based research skills and traditional library-based research skills are important. Many writers and authors also use digital recording equipment for conducting interviews or taking notes.

EDUCATION, TRAINING, AND ADVANCEMENT

High School/Secondary

High school students can best prepare for a career as a writer or author by completing coursework in English, history, and computer science. Advanced coursework in a field of particular interest can prepare students for writing knowledgably and coherently about that field. Participation in extracurricular activities such as debate clubs, school papers, or school television and radio programs can also help students develop the skills needed for a career in writing and editing.

Suggested High School Subjects
- Applied Communication
- College Preparatory
- Composition
- Computer Science
- English
- Journalism
- Keyboarding
- Literature
- Speech

Related Career Pathways/Majors

Arts, A/V Technology & Communications Cluster
- Journalism & Broadcasting Pathway
- Performing Arts Pathway

Business, Management & Administration Cluster
- Marketing Pathway

Information Technology Cluster
- Information Support & Services Pathway
- Interactive Media Pathway

Science, Technology, Engineering & Mathematics Cluster
- Engineering & Technology Pathway
- Science & Mathematics Pathway

Famous First

The first commercial jingle heard over the radio was in an ad for Pepsi-Cola in 1940. The jingle ran: "Pepsi-Cola hits the spot / Twelve full ounces, that's a lot / Twice as much for a nickel, too / Pepsi-Cola is the drink for you." Eventually the jingle was translated into 55 languages and ran worldwide.
Source: http://adage.com

Postsecondary

Postsecondary education is often a requirement for vacancies in the writing and editing field. Postsecondary coursework that can contribute to the numerous skills and vast frame of reference required of writers and authors includes education, literature, history, government, international business, economics, politics, and government.

Related College Majors
- Advertising
- Broadcast Journalism
- Business Communications
- Communications, General
- Creative Writing
- Journalism
- Playwriting & Screenwriting

Adult Job Seekers

There are numerous opportunities for adult job seekers interested in writing and editing. Working knowledge or experience in a particular field, such as education, marking, or retail, represent skills that can be transferable to writing and editing work.

Professional Certification and Licensure

Certification or licensure is not required to be employed as an author or writer. The majority of hiring companies and organizations require that applicants have at least an undergraduate degree with a concentration in either English or another field that pertains to the position needing to be filled.

Additional Requirements

Writers and authors must possess a love of the language and a commitment to quality writing. Writers and authors often work alone or from their homes, so individuals who want to explore this line of work should be comfortable in solitary settings.

Fun Fact

With the growth of social media has come the trend of unplugging for a time—or "digital detox." The Oxford Dictionary added the phrase in 2013.
Source: Virgin.com

EARNINGS AND ADVANCEMENT

Advancement for writers and authors is achieved by being successful within an organization or by moving to another firm. Larger firms usually give writing and editing responsibilities only after a period of entry-level research, fact checking and proofreading. Smaller firms give major duties right away, and competence is expected.

Median annual earnings of writers were was $61,240 in May 2016. The lowest 10 percent earned less than $29,380, and the highest 10 percent earned more than $118,640.

Writers and authors may receive paid vacations, holidays, and sick days; life and health insurance; and retirement benefits. These are usually paid by the employer. In addition, many writers and authors freelance to supplement their salaries.

EMPLOYMENT AND OUTLOOK

Writers and authors held about 131,200 jobs nationally in 2016. Employment of writers and authors is projected to grow 8 percent from 2016 to 2026, about as fast as the average for all occupations.

Online publications and services are growing in number and sophistication, spurring demand for writers and authors with Web and multimedia experience.

Some experienced writers should find work in the public relations departments of corporations and nonprofit organizations. Self-employed or freelance writers and authors may find work with newspaper, magazine, or journal publishers, and some will write books.

Related Occupations
- Actor
- Copywriter
- Electronic Commerce Specialist
- Journalist
- Online Merchant
- Radio/TV Announcer & Newscaster
- Technical Writer

Related Military Occupations
- Public Information Officer

Conversation With . . .
ALLISON VRBOVA

Communications Consultant
Two Willows Editorial
Bellingham, Washington
Communications, 10 years; consultant, 2 years

1. What was your individual career path in terms of education/training, entry-level job, or other significant opportunity?

I came to this career in a roundabout way. My bachelor's degree is in human services and after working in that field for a few years, I went back to get my Master of Fine Arts in creative writing.

My master's degree was initially more of a personal project, not intended as a stepping stone for a new career. However, during this same time, I helped my husband launch his own business and found that I really enjoyed PR, communications and content marketing. After that, I held a few in-house positions as a communications manager before launching my own consulting business in 2016. I focus on helping startups, small businesses and nonprofits clarify their messaging and create quality content in the form of blogs, e-books, videos, podcasts, and webinars, etc.

One of my clients is a sculptor who has always used salvaged wood, but never used that as part of his story. He recently relocated here to the Pacific Northwest, where locally sourced, sustainable materials are important to consumers. We wanted to emphasize this, but not be too heavy handed. We created a social media campaign (Twitter, Instagram, YouTube, and Facebook) that shows him at all stages of the process: searching for the wood, picking it up with his truck, delivering it to his studio, creating the final product, and delivering it to a happy client who appreciates the salvaged wood aspect of the sculpture.

2. What are the most important skills and/or qualities for someone in your profession?

It goes without saying that you must be an excellent writer. But above and beyond that, it's important to cultivate your storytelling skills. The buzzword these days is *storify*. In other words, my job is to help my clients take what are sometimes bland, technical topics and turn them into compelling narratives that people will actually enjoy reading.

The objective of writing for social media is largely the same as writing for a website: reinforce your brand's story and compel your audience to take some sort of predetermined action (retweet to spread the word, click through to a longer piece of content, sign up for an event, etc.) Style is where these two platforms really differ. Writing for social media needs to be more succinct, often pithy, meant to catch the reader's attention in a split second. On a website, your reader has already made the conscious choice to engage with the content, so your job is to keep them engaged. With social media, you have the additional challenge of standing out above all the noise to get that initial engagement.

Also, take the time to cultivate your interviewing skills. I often have to interview industry experts, so I need to feel comfortable asking lots of questions. I also need to listen well so people will feel encouraged to open up and share with me.

3. What do you wish you had known going into this profession?

Had I known I would end up in this profession, I probably would have gotten a journalism or marketing degree. With newspapers dwindling, a lot of journalists are going into the content marketing field.

4. Are there many job opportunities in your profession? In what specific areas?

Most mid- to large-sized companies have a content marketing team. Smaller tech startups often do, too. And growing companies often hire freelance content writers. I'd encourage people starting out to look for a full-time position on a content marketing team, either as a content writer, content coordinator, or content marketing manager. Wait to break out on your own as a consultant or freelancer until a few years into your career. You need the experience to be able to sell yourself to potential clients. (Plus, a steady paycheck is nice. Consulting can be up and down in terms of income. It works for me, but my husband also brings in a paycheck.)

Remote or telecommuting positions are often possible with this career.

5. How do you see your profession changing in the next five years? How do you see platforms evolving and what skills will be required?

Content is moving more toward video. That's not to say that content writers will ever be obsolete, because written content will always be part of the equation. But if you can gain skills and experience in video production, even if it's just writing video scripts, do so. It will become increasingly important over the next few years.

6. **What do you enjoy most about your job? What do you enjoy least about your job?**

I enjoy getting to be a perpetual student. Because I write about a wide variety of topics, I get to learn new things and be exposed to innovative people and ideas.

As someone who enjoys doing creative writing for fun, it can be hard to maintain that creative spark when I spend my workdays writing lots of words for other people. Sometimes at the end of the day, I don't have any words left for myself!

7. **Can you suggest a valuable "try this" for students considering a career in your profession?**

Start producing content of your own. This could be a blog about something you're interested in or a video series with tips about a skill you have or a podcast where you interview interesting people in your life.

MORE INFORMATION

Accred. Council on Education in Journalism & Mass Comm.
University of Kansas
Stauffer-Flint Hall
1435 Jayhawk Boulevard
Lawrence, KS 66045-7575
785.864.3973
www2.ku.edu/~acejmc

American Society of Journalists and Authors
Times Square
1501 Broadway, Suite 403
New York, NY 10036
212.997.0947
www.asja.org

American Society of Magazine Editors
810 Seventh Avenue, 24th Floor
New York, NY 10019
212.872.3700
asme@magazine.org
www.magazine.org/editorial/asme

Association for Women in Communications
3337 Duke Street
Alexandria, VA 22314
703.370.7436
info@womcom.org
www.womcom.org

Digital Analytics Association
401 Edgewater Pl # 600
Wakefield, MA 01880
(781) 876-8933
digitalanalyticsassociation.com

Dow Jones Newspaper Fund, Inc.
P.O. Box 300
Princeton, NJ 08543-0300
609.452.2820
djnf@dowjones.com
www.newsfund.org

Editorial Freelancers Association
71 West 23rd Street, 4th Floor
New York, NY 10010-4102
212.929.5400
www.the-efa.org

Interactive Advertising Bureau
116 East 27th Street
6th Floor
New York, NY 10016
(212) 380-4700
www.iab.com

International Association of Business Communicators
601 Montgomery Street, Suite 1900
San Francisco, CA 94111
800.776.4222
service_centre@iabc.com
www.iabc.com

International Bloggers Association
P.O. Box 193
Elizabethtown, KY 42702
internationalbloggersassociation.com

International Digital Media and Arts Association (iDMAa)
c/o School of Media Arts
Columbia College Chicago
33 E. Congress, Rm 600B
Chicago, IL 6060
www.idmaa.org

National Association of Science Writers
P.O. Box 7905
Berkeley, CA 94707
510.647.9500
director@nasw.org
www.nasw.org

National Newspaper Association
P.O. Box 7540
Columbia, MO 65205-7540
800.829.4662
briansteffens@nna.org
www.nnaweb.org

Newspaper Association of America
4401 Wilson Boulevard, Suite 900
Arlington, VA 22203-1867
571.366.1000
membsvc@naa.org
www.naa.org

Newspaper Guild-CWA
Research and Information
Department
501 Third Street NW, 6th Floor
Washington, DC 20001-2797
202.434.7177
guild@cwa-union.org
www.newsguild.org

Professional Travel Bloggers Association
contact@travelbloggersassociation.com
travelbloggersassociation.com/

Social Media Association
Atlanta, GA
socialmediaassoc.com

Social Media Managers Association
Chichester, West Sussex
UK
01243-601236
socialmediamanagersassociation.com

Society for Technical Communication
9401 Lee Highway, Suite 300
Fairfax, VA 22031
703.522.4114
www.stc.org

Society of Professional Journalists
Eugene S. Pulliam National
Journalism Center
3909 N. Meridian Street
Indianapolis, IN 46208
317.927.8000
cvachon@spj.org
www.spj.org

What Are Your Career Interests?

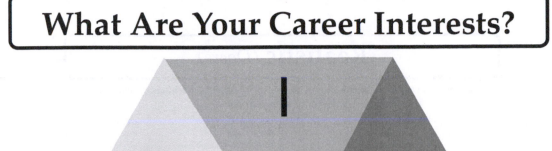

This is based on Dr. John Holland's theory that people and work environments can be loosely classified into six different groups. Each of the letters above corresponds to one of the six groups described in the following pages.

Different people's personalities may find different environments more to their liking. While you may have some interests in and similarities to several of the six groups, you may be attracted primarily to two or three of the areas. These two or three letters are your "Holland Code." For example, with a code of "RES" you would most resemble the Realistic type, somewhat less resemble the Enterprising type, and resemble the Social type even less. The types that are not in your code are the types you resemble least of all.

Most people, and most jobs, are best represented by some combination of two or three of the Holland interest areas. In addition, most people are most satisfied if there is some degree of fit between their personality and their work environment.

The rest of the pages in this booklet further explain each type and provide some examples of career possibilities, areas of study at MU, and co-curricular activities for each code. To take a more in-depth look at your Holland Code, take a self-assessment such as the SDS, Discover, or a card sort at the MU Career Center with a Career Specialist.

Realistic *(Doers)*

People who have athletic ability, prefer to work with objects, machines, tools, plants or animals, or to be outdoors.

Are you?		**Can you?**	**Like to?**
practical	independent	fix electrical things	tinker with machines/vehicles
straightforward/frank	ambitious	solve electrical problems	work outdoors
mechanically inclined	systematic	pitch a tent	be physically active
stable		play a sport	use your hands
concrete		read a blueprint	build things
reserved		plant a garden	tend/train animals
self-controlled		operate tools and machine	work on electronic equipment

Career Possibilities
(Holland Code):

Air Traffic Controller (SER)	Dental Technician (REI)	Laboratory Technician (RIE)	Property Manager (ESR)
Archaeologist (IRE)	Farm Manager (ESR)	Landscape Architect (AIR)	Recreation Manager (SER)
Athletic Trainer (SRE)	Fish and Game Warden (RES)	Mechanical Engineer (RIS)	Service Manager (ERS)
Cartographer (IRE)	Floral Designer (RAE)	Optician (REI)	Software Technician (RCI)
Commercial Airline Pilot (RIE)	Forester (RIS)	Petroleum Geologist (RIE)	Ultrasound Technologist (RSI)
Commercial Drafter (IRE)	Geodetic Surveyor (IRE)	Police Officer (SER)	Vocational Rehabilitation
Corrections Officer (SER)	Industrial Arts Teacher (IER)	Practical Nurse (SER)	Consultant (ESR)

Investigative *(Thinkers)*

People who like to observe, learn, investigate, analyze, evaluate, or solve problems.

Are you?		**Can you?**	**Like to?**
inquisitive	intellectually self-confident	think abstractly	explore a variety of ideas
analytical	Independent	solve math problems	work independently
scientific	logical	understand scientific theories	perform lab experiments
observant/precise	complex	do complex calculations	deal with abstractions
scholarly	Curious	use a microscope or computer	do research
cautious		interpret formulas	be challenged

Career Possibilities
(Holland Code):

Actuary (ISE)	Chemical Engineer (IRE)	Geologist (IRE)	Physician, General Practice (ISE)
Agronomist (IRS)	Chemist (IRE)	Horticulturist (IRS)	Psychologist (IES)
Anesthesiologist (IRS)	Computer Systems Analyst (IER)	Mathematician (IER)	Research Analyst (IRC)
Anthropologist (IRE)	Dentist (ISR)	Medical Technologist (ISA)	Statistician (IRE)
Archaeologist (IRE)	Ecologist (IRE)	Meteorologist (IRS)	Surgeon (IRA)
Biochemist (IRS)	Economist (IAS)	Nurse Practitioner (ISA)	Technical Writer (IRS)
Biologist (ISR)	Electrical Engineer (IRE)	Pharmacist (IES)	Veterinarian (IRS)

Artistic *(Creators)*

People who have artistic, innovating, or intuitional abilities and like to work in unstructured situations using their imagination and creativity.

Are you?
creative
imaginative
innovative
unconventional
emotional
independent
Expressive

original
introspective
impulsive
sensitive
courageous
complicated
idealistic
nonconforming

Can you?
sketch, draw, paint
play a musical instrument
write stories, poetry, music
sing, act, dance
design fashions or interiors

Like to?
attend concerts, theatre, art
    exhibits
read fiction, plays, and poetry
work on crafts
take photography
express yourself creatively
deal with ambiguous ideas

Career Possibilities
(Holland Code):

Actor (AES)
Advertising Art Director (AES)
Advertising Manager (ASE)
Architect (AIR)
Art Teacher (ASE)
Artist (ASI)

Copy Writer (ASI)
Dance Instructor (AER)
Drama Coach (ASE)
English Teacher (ASE)
Entertainer/Performer (AES)
Fashion Illustrator (ASR)

Interior Designer (AES)
Intelligence Research Specialist
    (AEI)
Journalist/Reporter (ASE)
Landscape Architect (AIR)
Librarian (SAI)

Medical Illustrator (AIE)
Museum Curator (AES)
Music Teacher (ASI)
Photographer (AES)
Writer (ASI)
Graphic Designer (AES)

Social *(Helpers)*

People who like to work with people to enlighten, inform, help, train, or cure them, or are skilled with words.

Are you?
friendly
helpful
idealistic
insightful
outgoing
understanding

cooperative
generous
responsible
forgiving
patient
kind

Can you?
teach/train others
express yourself clearly
lead a group discussion
mediate disputes
plan and supervise an activity
cooperate well with others

Like to?
work in groups
help people with problems
do volunteer work
work with young people
serve others

Career Possibilities
(Holland Code):

City Manager (SEC)
Clinical Dietitian (SIE)
College/University Faculty (SEI)
Community Org. Director
    (SEA)
Consumer Affairs Director
    (SER)Counselor/Therapist
    (SAE)

Historian (SEI)
Hospital Administrator (SER)
Psychologist (SEI)
Insurance Claims Examiner
    (SIE)
Librarian (SAI)
Medical Assistant (SCR)
Minister/Priest/Rabbi (SAI)
Paralegal (SCE)

Park Naturalist (SEI)
Physical Therapist (SIE)
Police Officer (SER)
Probation and Parole Officer
    (SEC)
Real Estate Appraiser (SCE)
Recreation Director (SER)
Registered Nurse (SIA)

Teacher (SAE)
Social Worker (SEA)
Speech Pathologist (SAI)
Vocational-Rehab. Counselor
    (SEC)
Volunteer Services Director
    (SEC)

<u>E</u>nterprising *(Persuaders)*

People who like to work with people, influencing, persuading, leading or managing for organizational goals or economic gain.

Are you?		**Can you?**	**Like to?**
self-confident	ambitious	initiate projects	make decisions
assertive	agreeable	convince people to do things	be elected to office
persuasive	talkative	your way	start your own business
energetic	extroverted	sell things	campaign politically
adventurous	spontaneous	give talks or speeches	meet important people
popular	optimistic	organize activities	have power or status
		lead a group	
		persuade others	

Career Possibilities
(Holland Code):

Advertising Executive (ESA)	Credit Analyst (EAS)	Foreign Service Officer (ESA)	Politician (ESA)
Advertising Sales Rep (ESR)	Customer Service Manager	Funeral Director (ESR)	Public Relations Rep (EAS)
Banker/Financial Planner (ESR)	(ESA)	Insurance Manager (ESC)	Retail Store Manager (ESR)
Branch Manager (ESA)	Education & Training Manager	Interpreter (ESA)	Sales Manager (ESA)
Business Manager (ESC)	(EIS)	Lawyer/Attorney (ESA)	Sales Representative (ERS)
Buyer (ESA)	Emergency Medical Technician	Lobbyist (ESA)	Social Service Director (ESA)
Chamber of Commerce Exec	(ESI)	Office Manager (ESR)	Stockbroker (ESI)
(ESA)	Entrepreneur (ESA)	Personnel Recruiter (ESR)	Tax Accountant (ECS)

<u>C</u>onventional *(Organizers)*

People who like to work with data, have clerical or numerical ability, carry out tasks in detail, or follow through on others' instructions.

Are you?		**Can you?**	**Like to?**
well-organized	practical	work well within a system	follow clearly defined
accurate	thrifty	do a lot of paper work in a short	procedures
numerically inclined	systematic	time	use data processing equipment
methodical	structured	keep accurate records	work with numbers
conscientious	polite	use a computer terminal	type or take shorthand
efficient	ambitious	write effective business letters	be responsible for details
conforming	obedient		collect or organize things
	persistent		

Career Possibilities
(Holland Code):

Abstractor (CSI)	Claims Adjuster (SEC)	Elementary School Teacher	Medical Records Technician
Accountant (CSE)	Computer Operator (CSR)	(SEC)	(CSE)
Administrative Assistant (ESC)	Congressional-District Aide (CES)	Financial Analyst (CSI)	Museum Registrar (CSE)
Budget Analyst (CER)	Cost Accountant (CES)	Insurance Manager (ESC)	Paralegal (SCE)
Business Manager (ESC)	Court Reporter (CSE)	Insurance Underwriter (CSE)	Safety Inspector (RCS)
Business Programmer (CRI)	Credit Manager (ESC)	Internal Auditor (ICR)	Tax Accountant (ECS)
Business Teacher (CSE)	Customs Inspector (CEI)	Kindergarten Teacher (ESC)	Tax Consultant (CES)
Catalog Librarian (CSE)	Editorial Assistant (CSI)		Travel Agent (ECS)

BIBLIOGRAPHY

Andersson, Barry. *The DSLR Filmmaker's Handbook: Real-world Production Techniques*. 2015. Print.

Bernardino, Jorge, and Pedro C. Neves. "Decision-making with Big Data Using Open Source Business Intelligence Systems." (2016). Print.

Black, Caroline. *The Pr Professional's Handbook: Powerful, Practical Communications*. 2014. Internet resource.

Brindle, Mark, and Chris Jones. *The Digital Filmmaking Handbook: The Definitive Guide to Digital Filmmaking*. New York: Quercus, 2014. Internet resource.

Briz, Brooks, and David Rose. *Getting a Social Media Job for Dummies*. Hoboken: Wiley, 2015. Internet resource.

Clarke, Adam. *Seo 2018: Learn Search Engine Optimization with Smart Internet Marketing Strategies*. USA: Simple Effectiveness Publ, 2017. Print.

Collier, Maxie D. *The Ifilm Digital Video Filmmaker's Handbook*. Hollywood, Calif: Lone Eagle Pub, 2001. Print.

Cotton, Kindra, and Denise O. N. Green. "Leveraging New Media As Social Capital for Diversity Officers." (2014). Print.

Foster, John, and John Foster. *Writing Skills for Public Relations: Style and Technique for Mainstream and Social Media*. London: Kogan Page, 2012. Internet resource.

Gingiss, Dan. *Winning at Social Customer Care: How Top Brands Create Engaging Experiences on Social Media*. 2017. Print.

Hyatt, Michael. *Platform - Get Noticed in a Noisy World*. 2012. Print.

Lamoureux, Louis. *Doing Digital Right: How Companies Can Thrive in the Next Digital Era*. 2017. Print.

Lazauskas, Joe, and Shane Snow. *The Storytelling Edge: How to Transform Your Business, Stop Screaming into the Void, and Make People Love You*. 2018. Internet resource.

Martin, Gail. *The Essential Social Media Marketing Handbook: A New Roadmap for Maximizing Your Brand, Influence, and Credibility*. 2017. Print.

McKee, Robert, and Thomas Gerace. *Storynomics: Story-driven Marketing in the Post-Advertising World*. 2018. Print.

Mohammadkazemi, Reza. "Sports Marketing and Social Media." (2015). Print.

Schaefer, Mark W. *Content Code : Six Essential Strategies to Ignite Your Content, Your Marketing, and Your Business*. Schaefer, Mark W, 2015. Print.

Schaefer, Mark W. *Known: The Handbook for Building and Unleashing Your Personal Brand in the Digital Age*. 2017. Print.

The Art of Social Media: Power Tips for Power Users. 2016. Internet resource.

Waldman, Joshua, and Sean Harry. *The Social Media Job Search Workbook*. 2014. Print.

Mohammadkazemi, Reza. "Sports Marketing and Social Media." (2015). Print.

INDEX

Photo credits: